State Farm Insurance is pleased

to present this beautiful

commemorative volume

celebrating one hundred years

of black college football

Like a Good Neighbor,

State Farm is There.

BLACK COLLEGE FOOTBALL

1 8 9 2 – 1 9 9 2

One Hundred Years of
History, Education, and Pride

by Michael Hurd

Foreword by Robert V. McDonald
Special artwork by Morrie Turner

For my dad, James D. Hurd, Sr., my sister Phyllis Hurd McKinsey, and my brother James D. Hurd, Jr.

For my two wonderful sons, the joys of my life, Jeremy William and Jason Michael ("the Paceman").
I cannot love you enough.

But, above all, for my late mother and best friend, Emily Jean Baxter Hurd —
"Polly" (Bishop College, Class of 1952), who always unfailingly believed in, encouraged, and loved me.
Her spirit will always live within me.

Title page photos:
Jackson State's Walter Payton, a.k.a. "Sweetness," is the NFL's all-time
leading rusher with 16,726 yards. Courtesy of the Chicago Bears

A rather glum-looking 1935 Johnson C. Smith team which, indeed, had
little to smile about. They finished 2–4–1, the fifth consecutive losing
season for the Golden Bulls. They would finish 2–3–3 in 1936 before
beginning a nine-season win streak. Courtesy of J. C. Smith University

Copyright © 1993 by Michael Hurd

For information, write:
The Donning Company/Publishers
184 Business Park Drive, Suite 106
Virginia Beach, Virginia 23462

Steve Mull, General Manager
Tony Lillis, Editor
Lori Wiley, Art Director, Designer
Robert V. McDonald, Project Director
Laura Hill, Project Research Coordinator
Elizabeth B. Bobbitt, Production Editor

Library of Congress Cataloging in Publication Data:

Hurd, Michael, 1949–
Black college football, 1892–1992:
one hundred years of history, education, and pride/by Michael Hurd.
p.   cm.
Includes bibliographical references.
ISBN 0-89865-882-9 : $29.50
1. College football—United States—History.
2. Universities and colleges, Black—United States—History. I. Title.
GV959.5.U6H87   1993
796.332'63'0973—dc20   93-20988
CIP

Printed in the United States of America

TABLE OF CONTENTS

Sports Illustrated

OCTOBER 14, 1985 $1.95

THE COACH

Eddie Robinson
Overtakes
Bear Bryant With
Win No. 324

GRAMBLING

Coach Eddie Robinson of Grambling always used to say, "America offers more opportunities to young people than any other country in the world." But opportunity comes at a price. "You have to be prepared. If opportunity comes and you're not prepared, you can't have it."

For a century, football has been a positive, motivating experience on Black college campuses. And Coach Robinson has exemplified not only the positive experiences of football, but of education, and life itself.

To this end, the Eddie Robinson Foundation has been formed to provide financial aid to the scholar-athlete whose eligibility has expired, and who desires to complete his undergraduate education. Its goal is to improve the visibility, support, and influence of the student-athlete through the development of an effective and positive education vehicle. The Eddie Robinson Foundation will benefit not only students at Grambling, but at all historically Black colleges and universities.

Cleve Abbott, Marino Casem, Jake Gaither, John Merritt, Ace Mumford, Billy Nix, Eddie Robinson—the common thread binding all of these great coaches—and many others—was their love of the game with the concept of living and working together to accomplish better opportunities for all people.

This Centennial Celebration book is the first of its kind. We hope you will enjoy reading of the rich heritage of Black college football. We are proud to be part of a tribute to those dedicated men and women who helped create an atmosphere and ambiance every fall, for a century, which was the Black college football experience and a truly magnificent one hundred years of history, education, and pride.

The only Sports Illustrated *cover ever devoted to a black college program pertained to . . . you-know-who from you-know-where.*
Courtesy of Sports Illustrated

Robert V. (Bobby) McDonald
Executive Director
The Eddie Robinson Foundation

PREFACE

"The problem of the Twentieth Century is the problem of the color line"
—W. E. B. Du Bois, *Souls of Black Folk*, 1903

Hold that line!—a popular football cheer

The nineteenth century's fade into history was comparable to a great broken-field run. It was dazzling, in its invention-crazed newness, its growth, and its near-lust for industry. However, by the century's conclusion, looking back to survey what it had wrought, it saw great disarray and divisive confusion, much like stunned defensive backs, strewn about the field, wondering where the runner went, and how he got there.

The dazzle of the century was: over $65 million in gold taken from California mines in one year (1853); Alexander Graham Bell patents the telephone, Edison patents the phonograph, George Eastman produces his first box camera, and communication would never be the same. Ditto for travel, as the East-West rail connection was completed (San Francisco to New York in 6 days and 20 hours!), and Henry Ford produced his first gasoline-powered engine. Also, among myriad other inventions, we are introduced to chewing gum, elevators, the electric light, and massed-produced cigarettes. In sports, Walter Camp selects his first All-American team (1889), Dr. James A. Naismith invents basketball (1891), and the first all-black baseball team (Chicago's Union Giants) was formed (1887).

Yet, the West was still wild, with settlers moving there in droves by covered wagon, shoving the Indians aside. In 1891, the number of lynchings in the United States is reported to be 112, the majority occurring in the South, with blacks the majority of the victims. And four years before the century turns, the U.S. Supreme Court will uphold the doctrine of "separate but equal" in *Plessy v. Ferguson*, paving the way for legalized racial segregation in all walks of American life. But the century's second half had already taken a decided turn for the worse in 1857 with the *Dred Scott* decision—a massive blow to anti-slavery forces—in which it was the court's Chief Justice Roger B. Taney's opinion that the Declaration of Independence was never intended to include (rights for) Negroes.

Four years later the Civil War began and raged until 1865.

While the government had pretty much solved the problem with the red man by putting him on reservations, now the business was what to do about the black man, the *free* black man. His reservations had been the Southern plantations, but with the signing of the Emancipation Proclamation September 1862, and later, with the ratification of the Thirteenth Amendment abolishing

In 1974, the Dallas Cowboys made Tennessee State's Ed "Too Tall" Jones only the second player from a black college the No. 1 overall pick in the NFL draft. Grambling's Buck Buchanan was the first (1963, Kansas City Chiefs). Courtesy of the Dallas Cowboys

slavery, December 1865, he was no longer confined—to plantations, at least, but there was no real hope that "the problem" would go away any time soon. The Civil War battlefields were quiet but the fight had changed face, assumed a multitude of disguises—all ugly—and escalated into a social war of physical and emotional acts of racial intimidation and suppression.

However, from the Civil War ashes rose most historically black colleges, and there was an ample supply of ready students, most illiterate, former slaves recently freed and looking to become mainstream, productive American citizens. Education has great catch-up speed, and if the newly-freed slaves were to make up for all of that lost time, learning would be the propellant to greater levels of achievement and empowerment. Since education had once been so staunchly denied in the South that there were laws against slaves learning to read, it is not surprising that most of the first schools were located in the Deep South, where entry to a white college was not even a remote consideration.

Some black colleges were designated "normal" schools, whose specific aim was training elementary and secondary school teachers. Religious groups (Presbyterian, African Methodist Episcopal Zions, et al.) were among many of the early school founders. However, some schools initially opened their doors through the financial aid of private individuals or philanthropic groups, or through legislative acts. (The soldiers and officers of the sixty-second U.S. Colored Infantry are credited with the founding in Missouri of Lincoln University, after giving $5,000 toward the school's incorporation.) The Land Grant Act of 1890 provided state aid, when no federal aid was to be given to any white agricultural and mechanical school unless the state had also provided for a similar school for blacks. The early black colleges focused on basic skills: reading and writing, but others also emphasized religion, vocational, and agricultural courses. Some classes were taught in one-room structures, perhaps a house, and student bodies of less than ten students—ranging from elementary grades through college—was not uncommon.

Come one. Come all. Come learn.

Humble beginnings, to say the least. Now, there are 105 historically black colleges and universities (HBCU) (total enrollment about 258,000), with Pennsylvania's Cheyney State considered the oldest (founded in 1837), and one of only three black colleges in existence prior to the Civil War. Lincoln (Pennsylvania) and Wilberforce (Ohio) universities are the other two—founded in 1854 and 1856. Wilberforce was the first coeducational college for blacks. Just over half the schools (54) today are private. The majority, overall, are four-year schools, with student bodies comprising just over 17 percent of the nation's black students in higher education. However, enrollments at HBCUs has shown an increase in recent years, and was up by 16 percent in 1990. The University of the District of Columbia, with an enrollment of 11,990, is the largest of the four-year HBCU's, and Southwestern Christian College (Terrell,

The 1922 South Carolina State team. Courtesy of South Carolina State

Texas) is the smallest with 225 students. The average black college enrollment is about 2,500, with twelve HBCUs having student bodies of less than five hundred. In 1990, black colleges awarded 27 percent of all bachelor's degrees earned by blacks nationwide.

Yet, there is a sentiment that historically black colleges, founded because of racism, are racist in themselves. Yet, as enrollment at HBCUs are on the rise, so is the racial and ethnic diversity of the schools' student bodies. The percentage of black students at HBCUs in 1990 was only 81 percent. And, black colleges have never turned students away because of color, ethnicity or religion.

"Black colleges perpetuate what the heritage is about," said Paul Collins, a graduate of Livingstone College and a retired professor of sociology at Cal State-Hayward and a former standout basketball coach and assistant football coach at Wiley College. "What you are, or are not, will be enhanced in that situation. Those kinds of relationships are not available at bigger colleges. You can't get involved with anybody like you."

Collins also offers one explanation of why many black colleges have been in such dire financial straits: Because of a desire to educate as many blacks as possible, regardless of the student's ability to pay tuition.

"If you showed any promise as a student, you were not pushed out of school," Collins said. "Schools went bankrupt because they would give so many kids educations for free. But how could you turn a kid away if he wanted an education? Black colleges are about educating people.

"Black colleges are about graduating!"

So, learning? No problem.

The color line? Problem.

But, hold on.

As bigger schools began recruiting black high school players, Florida A&M's great coach, Jake Gaither, was an outspoken critic of black high school coaches who stopped sending their best players to black colleges. Gaither produced thirty-six All-Americans, forty-two pro football players. Courtesy of Florida A&M University

"Where else do they make men quicker than on the football field? Football is the greatest classroom there is."
—Alonzo "Jake" Gaither, former head coach, Florida A&M

If the nineteenth century had been a football contest, the coach might have strongly considered burning the game film. "We did some good things and some bad things," he might say, generally meaning the bad outweighed the good. However, amid the century's industrial progress, change, and the ever-widening racial gap, in November 1869, twenty-five Princeton men travelled to nearby New Brunswick, New Jersey to meet a squad of twenty-five Rutgers men in what would be the first organized football game. From that, other schools would begin to field teams and a few would have black players, some of whom would go on to All-America fame. In general, these players were anomalies—one or two blacks on the few teams which accepted them, as some blacks, though totally excluded from attending white universities in the South, do find entrance into schools in the East.

But right away, football was a good thing and a bad thing. It seemed a fun thing, but many thought it was brutish and pandered to violence. Worse, a lot all of the school presidents disliked it. A definite bad thing. In 1873, Cornell President Andrew Dickson White offered this line in denying his team's request to go to Cleveland for a game against Michigan: "I will not permit thirty men to travel four hundred miles to agitate a bag of wind."

Unfortunately, the sport was not that simple. It was rough, appearing more a street brawl than a game, with possibly as many as fifty men per side. It was played without helmets and with very light padding for other parts of the body. Football would get so rough that in 1905, nineteen players nationwide were killed as a result of playing the game. President Theodore Roosevelt was a staunch football fan, once proclaiming: "In life, as in a football game, the principal to follow is: hit the line, don't foul and don't shirk, but hit the line hard!" That was being done all too well, and even Roosevelt could not totally ignore the game's violent nature and resulting deaths. In 1905, he held a conference with sixty-two college presidents and convinced them of the need to instate more humane rules, and curtail the barbaric play—or he would ban the game. That gathering was the first of what, five years later, would become the National Collegiate Athletic Association (NCAA).

At first, the few black colleges did not share in the football experience because of poor facilities, in general, and lack of money, in particular (aspects which have not greatly changed at historically black colleges). School administrators were not willing to spend portions of their already meager funds on games. However, as the schools began to grow, many presidents began to see the need for physical education programs, and from many of those programs intramural football teams were formed with students as coaches. Finally, the lack of enthusiasm toward football at black colleges changed on

December 27, 1892, in a Salisbury, North Carolina, cow pasture. There, in a snowstorm, Biddle (now Johnson C. Smith) takes on and defeats home team Livingstone, 4–0, marking the first intercollegiate football game between historically black colleges. A friendly rivalry, as well as an athletic history for an entire race, was begun. (Note: There are varying reports of the score— some list 5–0, however, in 1892, a touchdown only counted 4 points, increasing to 5 in 1898, and finally 6 points in 1912. There are no reports of an extra point being attempted.)

The timing could not have been better. According to the late Ric Roberts (Pittsburgh *Courier* sports writer and black sports historian), the game "eased misgivings of young black athletes who, during the infamous 'Black Nadir' of 1881–1900, had seen their kind banished from both baseball and football." Just before the turn of the century, George Williams, another black historian, noted: "The schools of the North have shut their doors in the faces of black children."

At black colleges, the doors were wide open, for academics and athletics. Two years after Biddle-Livingstone, Howard University (Washington, D.C.) and Lincoln (Pennsylvania) played the first black college game in the East, followed in 1897 by Tuskegee Institute (Alabama) and Atlanta University opening the game to black schools deeper in the South.

Now, one hundred years after Biddle-Livingstone, forty-three HBCUs are fielding football teams within the National Collegiate Athletic Association, with eighteen belonging to the NCAA's Division 1-AA, and several others in Division II. There are now four conferences comprised of HBCU teams:

— Central Intercollegiate Athletic Association (CIAA), the oldest (founded in 1912) and largest of the group, with eleven members.
— Mid-Eastern Athletic Conference (MEAC), seven schools.
— Southern Intercollegiate Athletic Conference (SIAC), nine schools.
— Southwestern Athletic Conference (SWAC), eight schools.

Both the SWAC and MEAC members are NCAA Division 1-AA schools, the SIAC and CIAA Division II. Several other conferences have existed at various times, but as schools de-emphasized football, unable to afford the costs, those leagues evaporated.

There were twenty-three bowl games played on January 1, 1947—six for black college teams, with another six black college "bowls" played in December. The Prairie View Bowl was a New Year's Day game, played in Houston, but the most popular of the bowl-type games for blacks was the Florida A&M-hosted Orange Blossom Classic. The OBC has been played continuously since 1933, and served for years as the unofficial black national championship game because of the powerful Jake Gaither teams in the 1950s and 1960s.

However, it was not until the Heritage Bowl was launched in 1991 (played at Joe Robbie Stadium in Miami), that black colleges had their first NCAA-sanctioned postseason game. In that game, Alabama State beat North Carolina

A&T, 36–13. The game is the only postseason bowl involving non-Division 1-A teams. The "Yam," "Pecan," and "Vulcan" bowls have disappeared, but in their place are "classics" galore. Some have been highly successful efforts at marketing black college football in major cities.

Yet, the product itself—the game—has maintained a large sense of purity, family, and hope. Never was that more evident than the weekend of February 19–21, 1993 in Baltimore, Maryland. Then, the Sheridan Black Network hosted its annual Black College All-American Celebration. What set that event apart from previous years was the recognition of the black college football centennial, and for that, SBN presented its all-time black college football team one night, the 1993 All-Americans the next. Stars of the past, stars of the future.

The stars of the past stole the show. Deacon Jones, Lem Barney, Donnie Shell, Mel Blount, and Robert Brazile were among the group tabbed the twenty-two best from one hundred years of black college football, though you knew every patron, in every black barber shop, who saw the list asked, "But, what about. . . ??" but you also knew you'd take this group and gladly challenge *all* comers. Collectively, from Willie Davis to Everson Walls, there was a sizable fortune in Super Bowl rings, but what price experience? The veterans passed along their war stories to wide-eyed, youthful warriors looking to ascend to similar heights of greatness.

More than anything, the weekend was an extraordinary reunion for a group of men who had achieved beyond even some of their wildest dreams. Practically all of them had college degrees and were successful beyond football, which had made them men.

"Just being here, among some of these guys and seeing all the greatness in this room, knowing they all came from historically black colleges, is wonderful," said Larry Little, a Pro Football Hall of Fame lineman who played collegiately at Bethune-Cookman (enrollment 800 during his career there). "You never forget where you came from, no matter who you are or how far you've gone. We all went through basically the same things and that's why I would always look at rosters and see how many blacks were on a team, then I would count and see how many went to historically black colleges.

"I still do that today."

ACKNOWLEDGMENTS

The honor of chronicling the rich history of football programs at historically black colleges was a formidable task, though one I have relished for several years. The initial proposal was drawn up in 1984.

I immersed myself in research on black college football, though very little was available in mainstream media publications. My research also included black history—American history, in general. The journey has been exhausting, exhilarating, frustrating, and fun! In the process, I have learned much about my country, my race, and myself.

Since beginning this project, I have weathered the anger and hurt from hearing, ad nauseam, about how blacks don't read or buy books. Yet, I have felt this book was needed, a large piece of American history that has never been documented, at least in a national medium. My prime concern was producing a book which would elicit pride from the black community for these athletes, coaches/teachers, and others who have molded the tradition of historically black colleges and their athletic programs, and through that, pride in ourselves as a people. This book speaks of perseverance and what can be done — continues to be done — though others may obstruct progress or instill doubt. And for many *of all colors* in our world, there is unfortunately still a great need for an abundance of perseverance, such as that held by the men in these pages. This book says, "You *can* do."

Never quit on your dreams.

In assembling the book, the paucity of records and other information on schools, teams, coaches, and players posed a huge problem. Many schools did not keep great records on their teams, if they kept them at all, and, as in the case of Grambling, much has been destroyed by fires or other damage, or just lost, as programs went under or schools were shut down. In those cases I have relied on newspaper articles (primarily the Pittsburgh *Courier*), the memories of players, coaches, alums, family members, black media veterans, and National Collegiate Athletic Association (NCAA) records.

For reasons of time or space, much of the volumes of information acquired did not make it to print. For that, the work is woefully, and no doubt noticeably, incomplete in scope. Space limitations also prevented more detailed profiles on dozens of great players, coaches, and their teams, all of whom deserved much more than just a mention. However, I would like to thank all who graciously consented to interviews or simply pointed me in the right direction. I wanted to interview many more people and could have easily produced a several-volume set of profiles alone. There was so much to be said by so many.

I had initially included a a chronology of black history events along with the All-America team listings, with three or four current event facts preceeding each year's team, but had to pull them, also because of space restrictions.

Without question, the completion of this project was greatly enhanced by the tireless efforts of Bobby McDonald, who diligently searched for a publisher and sponsor, was instrumental in researching and acquiring documents, and serving as marketing director for the book and related merchandise. Above all, he shared with me a deep belief in this project, despite the odds against its completion. Thank you Bobby.

Also deserving of thanks is the Bobby Mac Support Team. In particular, Sam Skinner, Michele Himmelberg and Don Steele; Willie Brown, Bill Seidler, and Louis Francisco from State Farm; and Steve Mull, Laura Hill, Tony Lillis, and Lori Wiley from the Donning Company.

For their marketing and promotional help, thanks also to Don Andersen, Ken Bentley, Douglas Black, Richard Boyle, David Brown, Herb Carter, Dr. Jewel Plummer Cobb, Thomas Coley, Matt Dawson, Wardell Davis, Peter Donovan, Henry Dyer, Dennis Farrell, Fred Hobdy, Roy Jackson, Owen Knox, Ed Lara, Stan Lewis, Aaron Lovejoy, Nelson Mason, Vernon-Rita-Linda McDonald and all the other McDonalds, Horace Mitchell, J. Penny, James Ramsey, Janet Redding, Charles Robinson, Coach Eddie Robinson, Denise Sprague, Rich Talmo, Harry Thompson, Paul "Tank" Younger, Vic Vavasseur and the rest of the Vavasseur clan, and Charles Whitcomb. Also to the ABSG, Cap Boy, AACA, SMI and to the Alphas and all of the other fraternities and sororities that make up the black college experience.

Thank you, too, State Farm Insurance, for entering this project as sponsor.

I was blessed with two hard-working research assistants, Melanie Neff and Sara Wakai. Melanie contacted most of the schools and helped compile the information for that chapter, in addition to transcribing tapes and other research duties, and helping me to maintain at least a shred of sanity. Sara spent many hours researching the *Courier* back issues on microfilm at UCLA and helped acquire the reproduced photos of the paper's All-America teams.

Lisa-Marie Aird, in New York, and Charles Vienn, Sr. (Ad Visor, Ltd.) in Houston, Texas were also instrumental in research and marketing.

I would like to specifically thank the following people for their immediate response and enthusiastic help in completing this book:

❑ All of the sports information directors and other publicists at the black colleges and conferences surveyed, including: Larry Barber, MEAC; Russell Boone, Fort Valley State; LeCounte Conaway, Hampton (and formerly CIAA information director); Joan Bahner (Fisk University Alumni Association); James Cuthbertson, Johnson C. Smith; Bill Hamilton, South Carolina State; James Hilliard, Langston; Alvin Hollins, Florida A&M; Clifton Huff, Livingstone; Jackie Madden, Jarvis Christian College; Martha Robinson, Meharry Medical School.

❑ Bill Nunn, Jr. and Eddie Jeffries, at the Pittsburgh *Courier*.

❑ Syndicated cartoonist Morrie Turner, for his excellent images on the Pro Football Hall of Famers.

❑ Journalists: Darrell Ardison, *The Houston Post*; Gregory D. Clay, *Newsday*; Howie Evans, *Amsterdam News*; Ivan Maisel, *Dallas Morning News*; Bret Moore, publisher, *Sports View* magazine; Ken Murray, *Baltimore Sun*; Roscoe Nance, *USA TODAY*; Russell Stockard; Lloyd Wells, *Houston Forward Times*.

❑ All of the archivists, historians, and librarians, who responded, including: Louise Rountree, Livingstone; Skip Mason, Atlanta's Digging It Up (an African-American historical research and consulting firm); Janice Bell and L.B. Smith, Southern University; Margaret Walker, *The Houston Post*; Fred Whitted, Fayetteville State.

❑ Alfred White, NCAA; Duane DaPron, National Association of Intercollegiate Athletics (NAIA); Dick Simpson, Negro League Historian; Keith Carroll, U.S. Department of Education; officials and/or publicists for the National Football League, NFL Properties, and NFL Alumni Association; The Canadian Football League; Amateur Athletic Foundation of Los Angeles.

❑ Arthur Ashe, for his extreme kindness, help, and encouragement at the outset.

❑ Lamar Rush, who designed the black college football centennial logo.

❑ Ron Bethea, Chairman and President Origins, Marketing, Management, Company.

❑ Annie Lucas and Marianne Williamson

❑ All concerned at *USA TODAY* for their support, especially the members of the Los Angeles Bureau *("Haya, the t-shirts are on the way!")*.

Finally, thanks to all my wonderful friends who have had to hear so much about this book, or just my quest to become an author, for the last few years, and who have been so supportive, encouraging, and tolerant of *me*, including: Sharon Alpert, Karen Allen, Kirk Bohls, Thomas and Marcia Bonk, Clyde Drexler (captain of the All-Human "Dream Team"), Nancy Gay, Terry and Linda Huffman, Tracy Dodds Hurd, Dianne King, Elaine Kluever, Gary Lenk, Leanne Reidy, Randy Riggs, Danny Robbins, Shelley Smith, Stan Spence, Cheryl Steele, Susan Steen, Dave Strege, and Ron Thomas.

Michael Hurd,
June 1993

INTRODUCTION

"In the East, college football is a cultural exercise. On the West Coast, it is a tourist attraction. In the Midwest, it is cannibalism. But in the Deep South, it is religion, and Saturday is the holy day."

—Marino Casem, Southern University athletic director and former head coach, on football in the Deep South.

Where else but the South, would you expect to find a player nicknamed, "The Lord's Prayer?" That would be former Tennessee State quarterback Eldridge Dickey. But through the years, there has also been "Shack" (Grambling's James Harris), "Big Train" (Morris Brown's John Moody), "Jazz" (Lincoln's Frank Byrd), "Bad News" (Buford, of Bluefield), "Tarzan" (Kentucky State's Joseph Kendall), "Satellite" (Mississippi Valley St. quarterback Willie Totten), "747" (Tennessee State quarterback Joe Adams), and now, "Air" (Alcorn State quarterback Steve McNair).

By any name, or any school, they would have played just as sweet, though few as well as "Sweetness," Walter Payton, the incomparable Jackson State running back and Pro Football Hall of Famer who is the NFL's all-time leading rusher. Of course old timers who saw Tuskegee's "Big" Ben Stevenson may beg to differ. But then, Willie Richardson, another Jackson State alum, was a four-time Pittsburgh Courier All-American receiver. Too, the NCAA Division 1-AA record book reads like a resume for Totten and his favorite receiver at Valley, Jerry Rice, an All-Pro with the San Francisco Forty-Niners and holder of the league record for most career touchdown catches (103).

Coaches? Casem is the "Godfather," but "Eddie" is the all-time winningest coach (381–136–15, .716), for the all-time (in name recognition, at least!) black college football program. Robinson and Grambling are marquee—Las Vegas-size marquee—but the Tigers are seldom a gamble at the gate. Ask college football fans what they know about black college football and they will answer: "Grambling," or "the Grambling band!" The program is on everybody's map because of Eddie Robinson, former school president (and baseball coach) Ralph Waldo Emerson Jones, "Prez," and former sports information director, Collie Nicholson, whose creative marketing efforts boosted the Tigers fame to worldwide proportions. In his zeal, Nicholson even went to the extent of learning enough Japanese to negotiate a contract for Grambling to play in the first regular-season collegiate game played outside the United States. And on September 4, 1976, Grambling clobbered Morgan State, 42–16, before 50,000 fans at Tokyo's Olympic Memorial Stadium.

The Grambling mystique is worldwide, and may have overshadowed Florida A&M and Jake Gaither, who has produced thirty-six black college All-Americans and six black college national championships. He retired after

Facing page: Willie Davis of the Green Bay Packers, an All-American at Grambling. Vince Lombardi said of Davis, "You look for speed, agility, and size. You may get two of these qualities in one man and when you have three, you have a great football player." Courtesy of the Green Bay Packers

Alcorn State quarterback Steve McNair said "No" to major colleges who wanted him to play defensive back, plus, McNair said, "I feel more comfortable at a black school. They care about me as a person, not just as a football player." Courtesy of Alcorn State

the 1969 season with a 203–36–4 mark and a winning percentage of .844, tops among all coaches with two hundred or more career wins.

In the Northeast, to talk black college football, you must begin with Eddie Hurt and Earl Banks at Morgan State and their separate winning streaks. Hurt's teams won forty-two games (six ties) without a defeat from 1932 and through 1937's 7–0–0 finish. In the 1960s Banks had a 32-game win streak (no ties) which remains a black college record. In the Deep South, Cleve Abbott had powerful teams at Tuskegee, led by the amazing Stevenson, in the Twenties. Billy Nicks made Prairie View a power in the Fifties and Sixties. Their successors are Willie Jeffries at South Carolina State, Houston Markham (Alabama State), Billy Joe (Central State), Joe Taylor (Hampton), Archie Cooley (now at Norfolk State after terrorizing Mississippi Valley opponents with his high-scoring version of the run-and-shoot offense which in 1984 averaged 640 yards a game). Joe Gilliam, Sr., former Tennessee State head coach (after many years as an assistant to John Merritt at Jackson State and Tennessee State), was lauded as being well before his time as a defensive strategist.

One hundred years of black college football has seen Grambling's Paul "Tank" Younger become the first player from a black college to break the NFL/black college line. He became an All-Pro running back and linebacker. Since then, black colleges have produced a steady stream of prize catches for professional football, from the NFL to the United States Football League to the World League of American Football.

There are twelve NFL Hall of Famers who played at HBCUs, including 1993 inductees Walter Payton and Larry Little, and Maryland State's Art Shell, the first modern day black head coach in the NFL (Los Angeles Raiders). Too, Marion Motley, former Cleveland Browns' running back is in the Hall. He started his collegiate career at South Carolina State, but finished at Nevada.

Until the 1960s, talent at black colleges ran thick. Curtis Miranda would become a three-time All-American center for Florida A&M, but, as a freshman, he was thirteenth (of fifteen) on the depth chart at his position, and those Rattler squads were primarily all Florida kids. Is there any wonder that three Florida Division 1-A schools (Florida State, Florida, and Miami) consistently rank among the top 20 teams in the country—at times all three in the top ten? Black kids make up the majority of those schools' better players, but imagine all of those caliber athletes going to one school—Florida A&M to play for "Jake."

The man had a true pipeline: he graduated his players, who upon returning to their hometowns and becoming high school teachers/coaches, sent their best players to him. One season, he had nine players who could cover 100 yards in 9.5 seconds, or faster. In 1960 and 1961, the Rattlers averaged 51.2 points a game (Mississippi Valley averaged 60.9 in 1984).

"We used to meet these Southern (white) schools at track meets and run them out of the park," Gaither said, at a time when the recruitment of black athletes to white colleges had heated considerably. "They used to say I had a farm system, and I told them they were right. My boys did come off the farm. Right here under their noses was the greatest talent in the world and they didn't want it. But, now you can't turn around without a scout from every white school down here beating the bushes for black players."

Yes, beat a bush and several future All-Americans and Heisman Trophy candidates hit the ground running, passing, and tackling. The talent pool had hardly been a secret to black schools, but white programs would not—could not—test the waters. They had to toe the line, and black colleges benefitted, though in the pre-Sixties, the players they uncovered had no glowing national credentials as prep players.

"We weren't able to get high school All-Americans," said Banks, who coached Willie Lanier and tight end Raymond Chester, among other standout players who went on to stellar NFL careers. "We got diamonds in the rough and watched them grow."

There were gems by the truckloads, refined in places like Itta Bena, Mississippi, Orangeburg, South Carolina, Princess Anne, Maryland, or Normal, Alabama. In earlier times, black kids in the South grew up watching and adoring black college athletes, many of whom were from their neighborhood or hometown. You wanted to run like Willie Galimore, catch like Otis Taylor, or hit like Mel Blount. Maybe you'd heard of coaches like "Big John" Merritt at Tennessee State, or "Pop" Long at Wiley. Maybe you went to Maryland State because of Art Shell or Johnny Sample, maybe to Grambling because of Buck Buchanan or, well, pick a G-Man, any G-Man. Maybe you wanted to be part of the Morehouse-Tuskegee rivalry, an eighty-year feud which is the longest running rivalry among black colleges. Maybe you thought it would be hip to be a part of Clark Atlanta's "Black Battalion of Death," a team which in 1928 ended Tuskegee's forty-eight game unbeaten streak. Or maybe you went to Texas Southern because you'd been in Houston's Third Ward on a Saturday night when Prairie View was coming to town and you felt that special charged

Program cover for inaugural game of what is now called the "Whitney Young Classic" and played at Giants Stadium. Proceeds benefit the New York Urgan League Whitney M. Young, Jr., Memorial Scholarship Fund. That first game drew 60,811 fans, with Morgan State winning, 9–7. Courtesy of Russell Stockard

Morehouse wide receiver Dextrel Smith makes a nice one-hand grab. Morehouse is among the oldest black college football programs—ninety-three years. Courtesy of Sports View

atmosphere around Jeppesen Stadium.

At one time, black prep stars wanted to be a part of all that. It was, in most cases, all they could be part of if they were looking at a collegiate athletic career. And, it wasn't a bad thing. There was camaraderie, fellowship, family, and the competition was as keen as you'd find anywhere.

But then a funny thing happened: integration, and it brought a classic good news/ bad news scenario. The good news was painfully obvious—increased opportunities and chances for stepping up in all facets of society. The bad news peered ominously from legislative caucus rooms and major college coaching offices. With integration, more schools, especially in the South, began admitting blacks, beefing up athletic programs. But as they bulked, black college teams began wasting away.

The pipelines dried. Some rusted.

For black college football, assimilation was an over-eager Grinch, grabbing most of the brightest ornaments from the high school football tree, leaving little glitter material for black college programs. It was a most cruel irony. Blacks had gained, as a whole, but what a setback for its colleges—athletically and academically.

"Negro high school coaches need to feel an obligation to Negro colleges," Gaither once said, expressing what many black college coaches were feeling. "The Negro high school coach turns his back on the Negro college and prefers to send his boys to a white college. In most cases these high school coaches attended a Negro college free on a full athletic scholarship. They were fed by their coach when they were broke, given clothes when they were ragged, but they think it's the greatest thing in the world to send their boys to a white coach."

Many think now that trend is reversing, but it remains a subject of debate. Some think the drop off in talent at black colleges has been minimal. Others, would say tragic. Still others say there has been no drop at all.

"We still get some of the better kids, but it's like planting a crop," said Willie Jeffries, head coach at South Carolina State (and formerly the first black head coach at a NCAA Division 1 School, Wichita State). "You don't know how it's going to grow. Black colleges are still recruiting the top athletes. We just don't get them all. It's hard to get a qualifier (academically). If he's worth anything as an athlete, he's gone (to a big school).

"We get good athletes who are not good test-takers. We got a lot more on GPA, but we do go after the best players. We don't want to ever say we didn't try."

Perhaps a player can gain more playing time at a black college—big fish, small pond, but others also point to a continued rise in black cultural awareness, and the feeling that thirst is best quenched in a black college environment. It's not just an athletic thing.

"More parents are sending their kids to black colleges," said Shell whose son, Arthur, Jr., decided to attend Morehouse. "He said, 'Dad, I want to find out about me. I want to find out what you've been talking about.' "

Still, all concerned with black colleges are focusing on the plight of the Mississippi and Louisiana HBCUs. Both states are looking at closing or combining the black colleges in their states or including them in the state university systems and further opening the schools to a more racially diverse student body.

"We are among the few groups of people in the United States who are willing to entrust the training of our best and brightest to others," said Dr. Arthur Thomas, president of Central State (Ohio) University. "The Catholics have Notre Dame, the Irish have Boston College, the Jewish people have Miami University, and the Mormons have Brigham Young. In addition to attracting the top scholars among their respective groups, it is interesting to note that each of these institutions boast athletic programs that consistently rank among the best in the country. We, as African-Americans, must develop ways to attract and retain our best—whether they be athletes or scholars—to our HBCUs."

That will take money, traditionally in short supply at HBCU's who seem to live eternally perched precariously on the brink of going out of business. To help allay those fears, HBCUs are attempting to bring many of their alums back into the fold, though a common problem is black college alums giving money to bigger schools, seeking perhaps to share in the national glow of high-profile programs. At black colleges, and most non-Division 1-A schools, that kind of glow is dimmed.

For all the rah-rah of college football, the underlying fact is the biggest cheers come from network and cable television board rooms. Big-time college football is big-time big business, funded greatly by television revenues, and shared primarily by the Division 1-A schools and all members of the College Football Coaches Association. College football programs generate millions of dollars per year from television appearances. The Bayou Classic (Grambling-Southern has been the lone black college game on network television. However, black college programs do not routinely play in 75,000-seat stadiums, and, in essence, do not exist for network TV heads: limited audience (though blacks, in general, watch more television than any other group), therefore limited sponsorship interest, therefore no deal.

Today, there is also a growing debate over whether or not black colleges should bolt from the NCAA and take a chance on their own. Not enough voice, not enough say-so, not enough money trickling down, it is said of their current relationship with the NCAA. Too, there is still an uneasiness over the NCAA's

In 1971, Thomas "Tricky Tom" Caldwell guided ECSU to its only CIAA title. Courtesy of Elizabeth City State University

23

Charlie Neal, "The BET Man," not the famous Dodgers baseball player. Neal does play-by-play for Black Entertainment Television, the primary television outlet for black college football games. Courtesy of Sports View

Propositions 48 and 42, which set eligibility standards for freshmen athletes, who must score acceptable minimums on standardized college aptitude exams. The concern there is whether the tests are culturally biased, but there also remains the question of how many potential student-athletes are denied entry—particularly those considered "at risk," many of whom are black and from low-income families.

Sounds bleak, yet a record 2,230,277 fans attended black college games during the 1993 season, though overall college football attendance was down. Fans of Southern's Jaguars (in Baton Rouge) have one of the most vaunted reputations for support among black colleges. In 1993, the Jags finished 5–6, but led NCAA Division 1-AA in average home attendance with 28,908. The SWAC, of which Southern is a member, led all NCAA Division 1-AA conferences, and also bettered the Division 1-A's Mid-American and Big West Conferences, with a 20,804 average (873,772 total).

Jackson State led Division 1-AA in average attendance from 1986 to 1989, including a Division 1-AA record average 32,734 in 1987. A hidden market?

"The evil that men do, lives after them. The good is oft interred with their bones."—Frederick Douglass, from *Julius Caesar* by William Shakespeare

This book is about remarkable human beings who just happened to be gifted athletes. A lot of their stories have never been told, and many of the players and coaches have passed on, unable to share in this recording of their glory. They took a lot with them, but the spirit they left endures.

What an outrageous one hundred years of great men, heroic athletic feats, fiercely proud academic institutions, and some dynamite bands!

Black college football may have its struggles, but it is very much alive.

And, teeming with pride.

CHAPTER ONE

"A Match Game of Ball"

It was the 1892 Christmas season and two tiny North Carolina schools were about to incidentally present Blacks with an historic athletic gift for the ages. Its presentation was heralded in this innocuous item, which ran in the AME Zion Church newspaper, *Star of Zion*:

"A game of foot ball (sic) will be played between Biddle University and Livingstone College Tuesday, Dec. 27, at the Livingstone College grounds. The Livingstone boys are sanguine of success, while the boys from Biddle are quite confident that they won't be beaten. The game promises to be interesting. There will be an open field, so a large crowd is expected. Both teams will do their best to carry off honors for their alma mater. Captain Walker has an excellent team and is well pleased with the work it is doing. Taylor, who plays center, is a fellow who weighs a little more than 200 pounds and is like a strong wall. Trent, Rives, O'Neil are good in their places. Everything is now in order for the game."

And the stage was set for history, despite the community's casual approach toward what would become the first football game between historically black colleges. Of course, there was little to get excited about. No strutting bands, dance routines, souvenir vendors, or even a blimp floating overhead. There was no reason for the fans to take the game that seriously. It was merely a break from studies, entertainment for the Christmas holidays, when most students remained on campus, unable to afford a trip home.

"Most of the people then had a struggle just getting an education," said Louise M. Rountree, former librarian and historian for Livingstone, and author of Blue Bear Trax, which documents the Livingstone football history. "They were hard-working people who didn't have that kind of (leisure) time."

Organized football had been a distant thought for black college officials. First, and utterly foremost, there was the business of education. The chains of slavery were off, and now the mind was also free—to learn. Varsity football? Its time would come, but before 1890, all sports at black colleges were intramural. Facilities and funds were meager and school officials were hesitant to invest more in athletics without appearing to be squandering their resources. Rather, the bulk of the school's money went toward books, teachers, and labs.

Livingstone's W. J. Trent, left, and J. W. Walker, who played in the first-ever black college football game, Livingstone-Biddle, 1892. Trent, who would go on to become the school's president, was manager as well as halfback. Walker, a fullback, was team captain. Courtesy of Louise M. Rountree, Blue Bear Trax

Biddle had been founded in 1867 in Charlotte, by black Presbyterian ministers, Livingstone in 1879 by members of the African Methodist Episcopal Zion Church in Salisbury.

Captained by L. B. Ellerson, the men at Biddle had banded their football team in 1890, calling themselves "The Bull Pen," studying and practicing (primarily by the rugby rules of England and Australia) the new sport, with students serving as coaches. After two years of intramural play, the Biddle team felt ready for an outside challenge, and their most likely opponent was just thirty miles to the north at Livingstone, which had only taken up the sport in the summer of 1892. Though two years behind Biddle in practice, Livingstone was also ready for outside competition. However, it is not clear just who initiated the idea for their historic game. The December 3, 1890 Indianapolis *Freeman* reported this from their Biddle correspondent: "Our football eleven has received a challenge from one of Livingstone College to play a match game of ball . . . the challenge will most likely be accepted, and the boys are now kicking the leather bag over the field."

The Livingstone team's start is recalled this way, according to the *The Blue Bear*, Livingstone's yearbook.

"In 1892, several young men . . . decided to inaugurate football at Livingstone. To that end, an order was placed for one of the regulation footballs from Spalding's . . . each man chipping in and paying for it. Then the fellows began to work putting cleats on their everyday shoes until after practice, when they would be taken off. Old clothes were patched and padded up and these constituted the togs (practice) of the first Livingstone varsity football team"

Given their two-year practice advantage, the game was a stroke of scheduling genius by the Biddle men, who departed by train for Salisbury on the morning of the ball game, occupying half of one of the "colored" cars. Overnight, snow had begun to fall, and by game time the field was heavily covered, and some accounts report a continuous snowfall throughout the game. Perfect football weather for the few intrepid fans who flocked to the "open field"—a cow pasture, actually—by wagon, buggy, surrey, on mule or horseback. Some walked.

The Livingstone players wore their new uniforms, made of ten-ounce ducking cloth, and sewn by the women of the Industrial Department. W. J. Trent, halfback and team manager (coach)—and, later, school president—proudly recounted, years afterward, that his uniform was best-looking because he was courting the director of the Sewing Department!

The Howard University team in 1894. Courtesy of Howard University

The mood surrounding the game was light, and that may have in part led to the lax attitude in keeping records, not just for the first game, but perhaps for many years afterward at other schools, as well. There was more a feeling of playing just for "fun." Records were not that important. Too, use of last names only was common in recorded references to players, even in newspaper articles, so the first names of many players are largely unknown. With that in mind, the first Biddle ("Golden Bulls") line-up was listed as:

Ends—H. H. Muldrow and J. J. Robinson

Tackles—Charles H. Shute and William Haig

Guards—C.E. Rayford and Captain L.B. Ellerson

Center—Hawkins Quarterback—G. E. Ceasar

Halfbacks—W. W. Morrow and Mebane

Fullback—William L. Metz.

The first Livingstone eleven (the "Blue Bears") was:

Ends—Henry Rives and Cornelius Garland

Tackles—J. B. A. Yelverton and Charles H. Patrick

Guards—R. J. Rencher and Jesse R. Dillard

Center—John J. Taylor

Quarterback—Wade Hampton

Halfbacks—John W. Walker (Captain) and William J. Trent

Fullback—F. H. Cumming

The squads took the field to play two 45-minute halves, and Biddle took a 4–0 lead at halftime. Unfortunately, there is no record of who scored the first touchdown in black college football history. However, the first player involved in a controversy was Livingstone's Trent, who, in the second half, recovered a fumble and raced in for an apparent score. Trent's touchdown was disallowed, however, by the game's umpire—Murphy, a white law student from the University of North Carolina (and a Livingstone manager). The Biddle players protested because they said their runner had stepped out of bounds. That was not easily discerned, however, because by that point in the game, snow had obscured much of the field marking.

Biddle, thus, took a 4–0 win. In those days, a touchdown was worth only 4 points, though many documents report the final score as 5–0.

The schools have maintained their rivalry, with JCSU leading the series 22-2-4. In 1923, Biddle was renamed Johnson C. Smith after the husband of Jane Berry Smith, who had established a major endowment at the school.

"It's always been a game you wanted to win," said Eddie McGirt, former JCSU player (2–0 against Livingstone) and coach (11–4–1). "I'm not bragging, but we always had a much better team. You could always get a rise out of them because they always got up for us. Sometimes, I thought it was the religious aspect of it as well as the athletic."

The teams would play annually on Thanksgiving Day before thousands of fans. After playing the first couple of games, though, Biddle withdrew from football competition, deciding to concentrate more on the school's debating team.

Ben B. Church made Who's Who in America *as a social worker, but his 1906 Livingstone team claimed the title: "The Colored College Champions." In eleven years, his teams won six North Carolina Interscholastic Association championships. Courtesy of Louise M. Rountree,* Blue Bear Trax

Livingstone's 1906 championship team. Courtesy of Louise M. Rountree, Blue Bear Trax

Said William Leak, an end and quarterback at Livingstone from 1934–1938: "During those days, the big event in the Carolinas was Smith-Livingstone on Thanksgiving and the Easter Monday baseball game (between the two schools). I don't think (the rivalry) has changed. You can't help but feel some special feelings about it."

And there were plenty of special feelings surrounding their 1992 meeting, the official black college football centennial game with Livingstone playing host once again.

This time, it was a sunny, windy October afternoon and ten thousand fans crowded into and around the tiny Alumni Field facility. It was no longer a cow pasture, though cleated Bulls and Bears would trample the playing field, set simply before modest concrete grandstands on one side, metal and wood bleachers on the other. The atmosphere was festive, with Black College Centennial and other racial pride and black college memorabilia in plentiful supply, and varieties of food running the gamut from freshly fried fish to Philadelphia cheese steak sandwiches to the usual football game fare, popcorn, peanuts, hot dogs. Kids chased each other up and down the grandstand steps. It was a beautiful community setting, and about as pristine as college football gets. It was as Norman Rockwell may have painted it. It was a community festival to commemorate what had been, to invoke the names of heroes past and present, to reaffirm brotherhood and family.

It was Livingstone's homecoming game, but spiritually, it was much more.

The 1913 Biddle squad. Courtesy of Johnson C. Smith

The roots of black college football had sprung from this patch of North Carolina earth and you thought of all the names that had gone before and wondered who would be the names to follow.

It was a grand, high-spirited day. At Notre Dame, they wake up the echoes. Here the family had gathered, for that is what black college football "games" tend to be much more about, family.

This time the fans knew what they had come for—a brush with history. They arrived in stretch limos and expensive cars. This time, there was seating—and a media presence. This time, there was no controversy.

Just fun.

Smith won the game, again, 14–6. Afterward, one Smith player congratulated his Livingstone opponents and friends. Then, remembering the importance of the day, shouted to no one in particular:

"That's two in a row!"

The 1921 Jarvis team, three years before the arrival of Arnett Mumford, who would go on to fame at Southern University. However, during his tenure at Jarvis (1924–1927), the team played only three games per season. Courtesy of Jarvis Christian College

The Lincoln-Howard game was one of the major social events of the season for Washington, D.C.'s black community. This game notice, from the Pittsburgh Courier, was for the opening of Howard's new staduim, of which Courier reporter L. A. Lauter wrote: "For the fashion show—the dazzzling display of fur wrappings—which has come to overshadow the game itself, the setting will not be brilliant. There are no boxes for the social elite." Courtesy of the Pittsburgh Courier

Morris Brown 1923 team. Courtesy of Skip Mason, Digging It Up

Clark versus Atlanta, 1923. Courtesy of Skip Mason, Digging It Up

Livingstone-Smith annual game. Courtesy of the Pittsburgh Courier

Coach Arnett Mumford, second row far right, with his 1926 Jarvis Christian team. Courtesy of Jarvis Christian College

Clark College, circa 1920s. Courtesy of Skip Mason, Digging It Up

33

Langston's 1921 team, of which it was written: "We hope that all the young men will return and bring others to help enrich the wealth of our foot ball [sic] material." Courtesy of Langston University

Big Train' Rolls Last Time

John (Big Train) Moody, 210-
and Morris Brown fullback, winds
his football career on New Year's
ay against Langston University in
ulcan Bowl in Birmingham. It
ay be many a year before another
ch player as Moody trods the
elds of this nation.
Already nominated on a number
all-time All-American teams.

has been national leader in scoring
among Negro elevens for the pa
two years and this will be his thir
time as All-American. He plunge
line, runs end, place kicks, punt
passes and just to get things goin
kicks off. He has averaged 41 yard
per punt for his career and h
scored 375 points. When Morr
Brown throws Moody to the Lio

Fullback John "Big Train" Moody, considered Morris Brown's greatest player. Moody was a three-time All-American. Courtesy of Skip Mason, Digging It Up

Elizabeth City State's football roots included a budding halfback/writer, No. 30 (second from left) named Palmer Haley, shown here, circa 1936–1938. He became much more familiar as Alex Haley, author of Roots *and* The Autobiography of Malcolm X. *Courtesy of Elizabeth City State University*

Livingstone quarterback Alfred "The Great" Tyler, who led the NAIA in passing in 1966 with 2,499 yards and 29 TD passes. Courtesy of Louise Rountree

Southern's 1947 cheering squad. Courtesy of Southern University

The 1958 national champions. Courtesy Prairie View

Several members of Prairie View's 1963 team with wide receiver Otis Taylor, third from right. Courtesy of Prairie View

CHAPTER TWO

The Coaches:
Something From Nothing

Many of the early coaches at black colleges were graduates of Ivy League schools. They played on those teams, then took their experience and wisdom to build black college programs. But, as the sport grew, the schools began producing their own coaches, many of whom played for then coached at their alma maters, or moved on to other black colleges.

The following is a look at a few of the prominent black college football coaches, past, and present.

EARL BANKS
Morgan State

The best way to follow a legend? Become one yourself.

That's what Earl Banks did at Morgan State, when he succeeded Eddie Hurt, who for one stretch of his thirty-one seasons with the Bears had six consecutive undefeated seasons. Hurt's record, from 1929 to 1959, was 173–51–19.

"The greatest coach at Morgan State was Eddie Hurt," Banks said. "You could never do better than him. I didn't try to equalize his record, but when I looked over the situation, I said, "What can I do different to distinguish myself?"

How about winning? That alone separates a lot of coaches, and that was the tack Banks took. From 1960 to 1973, he never had a losing season, finishing his career with the Bears with a 94–30–2 record. Hurt's winning percentage was .711, Banks .746.

Banks had three consecutive winning seasons from 1965 to 1967. That's thirty-two straight wins. That will generally get you noticed, as well. The National Football Foundation in December 1992, made Banks only the second black college coach named to their College Hall of Fame. Florida A&M's Jake Gaither is the other.

"There are a lot of great coaches who won't make the Hall, you have to be lucky," Banks said. "I have to attribute that to Eddie (Robinson). He gave us an opportunity to play them (Grambling), but Eddie would also tell people he was

"Papa Bear," Earl Banks, former Morgan State Bears head coach, was voted into the National Football Foundation and College Hall of Fame in 1922. In fourteen years as a head coach, 90 percent of his players graduated. Courtesy of the National Football Foundation

Facing Page: John Merritt holds his ever-present cigar as jubilant TSU football players carry their coach off the field following Merritt's 200th career victory. Photo by Frank Empson, courtesy of Tennessee State

Houston Markham, Alabama State, led his 1991 team to an 11–0–1 record and the national championship. Courtesy of Alabama State

too busy to do something and say, "Why don't you get a guy like Earl Banks?

"That's how you do it. Get on the banquet circuit and you get to be known."

Banks grew up in Chicago's south side, without a father and one of three kids. He played touch football with a tin can, and one of his classmates at Wendell Phillips High School was Claude "Buddy" Young, the great Illinois running back. Banks became an All-Illinois guard, then an All-American at Iowa, though only 5–7, 220. He played for the New York Yankees in the All-America Football Conference before a knee injury ended his career.

He coached first in Princess Anne, Maryland, at Maryland State before going to Morgan State.

"I used to say, these guys down here at Princess Anne are camping out," Banks said. "We had two showers, thirty players and very few uniforms. I learned to love it. I made a whole lot of comments when I went there. I didn't want to go, but I stayed nine years and cried when I left.

"Morgan was like another world."

At Morgan, "Papa Bear" Banks would produce, among others, tight end Ray Chester, running back John "Frenchy" Fuqua, running back Leroy Kelly, and linebacker Willie Lanier. Banks system was pretty basic.

"Our teams were something like (Vince) Lombardi and Green Bay," Banks said. "Do simple things, but do it well. We made sure we were moving like a machine and made it so there wasn't a whole lot of new learning.

"We just worked on fundamentals and tough football."

And a lot of wins.

"I had my heyday," Banks said. "One reason I retired, was to give someone else an opportunity to enjoy what I did and receive the benefits of being a head coach."

MARINO CASEM

Alcorn State

After graduating from Xavier University in 1956, Marino Casem hadn't given much thought to becoming a coach. He had given thought to living in Mississippi. At the time, neither idea had much appeal.

He had been among the first graduates of a corrective therapy program at the Veterans Administration Hospital in Tuskegee, Alabama, and that seemed an interesting career to pursue. But then, the man now affectionately known as "The Godfather," got an offer he couldn't refuse and it sparked a twenty-six year coaching career that ended after the 1992 season at Southern University.

Casem spent twenty-two years at Alcorn State and his 132–65–8 record makes him the top coach in Braves history. He was named Black College Coach of the Year seven times, and his teams won seven Southwestern Athletic Conference titles. Not bad for a career into which he practically stumbled.

"After Tuskegee, I went back home (Memphis) and was laying around doing nothing, mooching off momma," Casem said. "I was never one to be without a job. My fiancee (Betty McCain) had graduated early, and had a job at Utica (Miss.) Junior College. So, I borrowed my folks car and went down to visit her. The coach there had resigned, and she said 'Why don't you apply?'

"I didn't want to live in Mississippi, but interviewing for the job was an excuse to visit her, so I went back for the interview. I didn't want to go, but I was bored."

He signed on with Utica. So much for corrective therapy. And Betty can never complain about the trials of being a coach's wife because, as Casem fondly reminds her: "You got me into this."

In fact, she kept getting him into coaching. Casem went to the army in 1957 and served with the Fourth Armored Division, Fifteenth Cavalry. He also played and coached a lot of football. However, when he returned from the service, Betty had moved to Alcorn, as secretary to school president J. D. Boyd—the same guy who hired Casem at Utica.

"I came back to Alcorn and there was a position there," Casem said.

Casem, whose parents worked as domestics, had attended St. Augustine's Catholic High School in Memphis. Xavier, in New Orleans, is the only black catholic college in the country.

"I thought I was among the elite and I wondered why my friends were going somewhere else," Casem said. "I was somebody. Back then, we wanted education. We were well-prepped and hungry."

On the field, he learned about discipline from his Xavier coach, Alfred Priestly, then offensive style from E. E. Simmons, at Alcorn.

"He came back from Spring College, where he'd studied Forrest Evachevski and the wing-T," Casem said. "He made me master it, and that was the first controlled, organized offensive system I was forced to learn."

Alcorn had only two players drafted to the NFL before Casem's arrival in 1964, but during his tenure there, fifty-seven players were taken in the NFL draft, including defensive backs Willie Alexander, and Roynell Young, tight end Jimmy Giles, and defensive end Lawrence Pillars. The 1966 team produced a school-record nine players for the 1967 draft.

He was head coach at Southern in 1987 and 1988, both 7–4 finishes, and was interim head coach in 1992. His goal now is to produce as the Jaguars athletic director.

"Coaching is one of the last areas where you can touch kids and it means something," he said. "But the fire has to burn everyday. When it burns only when you stoke it, you've got to look somewhere else. The fire has to burn in your innards, when you're sleeping. My fire is burning now to do something to build this program, to make facilities better than anyone in the (SWAC), or state, and graduate kids at a level no one else is doing. The opportunities are here.

"As a coach, I've had a good run."

Marino Casem, now athletic director at Southern, made his mark as a head coach at Alcorn State, where he was 132–65–8 in twenty-two seasons. On coaching at black colleges, Casem said: "We've done so much with so little for so long, we believe we can do anything with nothing." Courtesy of Alcorn State

ARCHIE COOLEY

Norfolk State

The "Gunslinger" is reloading.

Archie Cooley's trademark cowboy hat is now hanging at Norfolk State, where he's looking to run-and-shoot his way back to a respectable reputation. At Mississippi Valley, Cooley, with quarterback Willie Totten and wide receiver Jerry Rice, made a joke of the NCAA record books with a merciless aerial assault that even his own defensive coaches found anything but funny. They had to practice against it!

Cooley moved on to Arkansas-Pine Bluff, but while his tenure there was also successful, it ended in tumult—140 allegations of impropriety in his program. That left Cooley about as dazed as the defenses his offense routinely shattered.

"I was a victim of success," said Cooley, who coached in 1992 as offensive coordinator at Southern. "I wasn't wrong. I was trying to sell my program. There were no recruiting violations, but clerical errors. I've been through a lot, and I took everything. I was doing too much too quick. They'd had six wins in eight years before I got there. Then we're 7–4, 9–1, and it was time for (me) to go. I don't want the stigma that I've got to cheat to win."

He won at Valley with an offense that redefined "wide open" football. He'd stack four receivers on one side (an idea he got from watching a basketball inbounds play), he used the no-huddle, double slots, sets with no running backs. Mostly, he let Totten throw, and throw, and when all else failed, he threw some more. So much so, the 1984 Devils averaged an NCAA-record 640.1 yards per game (496.8 passing, on 55.8 attempts per game, both also records).

That team also averaged 60.9 points a game. Yep, another NCAA record.

"No one was doing that at the time," Cooley said. "They called it playground ball and said it wouldn't work, that if Cooley succeeds he's a genius, if he fails, they'll run him out. But I never heard a reply when we were successful. In the end, you've got to say, 'Didn't Cooley start the no-huddle? Now, it's the 'hurry-up offense.' (Other teams) would run it for two minutes. We'd run it all game.

"We'd score sixty points a half and do what we wanted to do. In the first game we used it, we beat Kent State, 86–0, and we were in midseason form."

His defensive coaches sought relief.

"They said, 'You're going to have to stop scoring so fast, you're killing the defense.'" Cooley said. "I just told them they'd better get those (boys) in shape."

Cooley grew up in the Laurel, Mississippi, government projects and was recruited to Jackson State by the flamboyant John Merritt, to play fullback and center.

Archie "Gunslinger" Cooley, Norfolk State. Courtesy of Sports View

"[Merritt] was a great talker," Cooley said. "My momma fell in love with him, and he had this big, long, Mercury. Blacks in my town were driving Studebakers and Chevys, but he showed up in this big Mercury, and he was coming to my house. All the boys saw it."

At Jackson State, Cooley played fullback and center and "had the guts to talk back to Merritt. I'd say, 'Let's do this or that.' "

The Gunslinger's guns were drawn, cocked and ready to fire, early. He was hungry for action, hungry for success. Just hungry.

"My days at Jackson State, were the best four years of my life," he said. "There were girls and food. In the projects, we ate when we could. So, when I got to Jackson, I tried to catch up."

He's trying again.

George McElroy was the first black sportswriter at The Houston Post *and has covered black college football for most of his fifty years as a journalist. Currently, he is publisher and editor of the* Houston Informer, *a 100-year old newspaper serving the black community. He wrote the following story on Texas Southern football coach Alexander Durley which appeared in the February 25, 1973 Post.*

When Alexander Durley was a student at Douglass High School in Pittsburg, Texas, he had dreams of becoming an engineer or structural designer. He was an exceptionally good mathematician and an avid reader. But that was back in the late 1920s—during the Great Depression.

Durley never accomplished his goal, but he has spent all of his adult life engineering young men into the ranks of solid citizens by way of the gridiron. He has designed the course of success for scores and scores of his former collegiate footballers. As the portly athletic director at Prairie View A&M College puts it, his life has been a series of doing things he had no intentions of doing.

Durley entered Texas College in Tyler in 1931, two years after he graduated from high school, and graduated with highest honors and a triple major—mathematics, chemistry, and French. The late A. W. Mumford was Durley's coach the three years he played for the Tyler-based Steers. "I played guard for two years and my senior year I was a signal-calling, blocking back," Durley chuckled.

Immediately upon graduation, the scholarly Durley was hired as a mathematics instructor at his alma mater. He also served as an assistant football coach. After one year of teaching and coaching, he returned to his hometown to take over the principalship of the Union Chapel Elementary School. After several verbal clashes with the superintendent of schools about racial injustices, Durley resigned and enrolled at Atlanta University, where he earned a masters degree in mathematics.

He returned to Texas College as head librarian and assistant football

NCC's Herman Riddick who was 112–57–10 with the Eagles from 1945–1964. Here he is pictured with one of his prize pupils, Ernie Barnes, No. 64. Courtesy of Ernie Barnes

As an assistant head coach at Grambling, Doug Porter recruited and coached James Harris, Charlie Joiner, Sammy White, and Doug Williams. In four seasons as head coach (Mississippi Valley, Howard, and Fort Valley), Porter has had only four losing seasons. At Howard (1974–1978), he led the Bisons to a 30–21–2 record and produced the school's first pro player, Herman Redden. Porter has been head coach and athletic director at Fort Valley State since 1979, with only one losing season, 4–7 in 1990, and four Southern Inter-collegiate Athletic Conference titles. For his career, Porter is 137–81–4. He is president of the NCAA's National Athletic Steering Committee. Courtesy of Fort Valley State

coach. In 1942, when the head coach was mustered into the armed forces, Durley was given the head coaching chores. "An injury I received playing football kept me out of the service," he said.

From that point on, Durley became legend in black collegiate football circles. During the quarter century as a coach, his teams won 155 games, lost 80, and tied 13. Durley left Texas College in 1949 to assume the position of head football coach and athletic director at Texas Southern University. He resigned his athletic tasks at TSU in 1964, but remained at the Wheeler Street campus as a math professor.

However, during his absence from the coaching ranks, Durley kept athletically involved as a professional football talent scout. In 1969, he took over the head coach's berth at Prairie View. Two years later, because of illness, Durley abandoned his coaching duties.

"I have been fortunate to have coached many All-Americans," Durley smiled. He was quick to add, "Too many to name. I will just mention a few on that undefeated TSU team in 1952. They were a great group of fellows." Then, the former football mentor began to identify some of his all-time greats: Edward Smith, Adolphus Ford, and Clyde Tillman.

"They made the All-America team that year," Durley said with pride. "But," he said, "you cannot mention the 1952 Tiger team without mentioning Oliver ("Show") Brown and James ("Bo") Humphrey. They were the co-captains and the leaders. Who could mention 1952 without mentioning L. C. Roach, a great receiver and one of the greatest all-purpose players in my memory?"

He said Ed Smith was the type of ball carrier that could do it all, but for natural talent and explosiveness Ernest (Dumas) Lang, Johnny B. Felder and James Gardner were among the best he's had the pleasure of coaching.

Durley also founded the famed TSU Relays.

No, Alexander Durley never became an engineer as he once dreamed, but he is widely known in collegiate football circles as one of the great molders of manhood and citizenship this land of ours has ever known.

JAKE GAITHER

Florida A&M

Jake Gaither has been widely quoted on the qualities he looks for in a football player. "He must be *mo*-bile, *a*-gile, and *hos*-tile," Gaither said.

However, after his most mobile and agile player—Bob Hayes—had sprinted away from the 1964 Tokyo Olympics with two gold medals and the reputation as "the world's fastest human,' Gaither had to deal with a rather hostile Rattler squad. Hayes celebrity was bringing him the expected amount of media attention and there was growing resentment from his teammates.

"The boys got a little jealous," Gaither recalled. "They said (Hayes) had gone Hollywood. I said, 'Tell you how you can get just as much publicity as he gets.' They said, 'How, coach?'

"I said, 'Outrun him.' "

So much for that. Hayes was unequalled as a sprinter, and in coaching, few could run with Gaither, the son of a Memphis preacher man, who taught football and life with equal aplomb. In 1969, when Gaither stepped off the Florida A&M sideline for the last time, he left an enduring legacy that transcended black college arenas. One of the game's premier motivators, his teams won 203 games, losing only 36 times with 4 ties (.844, still the highest winning percentage among all NCAA coaches with over two hundred wins). He collected six black college national championships—three coming in a five-year span (1957–1961). He had twelve one-loss seasons.

Gaither, who would become the first black to serve on the Orange Bowl committee, won his two hundredth game (10–7 over Southern) in 1969 at a time when only three other coaches had reached that plateau: Amos Alonzo Stagg, Jess Neely, and Glen "Pop" Warner. In 1975, Gaither became the only coach in history to receive the "triple crown" of college football coaching awards, being awarded the Amos Alonzo Stagg Award (from the American Football Coaches Association) and the Walter Camp Award (Walter Camp Football Foundation), and by being enshrined in the National Football Foundation Hall of Fame.

In his thirty-six years at FAMU, Gaither also coached track and basketball, was chairman of the health, physical education and recreation department, was director of athletics,

Bill Bell, far left, and Jake Gaither, far right, led Florida A&M to eight of the school's ten national championships. Gaither was an assistant to Bell. Here in 1938, they are pictured with team captains, including All-America center Robert "Pete" Griffin, next to Gaither. Courtesy of Florida A&M University

and taught classes each semester. He sent forty-two players to the NFL, including Hayes, Hewritt Dixon, Willie Galimore, and Ken Riley. Gaither produced thirty-six All-Americans.

"He could sell himself to youngsters," said Woody Hayes, a legend in his own right as former head football coach at Ohio State. "He had a sense of humor with them, a sense of timing, and he was always willing to take the time with them. He didn't just regard them as a number on a jersey, they were human beings and he made the best men out of them, and those players respected him."

To the utmost. Gaither was a devout Christian who did not tolerate swearing, a concept difficult to associate with the macho, rough-and-tumble sport of football, where emotion is everything. But to swear within earshot of Gaither was to incur his wrath. Of course, that was tested on several occasions.

During one practice session, Dixon broke through a massive hole and sprinted off—untouched—on a long-distance scoring run.

"It was like he was shot out of a cannon," recalled former Rattler lineman

Grambling's Eddie Robinson, former New York Jets head coach Weeb Ewbank, and Texas Southern's head coach Rod Paige in 1974. Paige is now Dean of Education at TSU. Courtesy of Texas Southern University

Curtis Miranda, who was so impressed, he just stood there, and shouted, "Damn!" Then, knowing Gaither's distaste for swearing, Miranda feared the worse. "I was ready to pack my bags," he said. "But, he came over to me and said, 'That's okay, baby, I wanted to say something myself.'"

That time, he held his thoughts in check, but Gaither was not shy about expressing his coaching thoughts, and, when he did, a lot of people paid attention. His book, "Split-Line T," was a primer for his innovative offense, called at the time by Georgia Tech's Boddy Dodd, "one of the finest offensive ideas to come along in years." Woody Hayes called Gaither an offensive genius. Using that formation, Gaither's team's went 62–5 and averaged 41.7 points per game over seven years. It became the most popular offensive alignment in the country. The "split-line T" put pressure on the defense, reversing previous theory where the defense dictated what an offense could do.

Gaither's coaching clinics were widely popular, attracting black and white coaches alike. At one of Gaither's clinics, Alabama's Paul "Bear" Bryant questioned Gaither about the "split-line T" and said he doubted it would work in big time football. The exchange between the two great coaches went back and forth. Finally, Gaither, somewhat irritated, said: "I'll tell you what. I'll take my players and beat yours with it and take your players and beat mine with it."

Bryant was convinced.

Gaither, one of five children, had learned early about persuasion and hard work. Growing up, he dug ditches, was a bellhop, shoe shine boy, and coal miner. He learned motivation from his father, a minister in Kentucky and Tennessee (Gaither was born in Memphis), who could preach fire and brimstone, and the power of faith with the best of them.

"Some of the old people would hobble into church on canes, but the old man would get in the pulpit, and he had a tremendous voice," Gaither recalled. "He preached a powerful sermon. The old folks would throw their canes away and shout up and down the aisles. Then, when church was over, they'd hobble out of church. From that, I saw that under the stress of emotion, you can generate a powerful amount of physical strength.

"That's what I tried to transmit to my kids."

While attending Knoxville College he met Sadie, his spouse.

"He was very mischievous and a rebel," said Sadie Gaither. "If there was a strike, he'd be at the head of it. He was a good speaker, debater, and, incidentally, a football player. I never thought he'd coach. He was a good, solid student. I wouldn't say he was a troublemaker, but if there was trouble, he'd be in it."

Sadie taught English and many of her students were Gaither's players.

"She flunked more of my athletes than any other teacher," Gaither said. "But I never spoke to her about it. And the boys would come back, take the class under her again and pass. Then, 15 or 20 years later, they'd come back and thank her for flunking them."

To pass the test as a great team, Gaither told his players, meant giving "blood, sweat and tears," and, there was plenty of that to be spilled in streets as well as on the football field as the civil rights movement picked up steam in the 1960s. Here, the great coach came at odds with many in the black community for his seemingly passive, non-violent stance. Yet years later, after his retirement from coaching he was commended by the State of Florida as a great American who had "broke through racial barriers before it was fashionable."

"Jake epitomized that old Lions' Club toast: 'Not above you, not below you, but with you,'" said former Florida Governor Leroy Collins. "Jake always wanted to work with you. He wasn't thinking in terms of being subordinate or superior to anybody. His whole concept of life, and it came out in his citizenship and coaching, was working together to accomplish better opportunities for all people."

Despite his quiet, dignified manner, the reality of the times did not escape him, and at times, he vented his frustrations. His teams travelled to games by bus and were subject to the senseless rules of racism. There were towns where his team could not find places to stop and eat. There were highway patrolmen in some states who detained the team buses, denying them entrance to the state, because they did not have "proper" licenses—sending the buses back to secure the necessary traveling credentials for that state. Some service stations would not allow the team to use restroom facilities.

"It's hell to be a black man in the Deep South," Gaither said. "We tried to avoid hostility and things that were depressing and humiliating." Unfortunately, neither was in short supply. Yet, there was progress and the onset of integration signalled the beginning of the end for the glory days of black college football programs, and that may have been as troubling to Gaither as the civil unrest. He felt that black high school coaches—especially those who had themselves played at black colleges—had begun turning their backs on black colleges by sending their players to larger, white schools. However, Gaither's ultimate concern seemed more for the players headed for white colleges.

"They (high school coaches) think it's the greatest thing in the world to send their players to a white college," Gaither said. "A boy's education doesn't confine itself to the football field. In order to get a well-rounded education he's got to be integrated into every phase of university life. (At white schools), he's denied all the social activities of the university—can't join the fraternity and can't date the girl in the dormitory. He's forced to go across the railroad tracks for his social life and in most cases, across those tracks is worse than where he came from.

"They complain about discrimination and a lack of social life, but what did they expect? If they want a full university life, why didn't they go to a Negro school? I believe in integration, but as an undergraduate (a black player) is better off at one of our Negro schools.

Langston University coaches, left to right C. Felton "Zip" Gayles, Leroy G. Moore, Toby M. Crisp, William E. Anderson. Courtesy of Langston University

"A lot of these kids want a break because they're black. I don't want a break under those circumstances. I want a break because I can do the job. It's like I tell my players, 'The newspapers may say you're good. The alumni may say you're good. Your high school coach and your poppa and your momma may say you're good, but production is the only language I understand.'"

That production was not limited to the football field. Gaither's greatest joy may have been in seeing his players become productive citizens, though he prepared them for the frustrations in life.

"Your game here," he'd say, "wasn't worth a dime if it doesn't make better men of you. You can't win 'em all. The other guy is working just as hard as you are, and that's what makes the game of football so much like the game of life. Your momma's gonna die, poppa's gonna die, your best friends is going to let you down, sometimes you're going to lose your job and not meet your responsibilities financially. You're going to face constant reversal.

"You must learn to face those reversals, get up off the floor, and come back fighting."

Gaither rarely lost as a coach, even less as a human being. He ran with the best.

He outran most.

W. C. GORDEN

Jackson State

W. C. Gorden is the top coach in Jackson State history. He retired and became the school's athletic director in 1992, after a fifteen-year career in which he was 119–48–5. His teams won five SWAC titles outright and tied for two others. The Tigers won twenty-eight consecutive conference games from 1985 to 1989 and made nine trips to the Division 1-AA playoffs. In 1972, he guided Jackson State's baseball team to a SWAC title.

W. C. Gorden, Jackson State.
Courtesy of Jackson State

WALTER HIGHSMITH

Texas Southern

Walter Highsmith grew up in Lake Wales, Florida, wanting to be a Florida A&M Rattler and play for Jake Gaither. As an offensive lineman and middle linebacker he played on Florida A&M's 1961 national championship team. "I thought black football was *the* football," said Highsmith, now head coach at Texas Southern. "At the 1964 Orange Blossom Classic (FAMU-Grambling), there were 60–70 scouts and the two teams had twenty players drafted or go free agent, including Al Dotson and Bob Hayes. It was just a Mecca. Our kids really don't know what it was like back then. Jake would come in to meet the freshmen and say, 'If you came to Florida A&M for anything other than a degree, get the hell out of here!' " Highsmith stresses that, in black college

Walter Highsmith, Texas Southern.
Courtesy of Texas Southern University

programs, "You have to be in the hotel business and travel business. We may not stay in the Waldorf, but we can be in the nicest Days Inn."

BILLY JOE

Central State University

There's a mild debate as to where the first black college was founded. Was it at Cheney State, Lincoln (Pa.) University, or Central State?

"There's a fine academic tradition here," said Billy Joe, Central State's athletic director and head football coach. "This is the oldest black college owned, operated and founded by blacks. Cheney used to say they were the oldest, but Cheney was not founded by blacks, but by Quakers. Lincoln was the first to offer a degree."

For the record, in 1887, Central State originated as a separate department of Wilberforce University, founded in 1856. Cheney was established in 1837—as a high school, and Lincoln opened for business in 1854. So, who's No. 1?

Central State, at least in football. In twelve seasons with the Marauders, Joe's teams have been named Sheridan Network Black College National Champions five times—all coming in succession beginning in 1986. In that span, Central State was 52–7. In 1992, they finished 12–1 and won the National Association of Intercollegiate Athletics (NAIA) Division 1 national title. That was their second NAIA banner in three years. They won their first in 1990. In between, they played in the 1991 championship game, losing, 19–16, to Central Arkansas on a field goal with eight seconds left in the game.

Entering the 1992 season, the Marauders' .847 winning percentage in the last five years was the NAIA's fourth best, and, over the last ten years, the program's .797 winning percentage was ranked seventh. Joe has taken his teams to the NAIA playoffs in the last six seasons, and prior to that, four straight (1983–1986) in the NCAA's Division II playoffs, losing in the 1983 championship game, after going 10–0 in the regular season.

Billy Joe, Central State. Courtesy of
Central State

Obie O'Neill's 1960 Albany State team was 7–0–2 and unscored on. O'Neill coached the Rams from 1951 to 1967 with only three losing seasons. Courtesy of Albany State

Since 1983, Central State has lost only 9 regular season games. Before Joe's arrival they had suffered four consecutive losing seasons, and had winning records in only three of their previous eighteen seasons.

"We do some quality things here," said Joe, who was an outstanding running back at Villanova and then 1963 AFL Rookie of the Year with the Denver Broncos. "The program had been down, but I've gotten administrative support and I've been able to get the program off the ground. At first, we just wanted to make the program competitive in all games. We had to get out and do some serious recruiting. I tried to sell (recruits) on the opportunity to play right away, and we got a good freshmen group. A lot of them started. Our No. 1 guy was quarterback James Woody."

Joe, who also played with the Buffalo Bills, Miami Dolphins, and New York Jets, has been to two Super Bowls. He was a player on the Jets team which won Super Bowl III, and was running backs coach on the Philadelphia Eagles team which lost to the Raiders in Super Bowl XV. He began coaching in 1972 at Cheney, compiling a 44–25 mark in seven seasons, leaving there to join the Eagles coaching staff until moving to Central State in 1981.

As a player, he had thought being a coach was "the worst thing a person could do. You get fired and there's not a lot of money," he'd thought, but he reconsidered after working as a sales representative for a paper company.

"Coaching became a big deal when I discovered I was not happy working at any other job," said Joe, who grew up as the son of a steel worker in Coatesville, Pennsylvania "And I had had several jobs after retiring from the NFL (in 1969). It just wasn't exciting to go to work. I had played football since Midget League. I was sorry I hadn't gone into coaching right after retirement."

Joe was also named the 1992 Division I National Coach of the Year by the NAIA's Football Coaches Association. Previously, only Prairie View's Billy Nicks (1963) and Florida A&M's Jake Gaither (1969) had won that honor for black college coaches.

"I don't place my self in that category as somebody special or legendary," Joe said. "I didn't know a lot about black college football before Cheney. I was just excited to be a coach, irrespective of the venue, or the institution involved."

WILLIE JEFFRIES
South Carolina State

Having been an assistant coach to Hornsby Howell at North Carolina A&T and Johnny Majors at Pittsburgh, then head coaching jobs at South Carolina State, Wichita State, Howard, and now back at South Carolina State, Willie Jefferies has acquired a learned perspective on what it takes to make an athletic program successful, at any level.

He has achieved success, and is among those at the forefront of the campaign to strengthen black college programs, though improvement there takes on a different face—green. For all the rich tradition at black colleges, most of the institutions suffer from poor facilities, which in turn are a major hindrance in recruiting, not just for athletes, but for boosters as well.

"Black colleges are losing athletes because of facilities," said Jefferies, who from 1979–1983 at Wichita State, was the first black to head a NCAA Division 1-A program. "The problem at historically black colleges now is on the giving end. There's a quest about black people giving back to their institutions. We're not accustomed to giving, and the one's who are able to give, do not. That was a major difference at Wichita. It was major college all the way. We'd get $2 million a year from boosters.

"Here, we get about $20,000 from ours."

Robert Porcher pumped in $10,000 after becoming the Detroit Lions first-round pick in the 1992 NFL draft, and Jefferies said other former Bulldogs such as Harry Carson, Donnie Shell, and Dexter Clinkscale, have maintained strong ties to the school. Regardless of finances, Jefferies has not backed off recruiting top athletes.

"Some say, 'Why waste your time,' " Jefferies said. "But, sometimes, (the athletes) surprise you. Black colleges get about a quarter of the talent pool. Some schools are rich in tradition and the parents wouldn't have it any other way. But we go after the best players. We don't want to ever say we didn't try."

Effort has never been a problem for Jeffries, who played football and baseball for the Bulldogs in the late Fifties, and got a degree in civil engineering, then a masters in guidance and counseling. He came back to the Bulldogs as head coach in 1973.

"I've seen football evolve," said Jefferies, who in his first stint with the Bulldogs produced a 50–13–4 record, the top winning percentage (.746) all-time for the ninety-seven year-old school's history. During that time, the Bulldogs won five Mid-Eastern Athletic Conference titles, with Jefferies gaining four conference Coach of the Year honors. His 1976 team finished 10–1 and was voted Black National Champions. He was the Sheridan Network's National Coach of the Year in 1986. Since his return to Orangeburg, Jeffries is 23–20, with back-to-back 7–4 seasons in 1991 and 1992.

"Wichita State was a good experience," Jeffries said. "I could have had a lot of vertical movement from there. In 1982, I was a finalist for the Army job after we had gone 8–3 and beat Kansas. We played for conference titles three times. We had some pretty good years."

The Shockers were 8–3 in 1982, but the school dropped football in 1986, three years after Jefferies departure.

"I don't regret the move at all," he said. "The people out there were very cordial to me."

Willie Jeffries South Carolina State. Courtesy of South Carolina State

JOHN "BIG JOHN" MERRITT
Tennessee State

"Football gives a lot of black people hope. They want to win and be successful, so when we do win, it gives them a lot of pride. That's important."
—John Merritt

He called it "The Show," and few have directed football games or programs as the stogie-chompin', flamboyant John Merritt, who orchestrated a proud dynasty at Tennessee State. They called him "Big John," but Merritt, a heavyset 6–2, was as big in status as stature.

So revered is Merritt in Nashville they named a street after him. They wrote poems about him, and they still tell stories about him, but they still tell stories about Merritt just about anywhere he's coached. Merritt captivated Tiger fans for twenty-one seasons, winning 172 games (losing only 33, with 7 ties), and producing numerous All-Americans, including defensive ends Ed "Too Tall" Jones, Claude Humphrey, and Richard Dent, and quarterbacks Joe "Jefferson Street" Gilliam, and Eldridge Dickey.

However, his coaching career is understated. Many attribute a lot of his success to his two long-time assistants, defensive coordinator Joe Gilliam, Sr., and offensive wizard Alvin Coleman. But, it was Merritt's show and he led with character.

He *was* a character. Case in point:

As head coach at Jackson State, two of his star players were wide receiver Willie Richardson and quarterback Roy Curry. Richardson was a four-time Pittsburgh *Courier* All-American. One evening, the team was boarding buses for a road game. Earlier in the day, Merritt and warned, "The bus is leaving at 7:30, and I don't care who's not on it!"

As the appointed departure time approached, he noticed neither Richardson nor Curry were aboard. He also suddenly noticed he had forgotten his extra cigars. Merritt returned to his office for the cigars, but, for several minutes, could be seen peering through the drapes. Finally, Richardson and Curry arrived and boarded the bus.

Seconds later, here came Merritt: "Let's go, I don't give a damn who's not here!"

Yeah, let's get this show on the road.

"He was the best coach you'd want to play for," Richardson said. "He could get you to play. He was before his time. He'd come to recruit with a Bible in his hand and tell your mother, 'Every Sunday we'll have him in church.' "

And, then, back on the football field, but momma didn't need to know that. Sundays often found Merritt drilling his squads—particularly on the passing game. Said Richardson: "He'd say, 'I just love to see it in the air.' So, on Sunday, we'd just run pass patterns."

Two of college football's most well known coaches, Tennessee State's John Merritt, left, and Grambling College's Eddie Robinson share a few secrets prior to a Grambling-TSU football game in Nashville. Merritt was 11–9–1 against Robinson. Photo by Ricky Rogers, courtesy of Tennessee State

Hardly the kind of reverence you'd expect from a guy who had considered becoming a man of the cloth. Merritt, the son of a rock mason, grew up in Falmouth, Kentucky, during the Depression. He had thoughts of becoming a doctor or joining the ministry, but the gospel he wound up preaching was far removed from John the Baptist. Merritt had played linebacker and center at Central High School in Louisville.

"The first football game I ever saw, I was in," Merritt said. "My physics teacher my sophomore year was also the assistant football coach. One day he asked me if I'd like to play football. I had filled out to about 185 (pounds) by then. I said, yeah, I'd give it a try. I got beat up pretty bad that first year, because I had no idea what I was doing."

After a stint in the Navy, Merritt attended Kentucky State, playing noseguard and defensive tackle, and graduating in 1950. By then, he had a pretty good idea what was going on, or supposed to go on, in a football game and went into coaching at Versailles High School, while working on a graduate degree at the University of Kentucky.

After only three years at Versailles, Merritt came to the attention of Tellis Ellis, then Jackson State athletic director.

"A cousin recommended him to me," said Ellis, who, at the time, was trying to get the fledgling Jackson State program off the ground. "He had no college experience, but I was told that he was a good speaker. That first year, he was (3–5–1), but he grew into the job. He had a nice gift of gab, and a nice personality. A lot of his success was due to his assistant coaches, but he was a good organizer."

Two of his first three seasons at Jackson were sub .500, including 1–7–1 in 1954, his third season. His remaining eight seasons there were all winners, including 1961's 9–2 team which lost, 14–8, to Florida A&M in the Orange Blossom Classic. By then, his name was made, and Tennessee State president Walter Davis was looking for a coach to bring back the glory days the Tigers had enjoyed under legendary coach Henry Kean. Merritt, despite some problems with the Jackson administration, was content in Mississippi.

After several personal rebukes, Davis sent a team of Tiger representatives to talk with Merritt and let him know he was still the man Davis wanted to lead the program to major college heights. Merritt finally agreed, and off he went to Tennessee, taking Coleman and Gilliam with him.

"It was probably the biggest move in black collegiate athletics," Merritt said. "Never before had an entire coaching staff left a school and gone to another. There were a lot of mixed emotions about us coming to Tennessee State. But, later on . . . we sorta got married to the Tennessee State fans. It's been a good marriage ever since."

In twenty-one years of wedded bliss, Merritt never betrayed the TSU fans. He never had a losing season. His worst was 5–4 in 1975, but he also had five undefeated seasons, and five with only one loss. A list of his former players is a minor Who's Who among black college football and NFL greats. In addition to Jones and Humphrey, he also coached quarterback Joe "747" Adams, defensive back Jimmy Marsalis, tackle Vern Holland, and defensive end Cleveland Elam. Dent was the first black college player to earn Super Bowl Most Valuable Player honors (playing with the Chicago Bears in Super Bowl XX).

Six Tigers were taken in the NFL draft after State finished 10–0–1 in 1965 and was named black college national champions.

"I'd liken him to Al Davis, the way (Merritt) ran the organization," Adams said. "You'd see him two times a week—Monday and Thursday. He'd be out doing PR work, selling (Tennessee State football). He had more whites interested in what we were doing. The governor and the mayor would attend our games.

"But he always amazed us because he knew exactly what your responsibility was and what you were prepared to do that week."

And if you needed some prodding, he could, very smartly, motivate. Former Merritt assistant, Sam Whitmon, relates this tale from 1964: "We were playing a game against Kentucky State, and even though we were supposed to beat them by forty points or more, they were leading at halftime. Well, Coach Merritt is pretty slick, and he decided he was going to impress the players at halftime. Actually, he wanted to get in there and tear somebody up.

Mississippi Valley's Larry Dorsey, wearing a hardhat and ready to go to work. Courtesy of Sports View

"When we all got into the dressing room, Coach Merritt took off his coat, threw it to the ground and said, 'I'll whup anybody in here! I'll whup anybody in the house!'

"There were all these big 6–6, 6–7 boys standing around, but Coach Merritt grabbed assistant coach Alvin Coleman, Jr., a a little 5–11, 145-pounder, and said, 'I'll whup anybody here!' "

The Tigers went back out and whipped the Thorobreds, 31–30, and finished that season, 8–2.

Centennial Boulevard runs through the middle of the Tennessee State campus, and, in 1982, they renamed that street, "John Ayers Merritt Boulevard." A fitting tribute. His spirit ran through the hearts of Tiger fans.

"My staff and I operate like a committee—with me as chairman," he had said, "We feel that we can outwork each and every one of our opponents. We feel that those who start behind will have to run faster to catch up, or pass us. We might get beat a dozen different ways, but one thing they can't beat us at is outworking us. That's our philosophy at Tennessee State.

"We come here to work."

John Ayers Merritt died in December 1983. "The Show" goes on, without the great director.

It'll never be the same.

Cleve Abbott coached Tuskegee's powerful teams of the Twenties winning six national championships. Courtesy of Tuskegee Institute

ARNETT "ACE" MUMFORD

Southern University

Note: Arnett Mumford remains the most revered coach in Southern University history. Born in Buckhannon, West Virginia, Mumford graduated from Wilberforce University, then attained a Master's degree at the University of Southern California. He began his coaching career at Jarvis Christian College in Hawkins, Texas, then at Bishop College in Marshall, Texas, then Texas College in Tyler, Texas. He settled in at Southern University in Baton Rouge, Louisiana in 1936. In his first year with the Jaguars, his team was only 2–5–2. He retired following the 1961 season, having guided the Jags to a 169–57–14 record. Overall, in his thirty-six year career, he was 235–82–25, with eleven Southwestern Athletic Conference (SWAC) titles, six black national championships. His first came in 1935 at Texas College, the remainder at Southern, in 1948–1950, 1954 and 1960). He had four consecutive undefeated seasons (1947–1950), putting together a mark of 42–0–3 in the forty-five games during that span. He produced thirty-five All-Americans at Southern. Mumford died of a heart attack in 1962 at age 64. The following is an excerpt from a story written by Joe Planas for the Baton Rouge Morning Advocate in 1984 on the occasion of Mumford's posthumous induction into the Louisiana Sports Hall of Fame.

When they talk about football, they talk about "The Legend" and they

Long before Clarence "Big House" Gaines became the winningest coach in NCAA basketball history, he was a standout football player at Morgan State. Courtesy of Winston-Salem State

refer to Grambling's Eddie Robinson. They, however, err in number. They should really discuss "The Legends." One is Robinson, the other is Mumford, who elevated Southern football to a plateau where it became the envy of other Southwestern Athletic Conference schools.

"He loved Southern so much," said Mumford's widow, Rose. "And he loved to beat Eddie. Sometimes, I thought he needed to back up, but he never did. He was firm in his opinions. He was a disciplinarian and he was strict. Football was his life, he lived it, he loved it."

Mumford was dynamic. He believed in preparing his kids well for football and for life. He wanted them to be fit for making a contribution to life and consequently, he wanted them to be educated.

"I often thought of my father as the greatest man I ever met," said Emory Hines, former Southern coach and athletic director. "I think Mumford was the second greatest. He was straightforward and let the chips fall wherever they would. If he told you he'd do something, he did it. He didn't care who didn't like what he did, because he always felt he was doing the best for the most number of people involved."

Hines played guard for Mumford at Texas College.

"He taught me the quality of sticking with something until you perfect it," Hines said. "He was a perfectionist. We didn't have lights on the practice field, but Coach Mumford would get the players down by the end of the field near the street lights and work until he got what he wanted.

"Coach Mumford coached 30 or 40 years ahead of his time and his style and techniques were way ahead of his opponents. Some of the things I see in the NFL are things Mumford was doing back in the forties. He was on a par with Bear Bryant (Alabama) and Frank Broyles (Arkansas) and other great coaches of his time. Bryant and Broyles liked Coach Mumford a lot. I can recall Coach Mumford sitting down with them here at Southern moving soda water tops in offensive and defensive patterns until the wee hours of the morning.

"The times sort of victimized him."

When he couldn't officially learn more football at national coaches meetings because of his race, he would visit the hotels where the major coaches were staying for the All-Star Game. There, he would pick some of the finest minds in the country. Glen "Pop" Warner shared a lot of football secrets with Mumford.

"I'm telling you all this," Warner said, "because I know I'll never be playing you."

Halfback Odie Posey, an All-American and great open field runner who played at Southern from 1947 to 1950 saw genius in Mumford.

"His overall knowledge of the game and his ability to get his point over to his players were his strong points," said Posey, a member of the Jags 1948 undefeated National Championship team. "He not only gave you the play, he gave you the reason for calling that specific play. The wide receivers, flankers, men in motion, flanking and flaring, wing-T, and wideouts were all used by Mumford before the other guys got around to using them."

Robinson remembered Mumford. That's not surprising. You remember the lickings and the guys with the paddle.

"I wanted to play for Coach Mumford, but he had quite a few good quarterbacks, so I went to Leland (College)," said Robinson. "I beat him once, that's all. He was one of the finest coaches in football. He was then and would be now. He was a smart man who did a lot of research.

"He was a gentleman and good at everything he touched. If he had lived, he would have been closing in on three hundred victories and I might be still looking for that No. 300. He beat me so much, I thought I had stolen something."

WILLIAM J. "BILLY" NICKS

Prairie View

In 1965, William J. "Billy" Nicks retired as head football coach at Prairie and the program has not been the same since. Once revered, nationally, the Panthers have had twenty losing seasons, including four seasons where they won no games at all.

However, in Nick's tenure, from 1951 to 1965, Prairie View won five national titles.

Said Joe Booker, former Prairie View sports information director: "At that time, they called Prairie View the black Notre Dame, and it was because of Coach Nicks. We didn't have great facilities, but everybody wanted to play for Coach Nicks. We had so much talent. One year he sent a team to two different games on the same day, and we won them both by wide margins."

Nicks won ten SWAC titles and was the conference Coach of the Year four times. His overall record, at Prairie View and Morris Brown, was 184–55–9. In 1941, he guided his alma mater, Morris Brown, to a national title with a 9–0 record. Nicks was NAIA Division 1 Coach of the Year in 1963 and is a member of that organization's Coaches Hall of Fame.

At Prairie View, he also served as professor, head coach for football, basketball, and track.

"He was a classic coach," said Pro Football Hall of Famer Ken Houston, who played for Nicks. "He looked the part and he got his players to play. He didn't play favorites. If we were going on a trip, and there were star players missing when we got ready to leave, he'd say, 'We got eleven? Roll this bus.'"

William J. "Billy" Nicks (second from right) fielded powerful teams at Prairie View. In his twenty-one years with the Panthers, Nicks' teams were 184–55–9 and 11–1 in bowl games. Courtesy of Prairie View

Ken Riley, Florida A&M. Courtesy of Florida A&M

KEN RILEY

Florida A&M

Ken Riley was a scrambling quarterback for Florida A&M but played as a defensive back with the Cincinnati Bengals from 1969 to 1983, finishing with sixty-five career interceptions, fourth-highest in NFL history. He was All-Pro in 1975 and 1976 and took over the head coaching job with the Rattlers in 1986. Since, his record is 43–32–2. He was MEAC Coach of the Year in 1988 and 1990. As a student at FAMU, Riley won the team's scholastic award three years, was named in *Who's Who In Small Colleges* and nominated for a Rhodes Scholarship. "We competed in the classroom like we did on the field," he said. "Everybody wanted to make good grades. I didn't pursue the Rhodes Scholarship, but it was an honor to be nominated."

JOE TAYLOR

Hampton University

In his first year at Hampton University, Joe Taylor turned a 2–9 team from 1991 into a surprising 9–2–1 Central Intercollegiate Athletic Association champion in 1992. How'd he do it?

"It was simple," said Taylor, whose Pirates finished No. 3 in the Sheridan Network Black College Poll and sixth nationally in the NCAA's Division II, both all-time highs for Hampton. "We did a data base for each player in the program. We created a file that started with his grade-point average, then we went from there to his bench press, his vertical leap, his speed in the 40 and so on. We put together a psychological profile on each player so we could find out about his aspirations and goals.

"For instance, if you ask him where he would like to eventually live, and he said in a hut, you knew he had no ambition. If he wanted a home with a big fence around it, that may have indicated that he was insecure. We were able to learn a lot about this team in a short period of time.

"We've stressed winning as people, and tried to create an atmosphere conducive to doing that."

After wading through all those printouts, Taylor (the Sheridan Black Network's 1993 Coach of the Year) and his staff made eleven position changes, with primarily the same players from the 1991 season, and records began to tumble. The Pirates, operating from a Wing-T, set a CIAA single season mark for total offense (5,069 yards) and absolutely shattered the school record for scoring with 469 points, bettering the old mark by 129 points. That averaged to 42.6 points a game.

Running back Carlos Fleeks broke Hampton's season marks for rushing (1,312 yards), scoring (96 points) and touchdowns (16). Sophomore quarterback Matt Montgomery threw for two thousand yards and became the school's all-time leading passer (3,949 yards).

"We had used similar techniques at Virginia Union," said Taylor, who was 60–20–2 at Virginia Union, including a 1986 CIAA title. "Along with the physical body, you need a strong spiritual body. We've been able to put all of these things together and they've worked well for us."

Taylor also instituted mandatory study hall—two hours a day in the library, but also, players and coaches formed a gospel singing group.

"If you find a man's spirit, you'll find him," Taylor said. "The team's grade point averages went up and so did conduct. Everybody noticed a difference in the young men. We teach being a total person.

"My goal is to reach a national championship in an all–black setting, and it's possible, but I can't be the only one to think that. I have to convince guys that it's okay to be good in the 'hood, but don't be afraid to go uptown. And not just in football season, but year round. To think big, there must be power in your thinking.

"Don't let other people decide your world. It'll be too small."

In eleven years at Tennessee State (1944–1954), Henry Kean never had a losing season and was 93–14–3. To his right is assistant coach Lawrence Simmons; left is quarterback Dorsey Sims. "Call me a teacher of football, not a coach," Kean once said. "I'll tell you why. Just look at this list of my boys, the graduates. Many are coaching in high school and college. Others are educators. I like to think that I helped them establish a purpose in life. That's my reward. A teacher has so many advantages a coach doesn't enjoy." Courtesy of Tennessee State

Everson Walls. Courtesy of the Dallas Cowboys

CHAPTER THREE

The Players
Mobile, Agile, and Hostile

There are no black college football players in the College Football Hall of Fame because of the National Football Foundation's requirements for admission (you must have been named to at least one major All-American team, such as the Associated Press team). However, that has no bearing on the numbers of All-American-caliber players who attended black colleges. Their All-America credentials and recognition was, for years, chiefly chronicled by the Pittsburgh *Courier*.

From Ben Stevenson's dominance in the Twenties as an all-around player for Tuskegee, to Steve McNair's wealth of passing ability in the early Nineties, black colleges have produced Super Bowl heroes, Pro Football Hall of Famers, and dozens of other players with legendary status.

Here are a few profiles of some of those players.

Note: The following capsules of early black college players were compiled by Milton Roberts for *Black Sports* magazine in June 1976. Roberts was a black sports historian.

1900–1910

Floyd Wellman Terry (Talladega/Meharry/Howard): "Terrible Terry was, as his nickname describes him, a 'terrible' man on offense. he played for years. He knew every trick about running with the ball. He was a rugged player who could stop, start, spin, dodge, straighten, and had enough breakaway speed to make tacklers look foolish. He was strong, and had tremendous endurance."

1910–1920

Napoleon Rivers, End, Talladega: "Rivers had a fantastic pair of hands and was an excellent receiver. He was smart, efficient and steady on defense."

Franz "Jazz" Byrd, Halfback, Lincoln (Missouri): "Byrd was a lightning-fast, breakaway runner, small but super-quick. 'Jazz' could break a game open before the opponents knew what had happened. His end runs were picture plays. He had an amazing number of touchdown runs to his credit."

Edward L. Dabney, Center, Hampton: "Dabney was ahead of his time in center play. His size was awesome. He was a rugged defender, strong, and with great endurance. He was a leader who commanded great respect. When needed, he was a runner, his bull-like rushes accounted for many first downs and touchdowns."

1 9 2 0 – 1 9 3 0

John T. Williams, End, Langston: "A tall, rangy end, Williams was always alert on defense, a strong runner when needed, and a fine pass receiver. He was a heady player, with special talent as a punter. His kicks were high and long, some of the longest ever seen in a black college game."

Ted Gallion, Tackle, Bluefield Institute: "Gallion was an inspirational player. Often playing without a helmet, his flaming red hair could be seen from afar. He was in the opponent's backfield on defense, covered punts, nailed runners in their tracks. He was difficult to block on defense because of his quickness. On offense he was a machine, mowing down tacklers as he led the interference."

A. Louis Irving, Tackle, Morehouse: "Irving was a natural leader, durable, smart, and steady. His play gave confidence and encouragement to his team-mates, not with words—for he was a strong silent type, but with his solid play. He enjoyed the respect of teammates and opponents alike."

1 9 3 0 – 1 9 4 0

William Coger, Guard, Alabama State: "Coger was a giant with a body of iron. He was slightly older than most of his opponents and teammates, having worked in the mines before college. He was one of the most dependable linemen in the game. He is still remembered today as one of the greatest ever seen in the South."

Joe Kendall, Quarterback, Kentucky State: "Kendall was the first great collegian, black or white, to feature the forward pass, anywhere, anytime, on the field. His unbelievable arm could zing the ball long or short, with amazing accuracy. Receivers often dropped his bullet-like throws. The legendary Sammy Baugh came along a year after 'Tarzan' Kendall to stand the football world on its ear with the same pass barrage that Kendall had utilized before him. Not only could Joe pass, he also could kick for distance with the best punters in the game, and was a constant threat as a safety."

1 9 4 0 – 1 9 4 2

Herb Irawick, Guard, Kentucky State: "Irawick had exceptional size and grace, combined with quickness, and a love for the game. He was a devastating blocker and hole-opener, and a mountain on defense. Probably the best of

the guards in his time, 'Lord Herbie' would also rate with the best today."

John "Big Train" Moody, Fullback, Morris Brown: "Moody was one of the most natural football players ever. He had talent, brains, and the perfect temperament for the gridiron. His physique was perfect for his bull-like rushes, or wild gallops in the open. 'Big Train's' all around ability included unbelievable power for punting (with either foot) and of placekicking. He was the highest scorer in black college history at the time he played. His outstanding play in the service, against recognized stars from the big colleges did more to show the quality of black college football than anything else before."

The Sheridan Black Network Black College Centennial Team. Standing, left to right: Tank Younger, Robert Brazile, David "Deacon" Jones, Larry Little, Lem Barney, Rayfield Wright, Mel Blount, Jackie Slater, Ed "Too Tall" Jones, Art Shell. Sitting, left to right: John Stallworth, Everson Walls, Willie Davis, Willie Lanier, Donnie Shell, L. C. Greenwood. Not pictured: Doug Williams, Jerry Rice, Walter Payton, Ernie Barnes, and Harry Carson. Courtesy of Monroe Fredrick

JOE "747" ADAMS

Quarterback, Tennessee State

Football is ordered chaos and mayhem, sometimes enveloped in the din of several thousand screaming devotees, and a maniac coach or three. Yet, the huddle remains a lone symbol of order and discipline, unquestionably controlled by the quarterback.

That is greatly helped along if the quarterback is a man of some tenure. Given that, imagine Joe Adams surprise when as a freshman, he stepped into this first game huddle for the Tennessee State Tigers and was suggested several plays by various upperclassmen, all at once. Adams promptly put his foot down.

He was promptly punched in the mouth.

"But I let them know, even as a freshman, if I'm the quarterback, I'm the quarterback," Adams said, "I didn't back down."

And from that moment, he didn't back off, not that he ever had. Adams had grown up a rebellious sort in Gulfport, Mississippi. He read a lot about black power, about meditation, about defenses. He wanted identity. He wanted to throw the ball.

"Like most kids, at that time (mid-1970s), I was confused about a lot of things," he said. "It was a time to express myself. I always wanted to be an original."

He certainly was that when it came to throwing a football. After adjusting his mouthpiece, he spent four years with the Tigers, throwing for 8,653 yards and 75 touchdowns. That's more yards and TD's than Eldridge Dickey and Joe Gilliam, Jr., both TSU quarterback greats who preceded Gilliam. Big points for originality there.

His coach was the ever-colorful John Merritt, who once said that Adams could "throw a ball *around* a barn" (picture that!), or that Adams could throw "from goal line to goal line." But the tag that stuck was, "747," because, as then TSU sports information director Kendall Stevens put it, Adams put the ball in the air so much it was like "planes going up and landing."

"I thought (the name) was stupid, at first," Adams said. "I didn't feel comfortable, but I accepted it when my teammates started saying it. It was cool! Then, some guys would just call me '7' or '7–4–7.' "

Merritt, at first, was ready to call "411." Who was this kid? Adams had received recruiting letters from several large colleges (Southern Cal, Michigan, Ohio State) but wanted to attend Jackson State and play for Bob Hill, who liked the passing game. However, Hill was let go and W. C. Gorden, who favored a running game, took over. That left Adams looking for a program where he could pass the ball. He ruled out Grambling.

"They had Doug Williams," Adams said. "I knew I wasn't going there."

So, he would call Merritt three or four times a day.

"He told me, later, that he'd ignore my calls, because he didn't know who I was," Adams said. "My high school coach called Tennessee State in mid-August. I don't think they even knew what position I played. When I got there, I was so far down the totem pole, there were six guys in front of me."

Before Adams had committed to Jackson State (a commitment from which he was released by the NCAA), TSU offensive coordinator Alvin Coleman had made a recruiting visit to Gulfport, and drew up "Pattern 10" for Adams, the Tigers trademark passing attack, which featured five receivers.

"In 'Pattern 10,' we were constantly attacking the middle of the field," Adams said. "If they blitzed us, we'd hurt them, make them pay. It didn't matter what defense they were in, it was the wrong defense."

TSU was 8–1–1 in 1977, Adams freshman year, a season in which the

Tigers beat Williams and Grambling, 26–8, with Adams throwing for two touchdowns. Ironically, though Adams had grown up in a black college football hotbed, he had little knowledge of those schools before heading to Nashville.

"I didn't know there was such a thing as a predominantly black school," he said. "But, I got here and I was so excited. Hey, they've got a hospital here, Meharry Medical School, and most black doctors had gone there. That opened my eyes. I saw that blacks were progressing and there was some heritage."

That heritage would contribute to more confusion. What annoyed Adams most as an athlete was the label: "black quarterback."

"I resented that line, 'you're going to be the next black quarterback' (in the NFL)," said Adams, who was only a twelfth round pick by San Francisco. "But, that's what you were, a black quarterback. I was out-spoken, and I don't think a lot of people were willing to support me. I rubbed people wrong, and I challenged them to accept me for my merits.

"I wanted to prove I could be a black quarterback with a white mentality. I don't think people felt I was serious enough to make the transition. I always knew I had to be three times better, but I felt once I was on the field I could prove myself. But I was drafted so low it confused me. I didn't know what to think, and from that point, I made it worse, and I ran out of ammunition and fight. I was being immature, and it snow-balled.

"They were looking for reasons to cut you, and I gave them what they wanted."

Adams never made it to training camp with the Niners and ended up in Saskatchewan in the Canadian League. There, playing behind John Hufnagle and Joe Barnes, Adams voiced his frustration.

Said Adams: "They sent me home."

He did play on a Grey Cup championship team in Toronto, but wanted to come back to the NFL. No one called. He had subsequent stops in Ottawa and Memphis in the USFL, a franchise that folded. Now, Adams works in Santa Monica, California as a securities banker.

"I have a whole different perspective," he said. "(The pro experiences) jolted me. It used to destroy me, bring tears to my eyes, but now I can deal with it. That burning desire used to control me, now, I control it. At 22, I wasn't allowed to mature. I don't make a million dollars a year, but what I do make, I know I earned it."

ERNIE BARNES

Offensive Line, North Carolina Central

As a kid, playing football was such a remote thought for Ernie Barnes, he went to the extreme of making an agreement with his mother.

"If anybody asked her about me playing football, she was supposed to say, 'No, I don't want my son to play,' " said Barnes, who would grow to 6–2, 263

JOHN ARGUE   ERNIE BARNES   PETER UEBERROTH

After a professional career with San Diego and Denver, Ernie Barnes would get pretty busy with an art career, which, among other accomplishments, included getting named Official Artist of the XXIII Olympiad by the Los Angeles Olympic Organizing Committee, headed by John Argue and Peter Ueberroth.

pounds. "But I was the big guy who was sensitive and who everybody beat up—every single day from first grade through seventh, and I cried all the time and people said I was sensitive. I just grew up big.

"And, big guys, in a black community, are supposed to play sports."

There are circles where sensitivity has no place, where it is not understood or tolerated, especially in the physically imposing. For Barnes, such a place was Durham, North Carolina's mean streets—actually, dirt roads, stained with the sweat of workers who toiled, if at all, at tobacco factories. Blue collars, black skins. A double dose of machismo. Football, and the aura of toughness it generates, was understood. Music lessons? Reading poetry? Art appreciation? Alien concepts for many there, but, here came Barnes, this big kid who had physically grown faster than others in his age group, and who had to take, perhaps, more than his share of the cruelties of the greatest curse of youth— peer pressure.

A rough environment, to be sure. Barnes was in this setting, but certainly not of it. However, he nurtured his sensitivity into a lucrative art career, intertwined with a football career as an offensive lineman at North Carolina Central and in the AFL. He was the official artist for the 1984 Summer Olympic Games in Los Angeles. The paintings used in the television sitcom, *Good Times*, were Barnes' works, and another of his prints (*The Sugar Shack*) was used for the cover of the late Marvin Gaye's album, *I Want You*. Barnes recently finished a mural for Seton Hall University, but was also named, in 1993, to the Sheridan Black Network's All-Time Black College Football Team.

"I haven't thought of myself as an athlete in a long time," said Barnes. "Football prepared me in the sense that the dedication it takes to become an athlete, the perseverance and certain disciplines, carry over to real life. Those are the things I had to feed on to become an artist. I'm still playing the game, I just have a different tool."

He began playing football in high school in part because his mother, who worked as a maid for a wealthy Durham attorney, "reneged" on her agreement, but more because, "I had to."

"My mother was on the PTA and she had this little curly-haired kid that didn't fit in," said Barnes, who attended Durham's Hillside High School and was laughed at when he quit after his first brief attempt at making the football team. That sent him into hiding, literally, backstage in the school auditorium, in bathroom stalls, anywhere, during recess or the lunch hour, where they could not find him, torment him, victimize him. It was in these quiet, lonely places Barnes would pass the time drawing. One day, Tommy Tucker, Hillside's body building instructor, found Barnes, then a ninth-grader, hiding among the stage props.

Tucker, a former Olympic candidate in the javelin, befriended Barnes and put him on a weight program.

"When I went back to school in the tenth grade, nobody recognized me," said Barnes, who played center and eventually became team captain. "I gained respect."

Barnes was drafted out of Central by the Baltimore Colts in 1960, but would retire from the league as a Denver Bronco in 1965, after intermediate stops with the New York Titans and San Diego Chargers.

"My art experience became enriched through my athletic experience," said Barnes, who, in 1966, was named the official artist for the AFL.

Among the star-studded collectors of his works are: Bill Cosby, former Los Angeles Mayor Tom Bradley, Los Angeles Lakers owner Dr. Jerry Buss, Michigan Congressman John Conyers, Julius "Doctor J" Erving, actor Charlton Heston, and Ethel Kennedy.

LEM BARNEY

Defensive Back, Jackson State

In 1977, Lem Barney sang backup on Marvin Gaye's album, "What's Going On?" The album went gold and became a classic, as did Barney's football career.

"Singing on the album was as killing and thrilling as any football game," said Barney, who was joined in the background effort by Detroit Lions teammate Mel Farr.

In his eleven NFL seasons, all with Detroit, Barney thrilled fans and his hard-hitting style killed opponents. The Lions second round draft pick in 1967 intercepted ten passes in his rookie season and was named the league's Defensive Rookie of the Year. He played in seven Pro Bowls and was a 3-time All-Pro. Barney had 56 career interceptions, returning seven for touchdowns. He averaged 25.5 yards on kickoff returns (1 TD), 9.2 yards on punt returns (2 TDs), was inducted into the Pro Football Hall of Fame 1992 and named to the All-Time Black College Football Team in 1993.

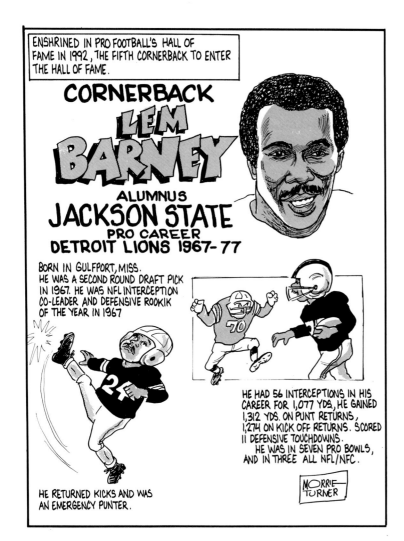

ENSHRINED IN PRO FOOTBALL'S HALL OF FAME IN 1992, THE FIFTH CORNERBACK TO ENTER THE HALL OF FAME.

CORNERBACK
LEM BARNEY
ALUMNUS
JACKSON STATE
PRO CAREER
DETROIT LIONS 1967-77

BORN IN GULFPORT, MISS. HE WAS A SECOND ROUND DRAFT PICK IN 1967. HE WAS NFL INTERCEPTION CO-LEADER AND DEFENSIVE ROOKIK OF THE YEAR IN 1967

HE HAD 56 INTERCEPTIONS IN HIS CAREER FOR 1,077 YDS, HE GAINED 1,312 YDS. ON PUNT RETURNS, 1,274 ON KICK OFF RETURNS. SCORED 11 DEFENSIVE TOUCHDOWNS.
HE WAS IN SEVEN PRO BOWLS, AND IN THREE ALL NFL/NFC.

MORRIE TURNER

HE RETURNED KICKS AND WAS AN EMERGENCY PUNTER.

Barney was a punt-returner par excellence.

"I turned it into a science," said Barney, who missed only eleven games in his pro career. In his first game, he intercepted the first pass thrown his way, by Green Bay's Bart Starr.

"I thought, 'This will be easy,' " Barney said. "Football never was work for me, just a labor of love. There were few guys doing what I could do. I wasn't cocky, but confident. I had the low back pedal, quick chopping feet, and always challenged receivers to turn me. If they couldn't, they couldn't beat me. I was a gambler, defiant, and relentless.

"If I didn't catch it you didn't either. I could take those choppy steps but maintain speed."

In high school in Gulfport, Barney sang in the glee club, but was also a 9.7 sprinter on the track team. He ran 9.5 at Jackson State where he was recruited as a quarterback, but made the squad as a freshman on special teams player. He was small, 185 pounds, but loved contact.

"I was an aggressive hitter," he said. "It was kill or be killed. They had to play me. But there were superb athletes in the SWAC. There were All-Americans stacked on top of each other."

And Jackson State had its share, including Barney, Ben McGee and Verlon Biggs. Barney became one of only ten defensive backs enshrined in the Hall. Four of those players are from Detroit: Barney, Jack Christiansen, Yale Lary, and Dick "Night Train" Lane. Barney is also one the four defensive backs from the SWAC in the Hall. (Southern's Mel Blount, Grambling's Willie Brown, and Prairie View's Ken Houston are the others.)

Yet, for all his decorations, Barney has never won a championship, at any level, and that does not rest easy with him.

"I was All-City, All-State, All-Pro, and Hall of Fame," he said. "But I never had a chance to be recognized as a champion. We were second and third for four years (in the SWAC), but never won against Grambling. I never beat the legend.

"If you find anything in my trophy case with 'Championship' on it, I stole it."

MEL BLOUNT

Defensive Back, Southern University

Being an NFL cornerback is one of the toughest jobs in all of sports. Almost by necessity, they are a cocky breed, bravado in large supply. Heaven help the corner playing with a shred of doubt, a lack of confidence.

Mel Blount entered the league in a third-round draft pick of the Pittsburgh Steelers in 1970 out of Southern University. There, he had been a unanimous All-American pick as a senior, but the complexities of playing NFL defenses saw him struggle in his first two seasons. He didn't feel ready for the league.

"I thought about quitting," he said. "I thought a whole lot about it."

Then, he came back for the 1972 season and defensive backfield coach Bud Carson made Blount a starter.

"I knew Mel was an outstanding prospect and had great ability and speed," Carson said. "He showed all the physical requisites to be as good as anyone in the league."

He would be better than most. From that point, Blount began shaping a Hall of Fame career in which he would miss just one of two hundred regular-season games and one play-off game in fourteen seasons. He played in six AFC title games and four Super Bowls. Blount had at least one interception every season and finished with a club-record 57 for his career.

"I owe it all to Bud Carson," said Blount, who was enshrined in the Pro Football Hall of Fame in 1989, and was named the All-Time Black College Team in 1993. "He gave me something no one else on the staff ever did— he helped me believe in myself."

Blount's play was hard to believe. He has been called the prototype cornerback of his era, but, with 4.5 speed, his era could be now.

"When you create a cornerback, the mold is Mel Blount" said Hall of Fame linebacker Jack Ham, Blount's former teammate. "I never saw a cornerback like him. He was the most incredible athlete I ever saw. With Mel, you could take one wide receiver and just write him off. Mel could handle anybody in the league."

In 1975, Blount was the league's Defensive MVP.

Mel Blount. Courtesy of the Pittsburgh Steelers

Robert Brazile. Courtesy of Jackson State

"If the scales were balanced, there was nobody I couldn't cover," he said. "That's what motivated me, drove me to be as good as I was. I played in front of 50,000 people in the stands and millions on TV. I didn't want to be embarrassed."

Opposing wide receivers had no choice. Blount perfected the "bump and run," so much so the NFL changed its rules limiting down field contact between defender and receiver. You could hear the sigh of partial relief from receivers league wide.

"I didn't want to be second to anyone," Blount said. "I wanted to set the standards for my position."

No doubt there.

***

ROBERT BRAZILE
Linebacker, Jackson State

Love and fear can be powerful motivators and partners. A youthful Robert Brazile learned that growing up in Prichard, Alabama.

"I had one girl friend in high school, and she lived across the graveyard," said Brazile, the former All-American linebacker from Jackson State and All-Pro with the Houston Oilers. "Half the time, I was scared to go through there, and it was a long walk if you went around. I think that had a lot to do with my speed. I'd walk back and forth through that graveyard—at night!

"But I had some cousins who knew I was coming through there. I knew they were there to scare me, and they knew I was scared. So it was like a footrace from one end to the other, and it was a good quarter mile. So I learned to sprint early—fast and low."

Which is how he played football, terrorizing runners and receivers with his hard-hitting style. He loved that.

"I was at Jackson State (as a freshman) with my mouth wide open, asking myself what I'd gotten into," said Brazile, a member of the Black College Football All-Time Team. "It was live. I thought, 'This is the kind of football I want to play.' It was physical and that was my game. If you stood in front of me you'd better be able to hit, because I'll bring it to you.

"On Saturdays, my momma don't mess with me on a football field . . .

Once I buckle up, it's lights out. But I never went on the field with an angry look. I was a smiler and coaches would say, 'This guy's having fun.' I've been described as a young pup in the backyard with an old shoe."

Brazile, a walk-on, was weaned at Jackson State by then defensive coach, W. C. Gorden. Brazile was impressed with Jackson State right away.

"I had gotten some calls from Bear Bryant, but I went to Jackson, not knowing there was a gold mine of talent there," said Brazile. "I never thought I'd be sharing the same halls and so forth with the leading rusher in NFL history (Walter Payton). We were freshmen, and I had walked into a dynasty.

"I had gone there for 'Pro Day,' " he said. "There were all these ex-pros, Lem Barney and people I'd read about, like Tank Younger. It was like a homecoming. They all looked like they cared about themselves, they were about something.

"And I hadn't seen that many black girls all in one spot, at one time."

He immediately got out of his commitment to Troy State (Ala.), and headed for Mississippi and Gorden's tutelage.

"W. C. liked jazz, so he sold me," Brazile said. "I could go by his house, and I think he adopted me more than I adopted him. That meant a lot to me, to be able to go to a coach's house and feel at home. It was family. He'd say, 'What are you doing liking jazz at your age?' But, my dad had played saxophone. So, we'd listen to jazz and talk. He'd put stuff in your brain."

Brazile started as a freshman, in his third game, and would become a two-time All-SWAC selection.

Now, the fear he deals with is not his. He works in Mobile in a "re-track" program for troubled youth in the Mobile public school system.

"It's so fulfilling, one day to another," he said. "It's in-house suspension. Kids come to see me and I give them a second chance. They have one foot in school, the other on the street, and I try to pull them back. Kids have different ways of crying, but they're all crying for attention."

That too is scary, but Brazile can relate.

"I've always seen football as a compass," he said. "I didn't have direction, but I knew if I wanted to get somewhere, football could take me. That was my compass. A compass doesn't tell you where you are or where you're going. It just puts you in the right direction."

And eases the fear.

ROOSEVELT BROWN

Offensive Lineman, Morgan State

Brown, from Charlottesville, Virginia, was a massive tackle (6–3, 255) for the New York Giants, after a career with the Bears in which he was twice named All-American (1951–1951). He was the twenty-seventh pick of the 1953 NFL draft, though only twenty years old. Started as a rookie and played for thirteen seasons. Brown, a classic pass protector,

Roosevelt Brown. Courtesy of the New York Giants

Harry Carson was a fourth-round pick of the New York Giants in 1975. A defensive end at South Carolina State, Carson's No. 75 has been retired.

made the All-NFL team eight consecutive seasons, and played in nine Pro Bowls. In 1956, he was the league's Lineman of the Year. He was inducted into the Pro Football Hall of Fame in 1975.

HARRY CARSON

Defensive End, South Carolina State

Harry Carson starred at South Carolina State, long before he started his impromptu, sideline victory showers for New York Giants head coach Bill Parcells, which have now become a sportswide trend. Carson would sneak up on Parcells, in the waning moments of games and douse the coach with a container of ice water. Carson's playing career, however, was pretty hot. He played defensive end at South Carolina State, but his NFL fame came as a linebacker—and sometimes soap opera actor, for the Giants. During his thirteen-year career Carson played nine Pro Bowls, tying a league record. He was All-NFL eight times. In 1980, he was named the NFC's Linebacker of the Year by the NFL Players Association. At South Carolina State, Carson did not miss a game in his four years, was senior class president, and was Kodak and Associated Press All-American. He was twice named MVP of the Mid-Eastern Athletic Conference. As a senior, he had thirty quarterback sacks.

L. C. GREENWOOD

Defensive End, Arkansas AM&N

It wasn't the gold shoes that made L. C. Greenwood a six-time All-Pro defensive end and integral part of the Pittsburgh Steelers' dominating "Steel Curtain" defense of the Seventies. He was tall, fast, strong, and had incredible range. Unbelievable range.

Unnoticed range.

"I'd be running all over the field making tackles on the other sideline," Greenwood said. "Then I'd hear the public address announcer say, 'Joe Greene on the tackle.' I'd get up and look around, and Joe was nowhere around. I'd tell people that was one of my pet peeves.

"That's my identity."

Or lack thereof. Greenwood, formerly an aspiring pharmacist, found a remedy for the I.D. mix-up in 1974, after fracturing an ankle—his.

"I had to play the next week and the doctor said to try some high-top shoes." Greenwood said. "I didn't like them. The equipment manager bought these plain black high-tops. I said, 'They feel good, but I don't like these ugly shoes.' He said he'd paint them white, but I asked him to paint them gold.

"I had intended to wear them only for that game, but I wore them twice because my ankle was still messed up. Then, I didn't wear them and we lost the game and we got all this fan mail that, 'L. C.'s got to wear the gold shoes, when he does, the Steelers win.' I had worn them for *two* games! So, I started wearing them, and then I got paid to wear them ($500 from Adidas).

"But Nike started rolling the thousands of dollars and I said, 'Okay, that's what I'll do.' Gold shoes. Yeah! They'd send me shoes by the case. I had grass shoes, rain shoes, any kind of sole they had —high-top, three-quarter, low-cuts.

"And after a while, I'd make a tackle and try to fall with my feet in the air. (The shoes) are my claim to fame. I just tried to put some color into the game."

Certainly didn't hurt what turned out to be a golden career. In 1993, Greenwood, who played at Arkansas AM&N, was named to the Sheridan Black Network's Black College Football Centennial Team. He led the Steelers in sacks four times in his thirteen-year career.

He had chosen to play football "as a means to an end," and most of the college scholarship offers he got in 1964 were academic, not athletic.

"I chose Arkansas because of their strong chemistry and biology departments," said Greenwood, the oldest of nine siblings. "The only schools I knew about to attend were black colleges."

He changed majors in sophomore year because "I was thinking of going to med school and competing with kids who had gone to Pittsburgh, Penn State or Notre Dame. I figured I'd better get real, I want to work, I want to have a job."

His degree is in vocational education. His avocation was football.

"I loved the game," said Greenwood, though he was a 6–4, 192-pound "rail" as a defensive end in high school. "I had no anticipation of playing more football. I only played two years in high school. I could run and hit and I didn't mind it.

"I chose football because I could get out some frustrations, and everything just kind of clicked. I never really thought about the NFL until the end of my first training camp with the Steelers. I realized I was faster and quicker— not bigger, but I could play in this league. I never feared anybody."

Bob Hayes, and Hayes with FAMU backfield mate Bob Paremore, an All-American in 1961–1962. Paremore played two seasons with the St. Louis Cardinals. Courtesy of the Pittsburgh Courier

BOB HAYES
Running Back/Receiver, Florida A&M

It was a spring day, 1964, when Jake Gaither answered his phone and heard the voice on the other end speaking with an authoritative Texas drawl. It was Lyndon Johnson. The president was calling and Florida A&M's Rattlers hadn't even won a national championship—yet. They would win their sixth under Gaither in the upcoming football season.

Now, that's foresight! But, Johnson, from a football state, much like Florida, was calling Gaither to talk . . . track(?).

Bob Hayes. Courtesy of the Dallas Cowboys

"We need (Bob) Hayes in the Olympics to represent his country," the president informed. Uncle Sam wanted Bob Hayes for the Summer Olympics, but Poppa Jake had him and, before letting the president know Hayes would indeed be a part of the Olympic effort, the coach wanted to set one thing straight about priorities.

Said Gaither: "Bob Hayes is a football player who just happens to be the world's fastest human."

He was a football player, all right, but man, could he run. Ironically, football purists thought him a track guy, and track folks thought him a football player who ran as though he were "stomping grapes." He proved them both wrong. Hayes won the 100 meters in the 1964 Olympics and anchored the winning 4 x 100m relay team in two performances that were—and, here, no other word will do—unbelievable. He followed that with an NFL career during which he became the Dallas Cowboys all-time leader in touchdown catches (71).

Could he run? Oh, yeah. Could he play football? No question. He introduced the league to speed and sent defensive coordinators scrambling to figure how best to defend him. Nothing really worked. Zones? *See ya!* Bump and run? *Wouldn't wanna be ya!*

Football was Gaither's frame of reference, and, being a Texan, Johnson, deep in his heart, probably understood. Besides, there are football fans who think the only thing worse than track is field, and to have that or anything short of a nuclear holocaust interfere with football season was sacrilegious, and the Olympics would do just that to the beginning of Florida A&M's season. Okay, this didn't happen to be just any lil' ol' track meet. And Bob Hayes did have extraordinarily gifted speed, first noticed when, as an eighth grader, he outran his high school's fastest sprinter, an upperclassman. As a freshman at Florida A&M, he ran 100 yards in 9.3 seconds. At the National AAU championships in 1963 he became the first man to run 9.1 over that distance.

You had visions of him being the first one-man passing combination, Hayes to Hayes. That incredible speed. That's what you remember about Bob Hayes, in a football game or a track meet.

"My track career overshadowed football,' he said, but after what he did at the 1964 Olympics in Tokyo, there would be little wonder about how you would recall his athletic career. His explosive performances in Tokyo, on a cinder track ("It was actually dirt," said Olympic teammate Richard Stebbins, then a freshman at Grambling) in the 100 meters and his anchor leg on the 4 x 100 meter relay lived up to his billing as "Bullet Bob."

Hayes won the 100 gold in then Olympic-record time, 10.0 (tying the world mark), despite running on a damp track and in the chewed-up curb lane. He won by *seven* feet, an unheard of margin. It was a tease. In the relay, where he ran with Paul Drayton, Gerry Ashworth, and Stebbins, the U.S. team trailed by about three meters when Hayes got the baton from Stebbins.

"In the last step before I gave him the baton, I put every effort I could muster in terms of speed," Stebbins said. "If I had to go one more step, I couldn't have given him the baton because he was really moving."

After taking the baton, Hayes made the jump to light speed, caught and dusted *(again!!)* some of the best sprinters in the world, winning by three yards. He had covered the distance in a mind-boggling. *8.4 seconds* (manually)—*8.6* electronically.

In 8.4 seconds?!

Said Hayes: "They talk about (Bob) Beamon, but that was no more incredible than my anchor leg." (Note: Beamon's awesome 29–2 1/2 long jump at the 1968 Olympics in Mexico City stood as the world mark until 1991, when it was bettered by Mike Powell.)

Few can argue Hayes' point.

"After the Olympics, I came back and told my coach: 'I'm not afraid to run against any human being.' " Stebbins said. "But Bob Hayes is in another dimension."

Gaither already knew that, and was happily plotting more ways to use Hayes. Speed was nothing new to the Rattlers, who would finish 9–1 that year, losing only to Southern, 43–20. Florida A&M averaged 33.7 points a game that season.

"We had two relay teams that could have gone national," Hayes said. "And we had nine guys (on the football team) that could run 9.5 or better. They used me in the deep slot, and I averaged ten yards per carry.

"Florida A&M was the only school I wanted to attend. They were scoring about fifty points a game, and Jake was legendary. He won, and he was smart."

And he cared, quite a bit, for Hayes.

"If he had had no mother or father, we (Gaither and wife Sadie) would have adopted him," Gaither said. "That's how much I love him."

Hayes rushed for 1,123 yards (6.9 yards per carry) during his career at FAMU, yet the questions about his football ability lingered. The Cowboys drafted him as a "future" pick in 1963, but he didn't join the team until 1965, But, was he just a trackman in football togs? Many sprinters had entered the league under that guise, none had stuck. Hayes did, for ten years.

Said Hayes. "We changed some minds."

KEN HOUSTON

Defensive Back, Prairie View

Ken Houston could always hit, and he did it so well he played center and defensive tackle at Lufkin's Dunbar High School, though he was only 6–2, 194 pounds. Then, he went to rural Prairie View.

"Those guys were huge," said Houston, who would eventually become a two-time All-American for Billy Nicks' Panthers, but not before a little shuffling. "My first year, there were five teams and 'the others.' I was on 'the

Kenny Houston. Courtesy of Prairie View

I'M WORTH ALL *YOU* GUYS?

80 94

IT MEANS "SUPER STRONG-SAFETY"

SSS

A 8TH ROUND PICK IN 1967 DRAFT, HE WAS TRADED TO THE REDSKINS FOR FIVE PLAYERS IN 1973

HE WAS ACCLAIMED N.F.L.'S PREMIER STRONG SAFETY OF THE 1970's

STRONG SAFETY

ENSHRINED IN THE PRO FOOTBALL HALL OF FAME, 1986

ALUMNUS PRAIRIE VIEW A&M

KEN HOUSTON

HOUSTON OILERS 1967-1972
WASHINGTON REDSKINS 1973-1980

MORRIE TURNER

PLOP!

BORN IN LUFKIN, TEXAS HE WAS NAMED TO TWO AFL ALL STAR GAMES AND 10 PRO BOWLS. HE WAS ALL-PRO, ALL AFC/NFC EIGHT OF NINE YEARS 1971-79

HE INTERCEPTED 49 PASSES FOR 898 YARDS

others.' There were about 140 players there and our starting center was 6–6, 290 pounds. They didn't even know my name.

"It was survival. We dressed outside, and if you got a sprained ankle, they'd give you a salt tablet, or something. And you couldn't run off if you wanted to. Prairie View was so isolated, it was four miles to the nearest bus stop. There was no where to go."

But up, which is the direction Houston took. As remote as Prairie View was, so were Houston's chances, at the time, for a pro football career. Yet, his awkward start with the Panthers was the foundation for a thirteen-year NFL career (six seasons with the Houston Oilers and seven with the Washington Redskins) as a strong safety. In 1986, he was inducted to the Pro Football Hall of Fame. He returned nine interceptions for touchdowns during his career, still a league record.

Houston learned about endurance, about chasing down "receivers" early at Prairie View.

"There were cows near the practice field and, if you made too many mistakes, an assistant coach would pick out one and say, 'Go touch that cow,' " Houston said. "Or, he'd say, 'Run to the Freeze King (a burger place) before I count to ten.' I spent most of the first year chasing cows and going to the Freeze King."

He survived that and, mercifully, was moved to linebacker, where he fared much better. Houston played on the powerful Prairie View teams with Otis Taylor, Seth Cartwright, Jimmy Kearney, Horace Chandler, Richard and Ezell Seals, and Alvin Reed.

"The (SWAC) games were tough," said Houston, who played on two SWAC title teams. "The referees would be cheating. You'd have to score 100 points to beat somebody 7–6."

Houston also played on two of Nick's national championship teams (1963 and 1964).

"Coach Nicks was a tremendous person for conditioning," Houston said. "We didn't have weights, but we'd get it done through natural exercises. We'd run three miles before and after practice. His whole things was, when you look across that line, a guy might be a better player, but he wasn't better conditioned.

"We were like a machine. We could have played two games the same night. You never worried about getting tired."

Houston was a ninth-round pick in the 1967 draft by the Houston Oilers, who rewarded him with a $6,000 bonus, a $13,000 contract and a new Dodge Polara.

"I was a project," said Houston, who did not move to safety until his senior year at Prairie View. "I could cover, but I'd never covered wide receivers. But they (Oilers) knew I would hit. I'd kill people. I was fearless."

If it hadn't been known, that ability was showcased in 1973 when the Dallas Cowboys and Washington Redskins renewed their biannual feud, before Howard Cosell and everybody. In that Monday night game, Dallas was driving toward a game-tying touchdown when Houston delivered "The Hit," stopping Cowboys fullback Walt Garrison, one-on-one, on a pass play at the goal line preserving a 14–7 Redskins victory.

"I have a lot to thank (Cosell) for, he made that play, because he talked about it so much," Houston said. "It was a dramatic game, and Walt was a great player. I don't think the hit was that great, but it was significant because of the situation. I thought I'd intercept, but I realized I'd overrun the play. Walt jumped up, and all I could do was just kind of stop. I caught him, and it seemed everybody was watching that one play, like time was standing still.

"That one tackle did more for my career."

DAVID "DEACON" JONES

Defensive End, South Carolina State/Mississippi Vocational

You're a rookie in the National Football League, and you're about to play your first game in the famed Coliseum, and lining up in front of you is a man you've only heard about. Now, you're about to hear from him.

He offers this ominous greeting: "Boy, yo' momma know you out here?"

Then, he offers his right hand, violently, to the side of your helmet, and as the sound reverberates you wonder why mom never told you there'd be days like this, opponents like this. But she couldn't have known, there was never anyone like Deacon Jones. His speed and agility revolutionized defensive end play. To say he was ahead of his time is gross understatement.

Jones invented the term "sack," because "I hated all offensive linemen and quarterbacks," he said. "I wanted to put them in a bag and beat it with a baseball bat. That's a sack."

Anybody got a problem with that?

They didn't keep sack totals during his playing days, but a 1992 CBS Sports study documented Jones total at 180.5. New York Giants linebacker Lawrence Taylor is the acknowledged all-time leader in that department with *only* 136.5. Jones is currently an advisor to Larry Ryckman, owner of the CFL Calgory Stampeders, and was enshrined into the Pro Football Hall of Fame in 1980. He was All-Pro from 1965 to 1970, and the league's Defensive Player of the Year for 1967–1968. He was named the Los Angeles Rams

ENSHRINED IN PRO FOOTBALL'S HALL OF FAME IN 1980

BY MORRIE TURNER

HE WAS AN OBSCURE 14th ROUND DRAFT PICK IN 1961

WE PICK "WHAT'S HIS NAME"!

HE WAS AMONG THE FIRST OF THE FAST, TOUGH, MOBILE DEFENSIVE LINEMEN

OOF!

HE WAS NOTED FOR HIS CLEAN BUT HARD-HITTING PLAYS, SPECIALIZING IN QUARTERBACK 'SACKS', A TERM HE INVENTED.

PRO CAREER
LOS ANGELES RAMS 1961-71
SAN DIEGO CHARGERS 1972-73
WASHINGTON REDSKINS 1974

DAVID (DEACON) JONES
ALUMNUS
SOUTH CAROLINA STATE
MISSISSIPPI VOCATIONAL

CLICK!

1967

BORN IN EATONVILLE, FLA. HE WAS DEFENSIVE PLAYER OF THE YEAR, 1967. HE PLAYED EIGHT PRO BOWLS.

"Most Valuable Player of All Time."

"The Secretary of Defense" rushed passers with a ferocity fueled by, more than anything, the rage in his heart against a system that down-graded him because of his color, a system he has never fully begun to understand. He is certainly not alone in that, but what set Jones apart, perhaps, was his ability to channel that anger toward a positive end.

"I didn't have a good training background, but I had a hall of fame attitude and drive that I haven't had since," he said. "My whole focus was defeating what the white man had said against us. It was not the way to go. Anger? Yes. It took me years to get that out, and I still don't understand (racism). Why do you hate me? No black man can answer that.

"But I had the will to succeed and anything that got in my way got hurt."

Jones came out of Eatonville, Florida, wanting, like most college-bound black football players in those days, to play for Jake Gaither at Florida A&M, but "Jake didn't think I was good enough. So, in 1957, Jones went to South Carolina State, played a season, but then sat out a season. The social climate—lunch counter demonstrations, sit-ins, etc.—had worn him down.

"It got too political and I had to leave the movement," he said. "I was too tired. You got spit on and all that, and I wondered, 'What am I living for?'"

He moved over to Mississippi Vocational. Compared to what he was about to experience, the days in South Carolina were harmless fun. Jones and a friend set out for Mississippi in a near-brakeless 1952 Plymouth station wagon.

"It was out of the frying pan, into the fire," Jones said. "They (police) stopped us going into Itta Bena."

And that harassment would continue, though Jones was well into doing a lot of that himself, on the field. He would have had to sit out a year, after transferring, but that had no appeal to him. So, he played under an assumed name: David Collier. No one blew the whistle. He played defensive tackle and receiver, though other accounts put him at offensive tackle. They'd run the tackle eligible play and throw him the ball.

"We played Florida A&M," Jones said, "and I (caught a pass and) dusted this defensive back for 66 yards on the first play."

Sweet revenge.

"I called Deacon 'Manster'—half man, half monster," said Bob Hayes, who played for the Rattlers and against Jones. "Everybody else would shower after a game, he'd just rip his uniform off and lick himself clean. That's how bad he was."

The Itta Bena sheriff and his deputies came to get Jones and a buddy late one spring night. They had not liked Jones radical attitude.

"I told my friend, 'I know the way to the bus station and you know the way to the bus station,' " Jones said. "If there's any deviation from that route I'm going for it. They drove us to the bus station."

The trip was without incident. Jones, back in Florida, worked serving at parties, but also, to keep in shape, he ran in heavy combat boots along the beach.

"I ran a 4.5 forty—at 260 pounds!" he said.

Then, he got a break, drafted in the fourteenth round by the Los Angeles Rams.

"I was in New Orleans visiting my brother and a scout for the Rams was there," Jones said. "He called me up and said, 'I've got a 45-minute layover, meet me at the airport.' I got out there and was as lean as a pin. I had my best stuff on. They must have known I was a desperate man. I thought the airline ticket was the bonus. I didn't know they gave bonuses! He said, 'We'll take a risk with you. I'll make you the highest paid player on the team, but don't tell anybody.' I said, 'Yes, I won't tell anyone.' He gave me $7,500."

"I was a rich brother! It was 1961. I used $2,000 to buy my mother a house and I'm thinking I'm on the team."

Well, not quite. The contract was valid only if he made the team. Like that would be a problem.

"What separated me from the other players was that I was physically and mentally ready," Jones said. "They're (NFL) constantly looking for opportunities to cut you. And as a black man, you're always proving yourself. They keep that doubt in the back of your mind, that you're not as good. You can't let your guard down.

"But I came out of a hellhole and I intended to cover that up before I died."

This is where the legend begins.

"I played crazy," he said. "I had to get their attention. I had to make noise. So, I'd jump on the badest sucker out there."

The famed head slap was born in practice sessions.

"In developing my game with the Rams, I started working on it against offensive tackle Charlie Cowan," Jones said. "It mixed well with my speed and quickness. It was a straight right, eighty times a game. After that, you forget pass protection. It was just a quick move off the ball."

Cowan retaliated by sharpening the point on his helmet where the facemask was attached, but that did not stop Jones. He continued to beat on Cowan's hat until his hand bled, but he'd come back the next day and do it some more.

Finally, he'd blunted the point. Jones still has a scar in the palm on his hand from the battering, and he proudly proclaims, "I knocked the edge off."

Through the years, he has maintained his emotional edge and when he speaks you can still feel the rage, though now it is almost a plea, for men to do right by each other, for black men—especially young black men—to stand tall. Deacon Jones can still head slap with the best of them. He delivers it verbally, but with the same force.

"I was a terrible student," said Jones, still a year from getting his undergraduate degree. "But I was so wrapped up in fighting the system, I forgot where I came from, and I apologize. I didn't fully understand (college). The one thing I resisted was education. I saw no movement. The same minds with education came back to menial jobs. Education meant nothing to me. But I got a Ph.D. in life. I was forced to get my education on the job. I'm aggressive. Yes, I made a mistake, but I found another way. I have walked with presidents and top businessmen and I challenge them."

He is a highly-sought and highly-paid motivational speaker. And, many times, his subject is the plight of black colleges.

"I don't like to get in the way of anyone else's choice," he said. "They're an absolute necessity and we don't get enough of us who support (them). But I have to figure that if I had had a choice, I would have gone to a Notre Dame. That was one of the things that (ticked) me off, walking by schools that had better equipment, better facilities, and I couldn't go to them. If I had had a choice, I sure would like to think I would have taken my shot at those turkeys."

Talk about waking the echoes.

ED "TOO TALL" JONES

Defensive End, Tennessee State

On the occasion of Ed Jones retirement from football in 1990, veteran Dallas *Times-Herald* columnist Frank Luksa wrote: "No one ever played as many (games) for the Cowboys. Few played better . . . We'll not see him again in a Cowboys uniform. No. 72 is 39 . . . He belongs to an era which has come and gone."

The "Too Tall" era in Dallas Cowboys' lore slowly began in 1974 when the team took the still raw but physically well-developed defensive end out of Tennessee State as the first overall pick in the NFL draft. Previously, Grambling's Buck Buchanan (Kansas City, 1963) had been the only black college player taken in that draft position.

Buchanan was a solid pick. Jones was not, having been recruited by over fifty colleges to play basketball out of Merry, Tennessee. He didn't play football as a high school senior.

"Ed was far and away our top-rated guy that year," said Gil Brandt, former

Cowboys director for player personnel. "We knew that he dominated that level (black colleges). But is he going to be as dominating in the NFL? It turned out the answer was 'yes.'"

Not right away, but after taking 1979 off to pursue a six-bout boxing career (6–0, 5 KO's), Jones came back and, yes, few played better. In his remaining ten seasons, Jones went to the Pro Bowl three times and would retire having played more games (224) than any player in Cowboys history. He also set a team-record with his 203 consecutive starts. In 1993, he was named to the All-Time Black College Football Team.

"I said that I'd like to play at least fifteen years," Jones said of a conversation he'd had with some friends early in his career. "Why I said fifteen I don't know, because at the time the average player was playing about five years."

Jones was nowhere near average and his durability became legend. "He takes shots on his knees, that would knock other players out for two weeks," said Dallas teammate Jim Jeffcoat. "He doesn't even tape his hands or his ankles. He was gifted with an unusual body."

That is what struck John Merritt when he first encountered Jones at Tennessee State. "One look at Ed, and we knew he fit the yard-stick we've always wanted our athletes to fit," said Merritt, who hadn't recruited Jones either. "He had the long muscles, he was tall, slightly pigeon-toed, had a great length from his crotch to his feet and had a fairly short body. We've always felt that a build like that made for good athletes.

"And to top it off, he had a square chin, that meant he would be a good hitter."

Jones had 105 career sacks, but his biggest hits came in boxing rings in a fight career that was not critically acclaimed. Why he took the year off for boxing remains a mystery.

"That's something I haven't told nobody why," Jones said. "I'll decide when it's time to tell. Tell you what, every (reason) I've heard, they haven't come close. I got out for reasons I had no control of. But when I left football, I didn't think I'd ever play again."

He did, and the benefits were not limited to himself.

"We had probably one of the most storied careers that two defensive ends could have," said Harvey Martin, Jones' defensive end mate with Dal-

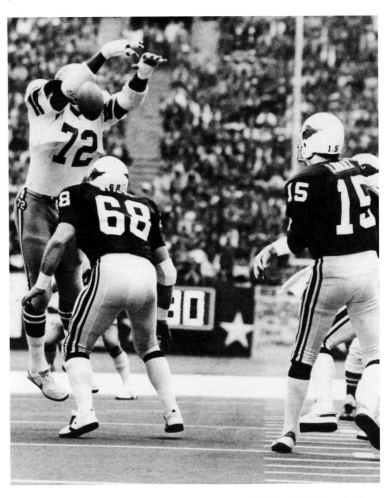

Tennessee State's Ed "Too Tall" Jones. Said Joe Gilliam, Sr., famed Tigers' defensive coordinator: "When he's rushing, we don't need to defend half the field. The quarterback simply can't see over him."

las and the team's all-time sack leader who retired in 1983. "Ed was more power. He withstood the brunt of the opposition because most teams are right-handed. I was the guy with the flash, flying around the end. We complemented one another.

"Ed Jones made Harvey Martin. If I didn't have Ed Jones to push me, I'd never have come alive."

Jones played on the Cowboys Super Bowl teams in 1975, 1977, and 1978. He made it a lively era.

WILLIE LANIER

Linebacker, Morgan State

Willie Lanier was going to Morgan State, and that was all there was to that. It didn't matter that he already had a full-scholarship offer from Virginia State, just south of Lanier's hometown, Richmond, Virginia. It didn't matter, either, that Earl Banks had no idea who Lanier was.

In mid-July 1963, Lanier was on the phone to the Morgan State coach, making arrangements to move to Baltimore.

"(Banks) said, 'Son, I've never scouted you, I don't have any film on you, and we don't have any more scholarships," Lanier said. "I told him, 'You need to understand, I didn't ask you for a scholarship. I said I wanted to attend Morgan State University.' "

Lanier asked for whatever financial aid he could get (work study, student loans).

"I've got to have that," he told Banks, adding, "Whatever deficit is there, I'll figure out some way to cover it. But, I want you to understand that the second semester will take care of itself from a scholarship standpoint, because I come to perform. I don't have any question about that at all."

Neither did anyone else, once they got a look at Lanier. Imagine Banks surprise, when he picked up Lanier at the bus station and feasted on the compact but imposing Lanier physique. He was enroute from 210 pounds as a high school senior to 245 for his freshman year at Morgan.

"Obviously, he saw a guy that was a little bit larger than he might have thought," Lanier said. "I did extremely well on the entrance exam and, from that point, it really became history."

Lanier had decided on Morgan because he felt the racial atmosphere in Richmond, at the time, would not allow him the business opportunities he desired after college graduation. And he did get a business degree and is working with a securities firm in Richmond.

"I remember when I left Richmond, my father told me not to be upset if I didn't play much (at Morgan)," said Lanier, who as a 155-pound 11th-grader, was cut from his high school team. "(Morgan) had a great team, and freshmen didn't play much. I told him he didn't understand. That I don't sit on anybody's bench, I don't ride the pine. Case closed. I don't remember anything about the first practices, but I started immediately. I don't know how my mindset was created, but I remember going through high school and my vision was, 'I believe I can do it.'

"I was on a mission to get something done, and it was not important to make it to the pros. My major focus was, in four years, to be employed."

He got a pretty good job when the Kansas City Chiefs chose him in the second round of the 1967 draft, as a middle linebacker. No blacks had ever played that position in the league. Lanier played eleven seasons. He intercepted 27 passes, recovered 13 fumbles and was All-AFL in 1969, All-AFC in 1970, 1972, 1973, All-Pro in 1971, 1974, 1975. He played in two AFL All-Star games, five Pro Bowls (Defensive MVP in 1971 game), and was inducted to the Pro Football Hall of Fame in 1986.

"It was a responsibility with opportunities, and that forced me to play what I consider an extremely high-quality game," Lanier said of playing in the middle. "In fact, if my memory serves me right, I know I didn't have any more than four or five penalties in eleven years."

That could be attributed to, perhaps his greatest edge, mental preparation. To make up for size or whatever physical shortcomings he might have had, he relied on mechanics, efficiency of motion, even when it came to his crushing tackles.

"In football, I had to understand one thing—angles," he said. "So, you can be faster, but if I adjust my angle of intercept I can make the play. It made sense."

So who needs film? "I don't need to study you" Lanier said. "I don't want to be bound by what you've done. I want to only be responsive to what you will do at that moment. I hated films, because that was history. You have to hurt me, once, in the game we're playing and then I will make an immediate adjustment. My point is that if I'm bound by the system and I'm not able to use my unique talents, then you've wasted me. If you pay me to perform, you pay me to make decisions."

And that's all there is to that.

LINEBACKER

BORN IN CLOVER, V.A. HE WAS THE CHIEF'S NO. 2 PICK IN THE 1967 DRAFT.

KANSAS CITY TAKES LANIER

MORGAN STATE

ENSHRINED IN PRO FOOTBALL HALL OF FAME 1986

BY MORRIE TURNER

WILLIE LANIER

ALUMNUS
MORGAN STATE

PRO CAREER
KANSAS CITY CHIEFS
1867-1977

VERY DURABLE, HE MISSED ONLY ONE GAME IN HIS LAST 10 YEARS

I'M TAKING THIS PASS

I'VE BEEN RUN-OVER BY A TRUCK NAMED "CONTACT"

HE WAS NICKNAMED "CONTACT" BECAUSE OF HIS FEROCIOUS TACKLING

HE INTERCEPTED 27 PASSES FOR 440 YARDS. HE PLAYED IN TWO AFL ALL-STAR GAMES, SIX AFC-NFC PRO BOWLS AND WAS DEFENSIVE STAR IN SUPER BOWL IV

LEO LEWIS
Running Back, Lincoln (Mo.) University

After being named an All-City running back for two years at St. Paul's (Minn.) Marshall High School, Leo Lewis wanted to go to Lincoln (Mo.) University to play football, but there were pressing obligations on the home front.

"My dad had died, and there were 11 of us kids," said Lewis, only 16 when he graduated high school and, initially, turned down Head Coach Dwight Reed's scholarship offer. "I thought it would be best to stay and help mother. So, I got a job as a supply manager for a drug store for a year. I got itchy pants the year I laid out, and mother said, 'I'd rather see you go to school, if you get the opportunity. Go, we'll make it.' "

He got the opportunity—again, when Reed returned the next year, and Lewis accompanied Reed back to Missouri.

"That first year, I got homesick," Lewis said. "My mother said, 'If you come back home, I'll shut the door on you. You stay in school and make something of yourself.' "

With those marching orders, Lewis, only 5–10, set about becoming a three-time Pittsburgh Courier All-American. In his four years at Lincoln, he gained 4,457 (8.5 yards per carry), scored 384 points and 64 touchdowns. All are still school records. Lewis was hailed, in some corners, as a better runner than Florida A&M's Willie Galimore.

They called Lewis, a 9.7 sprinter, the "Jet Express," and the "Locomotive."

"I had a loping style, and could change directions quickly," said Lewis, now 60, and assistant athletic director at Lincoln. "I could out run people, but they also used to say I hated to run out of bounds. I liked to punish people. I'd turn my back into them as they were coming, then break a crease. I had a lot of long runs, and I really liked kickoff returns."

Lewis had a Hall of Fame career in the Canadian Football League. In that league, he was a six-time All-Star, and rushed for 8,861 yards (averaging 6.6 yards per rush). He also returned kick-offs for 5,444 yards (29.1 average). He played on four Grey Cup Championship teams.

LARRY LITTLE
Offensive Guard, Bethune-Cookman

The first week Larry Little got to Bethune-Cookman as an undersized tackle, in 1963, the team practiced in the school gym for a week, running drills. Little had not been highly recruited and had to get someone's attention.

"They first noticed me in the gym," Little said. "I was playing guard and I was pulling around on the play and there was a guy holding a dummy. I hit the dummy and him so hard, I knocked him down some stairs. Back then, if you weren't good enough, they would cut you, just like in the pros. But, before we put on pads, they had me taking a picture for the newspaper, so I knew I was going to make the team. I started, on offense and defense, for four years."

He left Bethune-Cookman with a sociology degree and a yearn to play professional football. When he first got to the San Diego Chargers as a free-agent, the team practiced for a week before the rookie draft picks came in. Little had not been highly-sought by the pros. If he was going to make the squad, he had to get someone's attention, again.

"I had to play crazy," Little said. "I'd start fighting after the coach blew the whistle, just to be noticed."

Soon, you couldn't miss him, he wouldn't let you, and the need to duke it out became overshadowed by his extraordinary ability to pull out, and make a smooth path for running backs such as Larry Csonka, Mercury Morris, and Jim Kiick, who Little blocked for with Don Shula's powerful Miami Dolphins teams of the Seventies. Little played his first pro season with the Chargers before moving to stardom with the Dolphins, where he became one of the pre-eminent pulling guards in the history of the game.

Little was All-Pro for six consecutive seasons, played four-times in the Pro Bowl, and three times in the Super Bowl (two championships). He was inducted to Pro Football's Hall of Fame in 1993.

"I had great speed for my size," Little said. "A lot of people identified me as a pulling guard, but I was just as good inside at straight-ahead blocking. But that (label) didn't bother me. Now, you don't see teams doing what we did back then. What you have in the NFL now, with all the rules, is just a bunch of pushes.

"They don't really come off the ball and block anymore."

After his NFL career, Little coached his alma mater to two Mid-Eastern Athletic Conference titles (1984, 1988) and was MEAC Coach of the Year in 1984. One of his former players is Houston Oilers' defensive lineman Lee Williams. Little also had an aborted stint as head coach of the Ohio Glory of the World League of American Football.

"I love working with people," said Little, who also, for a time, ran a boys camp in Florida for underprivileged kids. "I love the camaraderie. As a player, I was a student of the game and I tried to learn as much as I could about the total game, as I did about my position."

With the Dolphins, his position coaches were former NFL greats Monte Clark, then John Sandusky.

Said Little: "If I couldn't learn from them, I had no business being in the business."

CURTIS MIRANDA
Offensive Lineman, Florida A&M

"As a kid, there was no other dream than playing at Florida A&M," said Miranda, a three-time All-American (1959, 1960, 1961) offensive lineman from Gainesville, Fla. "You wanted to see them play and we'd go to the games in Tallahassee. (Jake Gaither) came to my high school, and it was just a thrill. There was no other (school in my mind." Miranda, a 6–2, 235, was fast, strong, and quick, and needed most of all of those abilities to block for the varying styles of Rattler running backs, including Bob Hayes, Hewritt Dixon, Clarence Childs, and Bob Paremore. "We had so many great players," Miranda said. "We traveled four-deep. And there were so many guys who could run fast. If you didn't get out of the way, they'd run up your back. Dixon was straight ahead, hard, low, and fast. He was a guy you just didn't want to hit all day long. I did everything I could to get out of his way. But if you gave Bob a bump block, he was gone." Miranda played on two national championship teams (1959, 1960) at Florida A&M. "I don't think any school in the nation could have stayed in the park with us at that time. Most times guys just wondered how bad we'd beat a team."

WALTER PAYTON
Running Back, Jackson State

There was a cedar tree outside Walter Payton's dorm window at Jackson State and the future Pro Football Hall of Famer would put it to good use.

"He loved climbing down the tree more than walking down the stairs— and he would climb up the tree to get back in," said Robert Brazile, Payton's friend and former college teammate. "He was just . . . different, not strange, just different."

Payton climbed that tree, then he climbed into the record books, first at Jackson State, where he rushed for 3,563 yards (over 6 yards a carry) and scored an NCAA-record 66 touchdowns and 464 points and was a serious Heisman Trophy candidate, finishing fourth in 1975 (Ohio State's Archie Griffin won it). The Chicago Bears took Payton in the first round, the fourth player overall, and he began his climb to the Pro Football Hall of Fame, where he was enshrined in 1992.

Payton (5–10, 202) was NFC Player of the Year in only his second pro season, and NFL Player of the Year in 1977 and 1985. He played in 190 games, missing only one. He was All-Pro seven times and rushed for over 1,000 yards in 10 of his 13 seasons. For that, Payton not only is atop the NFL rushing tree, he owns the thing, finishing his career with an all-time best 16,726 yards.

"I never backed off a guy," said Payton, who grew up in Columbia, Mississippi. "There's always a time when you gotta put your head down and bang a guy in the gut. But speed and moves are my biggest assets."

That's only as a runner. Payton, at Jackson State and with the Bears, was also versatile. In college, he not only ran the ball, but also punted and place-kicked, he returned kicks, and he threw four touchdown passes. With Chicago, he threw eight TD passes, and was the league's KO return leader as a rookie. He had 21,803 combined net yards, and holds eight all-time NFL offensive records.

You'd need a sizeable tree to build a box to hold his records. Black college football had not seen such an all-around player since Tuskegee's Ben Stevenson. There have been few in the NFL with Payton's ability. Even his peers marveled.

"Earl (Campbell) was always inquisitive about the type of player Walter was," said Brazile, who was a teammate of Campbell's with the Houston Oilers. "He'd say, 'Dude, is Walter that good?' I'd say, 'Yeah. Walter can do anything he wants to do.' If Coach (Bob) Hill wanted us to run five miles, Walter wanted to run fifteen. If Walter felt he hadn't accomplished something in practice, we didn't leave the field.

"But, he was so inspiring with what he did on the field, he made me a better linebacker, just to be able to say to him, 'I got you.' I had to draw first blood from Walter, then they'd blow the whistle—it was time to go in!

"We (Oilers) played Chicago and he was averaging two hundred yards a game. He got thirty-five yards against us. After the game, he wouldn't speak to me. He was upset with Walter, not with me. He felt he'd let himself down. He knew if he came my way, bang-bang. Same thing, if I blinked an eye, Walter was going to score. That's how he was."

He was a lock for the Black College Football All-Time Team, announced

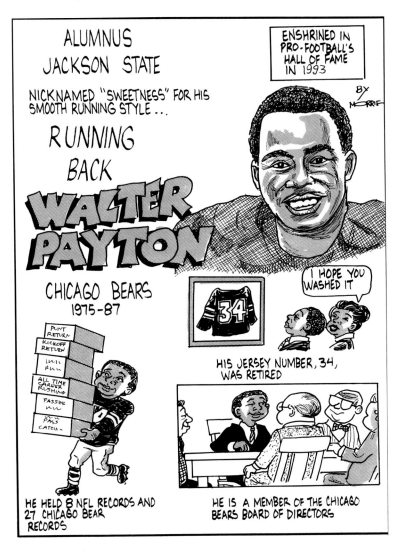

in 1993, and is involved with a group looking to acquire an NFL franchise. That could make Payton the league's first black team owner.

Greatness in Bears' runners have seen the team progress from Bronko Nagurski to Willie Galimore to Gale Sayers. Payton more than lived up to a boast he made as a rookie: "When I get through with this town," he said, "they're gonna love me. They ain't gonna have any choice but to love me."

He was right, and they do.

"If I have a character flaw, it's that I have a tendency to be too honest in public," he said. "I sometimes say things I believe about myself and my game when it would be better left unsaid. Maybe that's why I came on so strong about being the next Sayers and stuff like that.

"But what player doesn't think he's going to be the best at his position? You have to believe it. But maybe you don't have to say it out loud."

At times, that was just Walter, making the climb. He was different.

Just different.

WILLIE RICHARDSON

Wide Receiver, Jackson State

Willie Richardson's father didn't think his sons should play high school football.

"He was a minister, and football was not in line with what he was teaching," Richardson said. "He'd never played."

Yet, his sons, especially Willie, were blessed with athletic ability and developing into star football players. Once that got out, dad gave his approval.

"He saw me in the paper and he was just shocked," said Richardson, who grew up in Greenville, Miss. "But he met my coaches and got involved. And once I started playing, my brothers did, too."

Had dad not approved, he might have missed Willie's divine career at Jackson State, which birthed the original Jackson Five, the Richardson Brothers; Ernie, Charles, Willie, Gloster, and Thomas. Willie, the oldest of the group, really stood out, becoming a four-time Pittsburgh *Courier* All-American, and moving on to a nine-year NFL career, eight of those years with the Baltimore Colts.

John Merritt made Richardson a starter in only the second game of his freshman season.

"There were two receivers ahead of me," Richardson said. "We had lost to Prairie View, 52–6, in the opening game (1959) and he changed the whole offense. One thing helped me, no one knew me. I was fast and I'd just run by people. My sophomore year I got better, then, in my junior year, I started thinking that maybe I had a chance to play pro.

"When I was a kid, I caddied all day, but I wanted to get out of that. I practiced by myself. I wanted to be recognized and accepted. Every coach I

Willie Richardson. Courtesy of Jackson State

ever had was detailed and I learned early to run precise routes. I was in good systems that threw the ball."

A hand injury kept him from becoming a quarterback, but that worked for the best. As a senior, against Wiley College, Richardson caught four touchdown passes—in the first quarter, on five passes. He played on two SWAC title teams (1961, 1962) and the 1962 national championship team, and got a degree in health and physical education.

For the past twelve years, Richardson has worked for the State of Mississippi Department of Transportation as director of vehicle weight enforcement.

JERRY RICE

Wide Receiver, Mississippi Valley State

When Jerry Rice came out of MVSU the knock on him was that he did not have the speed to become a big-time receiver. So, as a first-round pick of the San Francisco 49ers in 1985, he quickly began racing his way past defenders and is now, simply, the best at his position. Maybe ever.

In only eight seasons. How's that for speed?

"It's tough getting a catch in this league, let alone a touchdown," said R.C. Owens, former Niners end. "But with him, it's almost like it's academic. He's the talent you look for to define all the skills of the position. He runs the field, pattern-wise, with great precision. He gets off the line. He has three speeds, and changes them at any time. He has great hands. He can react to the ball wherever it is.

Jerry Rice. Courtesy of NFL Properties

"Of all the guys I've watched in more than four decades, Jerry Rice epitomizes what the position is all about."

He has the hardware to prove it. Most notably, Rice is the NFL's all-time leader in TD catches (103), and holds league playoff records for most career receptions (75) and career TD's (13). He has played on championship teams in the 1989 and 1990 Super Bowls, getting Most Valuable Player honors for the 1989 game, and has appeared in seven Pro Bowls. He is a five-time All-Pro.

"I can think of nothing I'd like to accomplish in my career that I haven't already," he said. "The thing now is that I'm just enjoying the game."

Rice left college with eighteen NCAA Division II records.

"Going to Mississippi Valley was a blessing, because if I had gone to a major school, I don't think I would have been able to make as much progress in both academics and football," said Rice. "I was a shy kid coming out of high school. I might have been swallowed up by a big-time university."

But, never by a big-time defense.

ART SHELL

Offensive Line, Maryland State

Art Shell was destined to play at Maryland State. Had to be.

He had thought he'd play for Woody Hayes. Well, at least he wanted to, and had even gone to the extent of writing a letter to the venerable Buckeyes' head coach.

"I took typing my senior year in high school and, one day, I had some free time in class and I said to myself, 'I'll type a letter to Coach Hayes and ask for an opportunity to try out for the team.' I told him I enjoyed watching his teams and I gave him my size (6–5, 250). I don't know why I didn't send it."

Fate?

Later that same school year, Shell met Grambling head coach Eddie Robinson at a high school all-star basketball game. Shell was a two-sport star (center in both football and basketball) and played in both sports' all-star games.

"He said, 'If you can move on a football field like that you must be a pretty good player.'" Shell said. "He offered me a scholarship and, I thought, 'Boy, this is great.'"

It wasn't going to be that easy. Shell was convinced he was headed for Louisiana, but Maryland State's Roosevelt Gilliam was also hot on the trail, and when Shell found out Gilliam was coming by for a home visit, Shell left the house, having given his brothers explicit instructions not to tell Gilliam where he was.

"(Gilliam) had impressed me, and said he could have Johnny Sample (a Maryland State alum and by then, a prominent NFL defensive back) give me a call, but I had decided on Grambling and I didn't have the heart to tell him I wasn't going to his school," Shell said. "I left the house and told my brother if (Gilliam) came by to tell him that he didn't know where I was. I went down the street, but then my brother came and got me! 'He wants to see you.'"

Thanks, little bro'. Shell returned home, where Gilliam persisted he wasn't going home empty-handed.

"He said, 'I'm not leaving until you decide to go to Maryland State and he didn't move,'" Shell said. "My dad walked in and said the most important thing was education and, 'If you can promise me that, he's yours.' Coach said 'I guar-

I'M NUMBER THREE

HE WAS ALL-PRO; 1973, 1974 ALL AFC SIX TIMES

ALL PRO / ALL AFC

HE WAS NUMBER THREE DRAFT PICK IN 1968
HE PLAYED FOR THE OAKLAND RAIDERS (1968-1981) AND FOR THE LOS ANGELES RAIDERS (1982).
HE WAS LATER NAMED A RAIDERS' COACH

OFFENSIVE TACKLE

ART SHELL

ALUMNUS

MARYLAND STATE EASTERN SHORE

HE PLAYED IN 207 REGULAR SEASON GAMES AND 24 POST SEASON GAMES AND EIGHT PRO BOWLS
HE WAS BORN IN CHARLESTON, N.C.

MORRIE TURNER

ENSHRINED IN THE PRO FOOTBALL HALL OF FAME 1989

antee he'll get a degree.' The next thing I know, my bags were packed and I was going to Maryland State."

Fate has been kind to Art Shell. He had no real thoughts about a pro football career. But, he went on to a Hall of Fame stint with the Raiders as an offensive tackle (bulking to 285 pounds), with speed and devastating blocking skills. He was a third-round pick of the Oakland Raiders in 1968 and played in 230 games, including two Super Bowls and appeared in a franchise-record eight Pro Bowls.

He thought he'd get a degree, go back home and become a high school coach. Well, he got a degree, and he is a coach, but light years from the prep level. In 1989 he was named head coach of the Raiders, becoming the league's first (modern day) black head coach. He's won 36 of 63 games and was named the NFL's Coach of the Year in 1990 when the Raiders finished 12–4 and won the AFC Western Division title.

"I wasn't thinking NFL, but that's just the way it was, then," said Shell, who was twice named to the Pittsburgh *Courier* All-American (1966, 1967) team as an offensive and defensive tackle. "It was a different era. There was an importance on education because we knew without it you'd go nowhere. My father only made it to sixth grade, but he was street smart and he understood life."

And it was a hard life. Arthur Shell, Sr., worked in a paper mill, and his wife, Gertrude, died at thirty-five of a heart attack when Art, Jr. was fifteen— the oldest of five Shell children. He helped his dad raise the younger Shells. Art, Sr., a diabetic, died shortly after learning his son had made the Hall of Fame. His face partially paralyzed, among Art, Sr.'s last intelligible words were a reaction to his son's induction to the Pro Football Hall of Fame in 1989: "That's nice," he whispered.

"He died an hour before my plane landed," Shell said. "I went straight to the hospital and sat in the room with him by myself. I reflected on my life. I know I had made him happy.

"Now, I'm glad I didn't send that letter because of the experience I had at Maryland State. I was more of a person. Besides, in my neighborhood, black college football is what you knew. Those were the schools blacks were going to. Maybe we didn't have all the coaches that large schools had, but we had talent, and we had coaches that cared. They had to do a lot of teaching, and there might be only three coaches, and each of them had to work with maybe twenty guys.

"People said we didn't have coaching, but that's not true. Those were damn good coaches and they knew something. They instilled in us that you've got to work hard and people will notice."

Shell played offensive and defensive tackle and center. He was a three-time All-CIAA Conference lineman. He got a degree in Industrial Arts Education.

"I put pressure on myself to set an example for my other siblings." Shell said. "I had to set the tone and pace. Go to college, get an education. All of my brothers got (athletic) scholarships, too. (Kenneth to Maryland State, Bennie to Delaware State, Lawrence to South Carolina State.) My dad didn't have the money. So, we had to use our bodies."

It was destiny.

But Woody Hayes would have loved Art Shell.

DONNIE SHELL

Defensive Back, South Carolina State

Though an All-American for the Bulldogs in 1973, no NFL teams drafted Donnie Shell, but he earned a free agent tryout with the Pittsburgh Steelers, and quickly made a reputation as a ferocious special teams player, becoming the team's first-ever special teams captain.

However, in 1977, he won the starting free safety position in the pre-season, starting there for three regular season games, before moving to strong safety for the remainder of what would be a stellar fourteen-year career. He retired following the 1987 season as the all-time interception leader among NFL strong safeties with 51. He was named to the Pro Bowl squad five times. He led the Steelers with seven interceptions in both 1980 and 1984.

In 1982, Shell was named to the Steelers' All-Time team by Pittsburgh fans, and in 1993 was named to the All-Time Black College Team. Shell was a two-time MVP and All-MEAC player. He holds a bachelor's degree in health and physical education an masters degree in guidance and counseling, both from South Carolina State.

Donnie Shell. Courtesy of South Carolina State

JACKIE SLATER

Offensive Line, Jackson State

Jackie Slater was "just being a kid," not thinking about playing football though by tenth grade he had grown so much the teasing from his friends was inevitable.

"They'd tease me about going out for the team because I was so big," recalled Slater, now much bigger (6–4, 285) and a veteran offensive tackle with the Los Angeles Rams. "I had never played organized sports, but I was a fairly chubby kid growing up. I was above average size."

Slater took the challenge and made the football team, but also the basketball and track teams. He played defensive tackle at Wingfield High School in Jackson, Mississippi, but once he got to Jackson State, he was moved to the other side of the ball.

Hated it!

"I felt I was a defensive lineman," said Slater, "But they moved me to offense as soon as I got (to Jackson State). I was the biggest freshman recruit,

6–4, and about 265. I had never been around people who took pride in playing on the offensive line. I felt (offensive linemen) were just big people who got in the way. But, just being around guys like (tackle) Leon Gray and (guard) Emanuel Zanders, I was taught how to be a good offensive lineman. By my sophomore year, I began to develop."

Both Gray (Miami Dolphins) and Zanders (New Orleans Saints) also went on to NFL careers. At Jackson State, all three linemen had served as blockers for running back Walter Payton.

"It was a very rugged program," Slater said. "You look back and say you survived. It set the stage for (NFL) success. We were doing some things they were not doing in the pros, and when you're in the midst of that kind of talent, good athletes all the time, you anticipate good competition all the time. You get to the pros and it's not overwhelming."

Drafted in the third round by Rams in 1976, Slater has played in more games (238) and for more seasons (17) than any player in Rams history. His total games tie him with former New York Jets and Denver Broncos kicker Jim Turner for thirteenth all-time in the NFL. He has been selected to six consecutive Pro Bowls, seven overall.

Jackie Slater. Courtesy of Jackson State

JOHN STALLWORTH

Wide Receiver, Alabama A&M

After playing a couple of seasons at Alabama A&M John Stallworth began to think he might be able to play professional football and told his roommate so. Stallworth got a surprising reaction: "He kind of chuckled."

Thanks, roomie. But, even Stallworth understood.

"Pro athletes just didn't come out of Alabama A&M," said Stallworth, who, along with running back Ronnie Coleman (Houston Oilers) began to change that attitude. "In the history of A&M, maybe two guys had gotten drafted and they didn't make their teams. Professional football players just didn't come out of this school. They came out of Grambling, Tennessee State, Florida A&M."

"Not Alabama A&M."

Stallworth played fourteen seasons (1974–1987) with the Pittsburgh Steelers, including their dominating teams of the Seventies. He caught 3 TD passes in four Super Bowl games (that's him making that nice over-the-shoulder highlight catch for a 73-yard score in Super Bowl XIV, January 1980, in Pittsburgh's 31–19 win over the Rams). His career average gain of 24.4 yards per catch is the highest in Super Bowl history, ditto for his 40.3 yards per catch against the Rams, coming on just three receptions.

"I was just trying to promote within myself a positive attitude," Stallworth said of the conversation with his roommate. "I had a decent junior year and a pretty good senior year."

John Stallworth. Courtesy of the Pittsburgh Steelers

Pretty good? His final year at A&M, Stallworth was an All-American after catching 48 passes for 925 yards and seven touchdowns for Louis Crews' team, which played only nine games that year.

Stallworth had attended predominantly white Tuscaloosa High School but was not heavily recruited for a college scholarship. He initiated contact with Alabama A&M in 1970, his senior year.

"My choices were A&M, A&M, and A&M," he said. "The first black college game I saw, I played in. But I came into my own at A&M. I came out of high school from a team that for two years won only two football games. We didn't have a lot of enthusiasm. At A&M, I saw guys clapping their hands and singing at practice and having a great time.

"I thought, 'This is fantastic.' But, the first three years there, I didn't think football. I was there to get an education and didn't think any further than that."

Stallworth now sits on the school's board of trustees and runs Madison Research Corp., a firm of electrical and mechanical engineers and physicists in Brownsboro, Alabama, which does work for the federal government. He is also a member of the National Black College Alumni Hall of Fame.

BENJAMIN "BIG BEN" STEVENSON
Tuskegee Institute

Note: Ben Stevenson was the best player of his time, maybe all time. His son, Major, was also a pretty good football player at Yates High School in Houston, then at Texas-El Paso and in the Canadian Football League. Of growing up the son of a legendary athlete, Major Stevenson remembers: "As the years went by, Dad's mystique appeared to grow. I still remember summers at my grandmother's in Liberty, Missouri. All the townfolk—merchants, sheriff, clerks, and the like, of Liberty and many from as far away as Kansas City, were poised, awaiting "Big Ben's" return. Streets were lined on both sides with cheering fans, friends and relatives. It was as though we were traveling some mystical parade route to grandma's house. Their hero was home. For me, that was one of the most heartwarming encounters I have ever witnessed."

Major Stevenson, who lives in Austin, Texas, is now an aspiring writer and has been conducting research into his father's famed career. The following account of Ben Stevenson's career was written by Major.

Selecting college football's greatest performers indeed is an arduous task. Among that magnificent list of talents is,

After his legendary career at Tuskegee, Ben Stevenson coached at his alma mater then at Booker T. Washington High School in Houston, where he coached state championship teams in basketball, football, and track. Courtesy of Tuskegee Institute

however, one player who many felt incomparable—Tuskegee Institute's Benjamin "Big Ben" Stevenson, who was discovered by a retired Army officer, Major Cleve Abbott, who had accepted the head coaching position at Tuskegee shortly after World War I.

In 1924, on a return trip from South Dakota State, where he had previously coached, Abbott found 18-year-old Stevenson, born and raised in Liberty, Mo., working as a farm laborer, in Kansas. Abbott persuaded the young prospect to return with him to Tuskegee.

Once there, Abbott kept a watchful eye on Ben, and a great father-son relationship grew between them. Stevenson studied industrial arts, and later majored in animal husbandry. A diligent student, he was taught and mentored by Dr. George Washington Carver and received his Bachelor of Science degree in 1931.

Tuskegee combined its course curriculum to include what was called "underclassmen," or prep schoolers, and these students were allowed to participate in extracurricular activities on the collegiate level. That was later revised by the Central Intercollegiate Athletic Committee, limiting the years a student could participate athletically at the college level. That rule came in response to Stevenson's playing longevity, eight years!

In 1924, Abbott had given young Stevenson a crash course in football, then unleashed "Big Ben" (6–2, 210 pounds), who stormed through opposing defenses with the fury of a Kansas tornado. He would lead the "Golden Tigers" on a championship campaign that remains unequalled today. The unknown teenage phenomenon ran, received, scored, defended, and kicked as Tuskegee designed a 9–0–0 record, winning its first Black College National Championship for the school and Abbott. Ben combined speed (9.8 100-yard dash), strength, and durability. He outran many opponents, but is most remembered for his finesse and power.

Stevenson played halfback in a backfield that featured a shifty, ball-handling quarterback named Paul Smith and fullback (blocking back) Ernest Bailey. "Big Ben" scored on runs of 84, 77, 63, 55, 49, and 44 yards in his rookie season. Using the drop-kick, he booted field goals of 40, 43, and 39 yards. Stevenson thunderbolted Tuskegee to an all-time record, as they outscored opponents 301–25. As a defensive backfield specialist, he made tackles with

World of Sports

(By F. M. Davis for A. N· P·)

SPEAKING OF ALL-TIME ALL-AMERICANS

Chicago—In the Novmber issue of Frank G. Menke's All-Sports magazine, Paul W. L. Jones, superintendent of the colored industrial school of Cincinnati and ranked as one of the gratest students of Negro athletics in the nation, picks an All-Time, All-American football team from Negro colleges.

Here it is:

Ends—Williams (Langston) and Rivers (Talladega)
Tackles—Gallion (Bluefield and Irving (Morehouse)
Guards — Miller (Greensboro A. and T.) and Scott (West Va. St.)
Center — Dabney (Hampton)
Quarterback — Ritchie (Wilberforce)
Halfbacks—Johnson (Fisk) and
Halfbacks — Johnson (Fisk) and Kendall (Kenfuck State)
Fullback — Stevenson (Tuskegee)
Williams, says Jones was the greatest wingman produced in Negro college football," Kendall the most accurate and dangerous passer," Tubby Johnson "the most consistent ground gainer of his day" and Ben Stevenson, "the greatest all-around football player."

Byrd, of Lincoln; Cogar, of Kams State, and several others that rabid fans will tell you are the best who ever did it.

Of course this will start an argment in some centers. But in order to make it really worthwhile, your columnist expectorates upon his hands r'ars back, and lets fly on the typewriter with his conception of an All-Time, All Negro All-American from colleges of both races.

Ends — Paul Robeson (Rutgers) and Willis Ward (Michigan)
Tackles — Duke Slater (Iowa) and Hollingsworth (Iowa State)
Guards — Brice Taylor (Southern California)and Cogar (Alabama State)
Center — Bill Lewis (Harvard)
Quarterback — Fritz Pollard (Brown) and Oze Simmons (Iowa)
Fullback — Ben Stevenson (Tus-

To Stevenson, the greatest honor he received was getting named to Paul Jones All-Time, All-American football team for black players at any college. Courtesy of Tuskegee Institute

Tennessee State quarterback Eldridge Dickey was known as "The Lord's Prayer." A three-time All-American, he threw for 6,523 yards and 67 touchdowns with the Tigers. Dickey came close to attending Southern, and in 1965, as a sophomore at TSU, he had his one of his finest games against the Jags. That night, in Baton Rouge, Dickey rallied the Tigers from a 36–7 halftime deficit to a 40–36 win. Dickey was a first-round pick of the Oakland Raiders in 1967, ahead of Ken Stabler, but Dickey's career lasted a brief four seasons after getting switched to wide receiver. Courtesy of Tennessee State

reckless abandon, and became a master of interceptions. The *Crisis* magazine featured him as, by far, the top pass thief in the Southern Intercollegiate Athletic Conference, one of the greatest football players, adding "young Stevenson seems impervious to injury."

The 1925 team outscored opponents 224–6, and produced another 9–0–0 record, the second of six national championships (1924, '25, '26, '27, '29, and '30). Only Bluefield State, in 1928, broke the Golden Tigers streak. The iron-willed Abbott had transformed an unsuspecting group of young men into perhaps the greatest college machine this country has ever seen.

Tuskegee's 1926 game against Lincoln (Mo.) Institute was the highlight of the black college season. Billed as the showdown of the year, Abbott's Tigers faced a very determined squad of Lions, who built an early 16–10 lead when, unfortunately for "Skegee," Stevenson was knocked unconscious and missed a good portion of the game. "Big Ben" had already scored a touchdown, extra point, and field goal, but Abbott grimaced as his star sat dazed on the bench. After several doses of camphor under the nose, Ben was lifted out of his fog, and Abbott returned him to the game. Soon, Tuskegee's famous "Skegee single reverse" (forerunner of the Green Bay Packer sweep), with two pulling guards as convoy, sprang "Big Ben" past several diving defenders as he maneuvered his way to a 90-yard TD run. Stevenson converted the PAT for a 17–16 reversal. In the fourth quarter, he booted a 32-yard field goal as Tuskegee won 20–16. Stevenson had scored all of his team's points, and the victory assured Tuskegee would either win or share another national title. They ended the season with a 9–0 record, outscored their opponents 286–84, and were regarded as national co-champions, along with Howard (7–0).

While Knute Rocknee led Notre Dame and "Red" Grange romped at Illinois, Stevenson sparked a Tuskegee squad that dominated black college football throughout the 1920s. No team matched Tuskegee's 1924, 1929 (9–0, 249–26), or 1930 (11–0–1, 338–38) records. By 1928, Abbott's teams had compiled a 48-game win streak.

During an eight-year span (1923–1930), Tuskegee recorded an unduplicated 69 wins, 1 loss, and 6 ties. The one defeat came at the hands of Clark Atlanta in 1928, 13–9. During this reign "Big Ben" received seven consecutive, unanimous All-American awards (1924–1930). In doing so, he led his team and the SIAC in rushing, scoring, and interceptions, and was near the top in receiving each year.

Stevenson's career ended with the 1930 season, having tallied 42 runs of fifty yards or more for touchdowns. For Abbott, his Tuskegee teams would never again reach the pinnacle of success they had experienced during the Stevenson era.

Inevitably, the comparison between Illinois' Red Grange and Stevenson would surface. Many sports enthusiasts said Grange was a better long distance threat, but 80 and 90 yard runs were common with Stevenson. Grange carried more offensive load, but Stevenson was a phenomenal two-way starter, who scored many times on interceptions.

"Big Ben" also excelled at track. As captain of the team (1925–1927), he won national acclaim in the 100 and 200-yard dashes. He broad jumped over twenty two feet, and anchored the Golden Tigers sprint relay team. Several times he received the most outstanding athlete award at the Tuskegee Relays, one of the largest track events on the black college circuit.

Frank G. Menke's *All Sports* magazine recognized a team of Negro All-Time All-Americans, as selected by Paul W. L. Jones (one of the great students of Negro athletics). Jones' team included end Paul Robeson (Rutgers), tackle Duke Slater (Iowa), and quarterback Fritz Pollard (Brown). Stevenson was selected at Fullback, and voted the game's greatest all-around player. That was Big Ben's most memorable award, for it rated him with major college players, erasing much of the myth of inferiority associated with black college teams.

Stevenson's heroics may never again be matched. The endurance and stamina required to complete seven full seasons of two-way football is unimaginable today. Long before Grambling College showcased Paul "Tank" Younger, before Willie Galimore rocketed to fame at Florida A&M, Stevenson took Tuskegee on a whirlwind ride to greatness.

OTIS TAYLOR

Wide Receiver, Prairie View

Otis Taylor grew up a self-described "momma's baby." She was a domestic and he would follow her to work, he would follow her everywhere.

But he was also a great high school athlete, at Houston's Evan E. Worthing, in football, basketball, baseball, and track. Texas Southern recruited him, but he chose Prairie View and coach Billy Nicks and, at first, Taylor didn't like it at all. Prairie View is less than an hour's drive from Houston, but it seemed light years from home.

"I was very lonesome," Taylor said. "I was the youngest of three kids (two sisters). I didn't want to go too far away. We were just that close. Prairie View was homey, and, if anything happened I could walk home."

Figuratively, he did, "but my mother made me come back."

Mother's know these kinds of things, and, Taylor's mom knew it was time he sprouted wings and flew on his own. He went back and he soared. Taylor became one of the great receivers in Panthers history, then joined the AFL Kansas City Chiefs in 1965 as a fourth-round draft pick.

"I started meeting guys like myself, poor," he said. "We could stuff all of our clothes in a small box."

There were no buses large enough to fit all the talent at Prairie View. The Billy Nicks years there saw an abundance of choice players pass through the

Otis Taylor. Courtesy of Prairie View

tiny school. Taylor was an outstanding quarterback in high school and went to Prairie View to play that position.

"But, in the fall, I saw Jimmy Kearny throwing the ball, and I knew I had to find somewhere else to play," Taylor said. "I switched to end, and he and I became a combination. If things had been right in this country, Jimmy Kearney would have been a quarterback in the pros. He had a 4.0 GPA. The timing was bad, though he turned out to be a great defensive back.

"The Southwestern Athletic Conference was as strong a name as any conference in those days. You look at the players. The SWAC had players of great ability."

And perseverance.

"We were a little school and it was hard times," Taylor said. "We didn't have enough money to stop and eat on road trips, so we took baloney sandwiches. We'd leave on the bus about midnight, and get where we were going about 2 or 3 hours before game time. When we got back, we'd circle campus on the bus, honking the horn, waking people up to let them know we'd won."

WILLIE "SATELLITE" TOTTEN

Quarterback, Mississippi Valley State

In the sweltering Itta Bena, Mississippi heat, in the late summer of 1984, Archie Cooley made a suggestion to his quarterback, Willie Totten.

"Let's try something," the Mississippi Valley head coach began. "Just call the plays at the line of scrimmage."

As in, no huddle?

"I thought he was crazy," recalled Totten, who, from that point, began driving defenses insane. The heat had not gotten to Cooley, but the Delta Devils were about to light up the nation with a passing game that left all concerned—receivers, defenders, officials, stat crews—gasping for air. Totten was the trigger man in Cooley's version of the run-and-shoot offense, in which there was little running but a whole lot of shooting. Rapid fire. Some called it "fastbreak" football.

They were right.

"It was so easy, it was amazing," Totten said. "People would say if they walked to the restroom, when they came back, we'd have two touchdowns."

Or more, and after guiding that offense for his final two seasons at MVSU, Totten departed with 56 NCAA and 36 Southwestern Athletic Conference passing records. That first year, in ten games, he threw 518 passes, completed 324 (63 percent), for 56 touchdowns, 4,558 yards. He followed that in 1985 with 492 attempts, 295 completions (60 percent), for 39 TD's, and 3,695 yards.

During one game, a radio announcer, noted: "The Devils just pass and pass. The ball looks like it's floating in air like a satellite." A nickname was born. For his career, "Satellite" Totten completed 952 passes (1,629 attempts) for 141 TD's, and 13,170 yards. Roughly, that's 7.5 miles.

"The first week with the no-huddle, I passed out, running up and down the field, it was so hot," said Totten, now an assistant football coach and head tennis coach at Valley. "A lot of guys passed out. We'd score 15 or 20 touchdowns a day in practice. We thought, if we can do that to our teammates—who see it everyday, what do you think we can do to a team which has only three days to practice for it?

"It was exciting to go to practice. Our first game was against Kentucky State, and we won 86–0. We knew we had something."

What they had was one of the most prolific offenses in college football history. Totten threw, his main receiver, Jerry Rice, caught and ran, and caught and ran, and scored—ad infinitum.

"I could shift my guys around and the defense couldn't do a thing about it," Totten said. "The only one who could stop that offense was me. The receivers were catching everything."

And what they didn't catch, defenders did. Totten threw 22 interceptions in 1984, 29 in 1985. Didn't phase him a bit.

Said Totten: "I'll give up three interceptions for six or seven touchdowns anytime."

Totten, from Coila, Mississippi, seemed poised to pass the NFL dizzy, but was not drafted. There were questions about a knee injury he'd suffered during his sophomore season. There were questions about his mobility, speed, arm strength. Lots of questions. But he played in Canada with the British-Columbia Lions and Toronto Argonauts. And, he did play with the Buffalo Bills in the 1987 season's strike games.

"I didn't want to accept (not getting drafted)," he said. "I can point fingers, but that won't solve anything. What happened happened. The records will always be something I can look back on and say, 'I did those things.' It'll take time to break those records, though more teams are throwing a lot. Now, coaching is real rewarding. Maybe I'll become a head coach and create my own 'Satellite Express.' "

EVERSON WALLS

Defensive Back, Grambling

Everson Walls was practically hand-delivered to Grambling. He had not played football until his senior year (becoming an all-district safety) at Berkner High School in Dallas, but his girlfriend (now wife), Shreill, was headed for Grambling where her uncle, Ernest Sterling, happened to be an assistant coach.

Head Coach Eddie Robinson had one remaining scholarship and Walls took it.

"I knew nothing about Grambling," Walls said. "I was going to an entirely different world. But it was a positive, all-black environment with challenges and opportunities. But I had my doubts. Those were some of the biggest guys I'd ever been around."

Walls was a big man when he left Grambling as an All-SWAC selection, leading the nation in 1980 as a senior with a school-record eleven interceptions. He entered the NFL as a free agent, but is the only player to lead the National Football League in interceptions in three seasons (1981, 1982, 1985).

Too, in 1993, he was named to the Sheridan Black Network All-Time Black College Football Team.

At Grambling, he spent his freshman year (along with other freshman defensive backs Mike Haynes, Robert Salter, and James White) trying to frustrate Heisman candidate, quarterback Doug Williams, in practice.

"That was our main goal," Walls said. "We were always so pumped up and brash. Doug would complain to coach, 'They're not playing the defense right.' But, every practice was our game day. At times, we wouldn't end practice until he had scored a touchdown. A lot of times we'd go to overtime. He'd throw a TD pass and yell: 'That's six!'

"But, with the success I had on the field, I was motivated to go to class and I looked forward to the future. It gave me hope, and a lot of black kids don't have that. And if I could stop Doug Williams 25 percent of the time, once I got to the pros, those balls looked like volleyballs.

"I had seen every passing situation, because Eddie had shown us."

Walls father, Wellon, had been a running back at Prairie View and held the school record for freshman rushing.

Joked Wells: "But, they've probably broken it about eight times."

Walls got a degree in accounting and, in 1990, joined several other Cowboys players in opening "Cowboys Sports Cafc." Hc is also an aspiring stockbroker.

"I was the youngest player on Dallas' Twenty-fifth Anniversary Team, and I'm the second-youngest on the Black College Team, and I look around at those other faces and it's the proudest moment of my career," Walls said. "I haven't stopped talking about it yet."

RAYFIELD WRIGHT
Offensive Line, Fort Valley State

The first time Rayfield Wright set up as right offensive tackle for the Dallas Cowboys, Craig Morton got dumped on his behind. He did not like that.

"I had gotten picked up and thrown into him," Wright said. "He cussed me out."

Wright did not like that.

"I said, 'This ain't right,' " Wright recalled. "I was embarrassed."

Wright set out to right himself by studying film of some of the NFL's great offensive linemen: Bob Brown, Forrest Gregg, and Ernie McMillan. "I found out I couldn't block like any of them, they were all different. I had to develop something of my own."

What he came up with was using his talented skills of quickness and agility. He honed them and went on to a thirteen-year career with the Cowboys for which he was lauded as one of the best offensive linemen ever. He had four All-Pro seasons and played in six consecutive Pro Bowls.

"I blocked Deacon (Jones), Bubba (Smith), Willie Davis, L. C. Greenwood, Claude Humphrey, Jack Youngblood, Carl Eller. All the baddest defensive ends were on the (right side of the line)," Wright said. "I give credit to my God-given ability."

He'd been pretty generous with Wright, who, at Fort Valley State, played tight end and, at 6–6, was also the world's tallest safety. His first love was basketball, where he averaged 28 points a game and was highly-sought by the Cincinnati Royals.

He had only one year of high school football, and had received no attractive collegiate athletic scholarship offers. But knowing his mother did not have the funds to send him to college, he paid a visit to his Griffin, Georgia, Air Force recruiter and signed up. He even coaxed about nine of his buddies to join him.

"My mother and grandmother had raised us," Wright said. "They were domestics. My dad left when I was three. I was the first to graduate from high school. I volunteered because I wanted to play basketball and I could do that in special services.

Rayfield Wright. Courtesy of the Dallas Cowboys

Much too simple. A cousin at Fort Valley State told basketball coach Leonard Lomax about Wright and the coach offered Wright a scholarship but Uncle Sam already had the recruiting edge.

"I hadn't been sworn in, but I had taken a physical," Wright said. "So, I set up a meeting with all those people: my mother, grandmother, recruiting officer, the coach, and our minister. They met for two or three hours, while I sat outside waiting."

He was released from his Air Force commitment, after his recruiter had warned him if he left college he would immediately get drafted into the Army. Wright did make a commitment to his family.

"I told that them I wouldn't leave under any circumstances," he said.

There were temptations. After averaging 28 points a game in his junior season, the Royals started calling, asking if he'd like to go hardship.

"I could have used the money," Wright said, but by his senior year, he had blossomed into a pretty good football player, making the All-Southern Intercollegiate Conference team and, one day, he got another call from another professional team.

"Gil Brandt (of the Dallas Cowboys) called, and I was floored," said Wright, who was so shocked, he asked for Brandt's number, hung up and

Texas Southern wide receiver Warren Wells was a major reason Oakland Raiders quarterback Daryle Lamonica became known as "The Mad Bomber." Said Ken Houston, former Houston Oilers and Washington Redskins defensive back: "Warren was the original 'Dr. Doom.' He was cold-blooded. He had a staccato step like (Paul) Warfield." Courtesy of the Pittsburgh Courier

Tennessee State was 10–0 in 1966, averaging 40.6 points a game, including an 83-0 trouncing of Kentucky State. Here, left to right, defensive end Claude Humphrey, quarterback Eldridge Dickey, and punt return specialist Nolan "Super Gnat" Smith, hold the Pittsburgh Courier national championship trophy awarded the Tigers. Courtesy of Tennessee State

Dennis Mahan, No. 44 holds the career touchdown record (35) for Hampton University. He scored 212 points in his career (1979–1982). Courtesy of Hampton University

called him back. "I thought it was a joke my friends were playing. I apologized to him. But at the time, I wasn't interested in pro football, but pro basketball."

Dallas took Wright in the seventh round.

"Then, (pro) basketball started in August, football in July," Wright said. "I told my mother, 'I'll give (football) my best shot, but if I don't make it, I'm not coming home, I'm going to Cincinnati.' "

The next time he went home, it was as a Dallas Cowboy. There were 135 rookies in his first camp with Dallas. Wright was one of only five who made the team.

"I was ecstatic," he said. "A lot of my friends tried to discourage me: 'You're a basketball player. Stay here and work with us at the (paper) mill.' I wanted more than that."

Wright, who could cover 40 yards in 4.8 seconds, played tight end and

defensive end for the Cowboys before moving to offensive tackle in his second season. His big break came when Ralph Neely broke an ankle. Wright was No. 2 on the depth chart, going into a game against the Los Angeles Rams, and Deacon Jones.

"He was big, strong, and fast," Wright said. "He'd go by and I was still in my stance. He was awesome. He'd knock me completely over, then help me up. 'Hey, rookie, welcome to the NFL.' He was teaching me something—pay attention, don't lose focus. But I got a game ball for that game. He was the best, but I had a good game."

He liked that.

Rufus Porter was a four-year starter at linebacker for Southern's Jaguars, and has been a two-time Pro Bowler for the Seattle Seahawks. Courtesy of Southern University

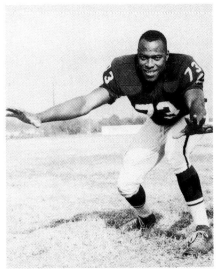

Jackson State's Ben McGee, a two-time All-SWAC defensive lineman, was drafted by the Pittsburgh Steelers in 1964. Courtesy of the Pittsburgh Courier

John "Rough Raider" Brown, 1946 All-American center for North Carolina Central. Courtesy of the Pittsburgh Courier

Several of Robinson's former players admire the coach's Heritage plaque. Left to right: James Harris, Essex Johnson, Robinson, Henry Dyer, Willie Davis, Ben Williams, Tank Younger. Courtesy of David Hoply and Orange County Sports Association

CHAPTER FOUR

Grambling
"The G-Men Are Coming"
By Robert V. McDonald

"First of All; Servants of All; We shall transcend all."—Alpha Phi Alpha Fraternity Motto

The story of Grambling football is actually rooted in a story about baseball.

In 1941, Eddie Robinson was twenty-two years old and just out of being a star quarterback at Leland College, which was in Baker, Louisiana (just east of Baton Rouge). Robinson was working in a feed mill in Baton Rouge when he heard about a football coaching job at Louisiana Negro Normal and Industrial Institute in Grambling, Louisiana. Quicker than it took him to pronounce the school's name, Robinson was headed there to interview for the job with Dr. Ralph Waldo Emerson Jones, school president.

The school at the time was long on names, short one football coach. Robinson was eager to change that when he visited Jones, affectionately known as, "Prez."

"The talk rambled to baseball and I admitted I was one heck of a hitter," Robinson said. "Dr. Jones said he was the best pitcher these parts had ever seen. I said I could hit any pitcher I faced. He said, 'Let's get a mitt and we'll see.' So, we went outside. His brief warm-up told me that the man could throw. But I could hit.

"Suddenly, I remembered it was a job I was after. I went down swinging on three straight pitches—and got the job."

It was the only time Robinson would strike out at Grambling. He tossed his bat aside, picked up his coach's whistle and became a big hit in football. Jones would go about the business of running the university, and coaching baseball. The two were the first elements of a triumvirate that would elevate Grambling football to icon status for black college football. Joining them would be Collie Nicholson, a former Marine combat correspondent, who became the school's sports information director and "idea" man after returning from the South Pacific to finish work towards his education degree. Nicholson, was a Grambling junior at the time (1946) he took the job. He was

"Prez," Dr. Ralph Waldo Emerson Jones, former Grambling president (and a Southern grad), who was also the school's first football coach (1926-1932). He also coached baseball from 1926 until 1977. One year, he lobbied with his athletic director — Eddie Robinson — for an extra baseball scholarship. Robinson relented after Jones agreed the recruit could also play football. Jones later convinced Robinson the player should be limited to baseball, after Robinson wanted to put the kid on a weight program. The player went on to star with the 1969 New York Mets. The player was Tommie Agee. Courtesy of Grambling

103

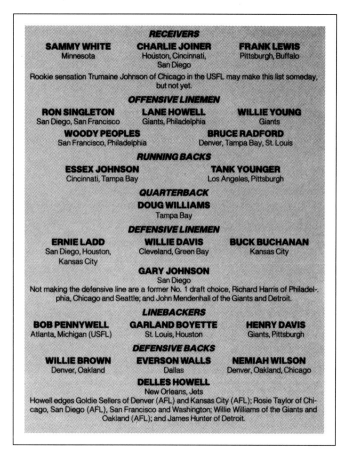

RECEIVERS

SAMMY WHITE	CHARLIE JOINER	FRANK LEWIS
Minnesota	Houston, Cincinnati, San Diego	Pittsburgh, Buffalo

Rookie sensation Trumaine Johnson of Chicago in the USFL may make this list someday, but not yet.

OFFENSIVE LINEMEN

RON SINGLETON	LANE HOWELL	WILLIE YOUNG
San Diego, San Francisco	Giants, Philadelphia	Giants
WOODY PEOPLES		**BRUCE RADFORD**
San Francisco, Philadelphia		Denver, Tampa Bay, St. Louis

RUNNING BACKS

ESSEX JOHNSON	TANK YOUNGER
Cincinnati, Tampa Bay	Los Angeles, Pittsburgh

QUARTERBACK

DOUG WILLIAMS
Tampa Bay

DEFENSIVE LINEMEN

ERNIE LADD	WILLIE DAVIS	BUCK BUCHANAN
San Diego, Houston, Kansas City	Cleveland, Green Bay	Kansas City

GARY JOHNSON
San Diego

Not making the defensive line are a former No. 1 draft choice, Richard Harris of Philadelphia, Chicago and Seattle; and John Mendenhall of the Giants and Detroit.

LINEBACKERS

BOB PENNYWELL	GARLAND BOYETTE	HENRY DAVIS
Atlanta, Michigan (USFL)	St. Louis, Houston	Giants, Pittsburgh

DEFENSIVE BACKS

WILLIE BROWN	EVERSON WALLS	NEMIAH WILSON
Denver, Oakland	Dallas	Denver, Oakland, Chicago

DELLES HOWELL
New Orleans, Jets

Howell edges Goldie Sellers of Denver (AFL) and Kansas City (AFL); Rosie Taylor of Chicago, San Diego (AFL), San Francisco and Washington; Willie Williams of the Giants and Oakland (AFL); and James Hunter of Detroit.

In 1983, Paul Zimmerman, Sports Illustrated's *pro football writer, picked Grambling's All-Pro team. Courtesy of* Sports Illustrated

the first full-time publicist for a black college.

"Prez said, 'I'll find the money to do what needs to be done,' " said Nicholson. "We met every two weeks. He said, 'Your job is to get us local, regional, then national attention. Your job is innovative ideas, Eddie's job is to coach, mine is to get the resources.' "

Each man did his job, but always out front was "Eddie." At Grambling, "everybody is somebody," but Robinson is the football coach. There is no dispute there. His 381 wins (all-time collegiate best) say so. The more than three hundred players he has sent to professional football say so. Most important, the respect he has garnered says so.

Said Joe Paterno, noted Penn State football coach: "Nobody has done or ever will do what he has done for this game."

In fifty-two years at Grambling, a small, out of the way, black college, Robinson has transcended the bounds of size and ethnicity, elevating the program to unimagined heights and worldwide celebrity. His first Grambling team (1941) was only 3–5, but the next season, the Tigers were 8–0 and unscored on. He has not had another losing season, has won six black college national championships, and won sixteen Southwestern Athletic Conference titles. Also, he has:

—Received the National Football Foundation and College Hall of Fame "Outstanding Contribution to Amateur Football Award."

—Had a street in Baton Rouge (Southern Jaguar territory) named after him.

—Served as president of the American Football Coaches Association.

—Mowed and lined the Grambling football field, sewed torn uniforms, taped ankles, groomed the cheerleader squad, directed the band, and written game accounts for Louisiana newspapers.

He's done it all.

"The word coach covered a lot more in those days," Robinson said of his beginning at Grambling, when he made $64 a month to support his new bride, Doris Mott Robinson, who was expecting the couple's first child. Robinson's was also coaching men's and women's basketball and running the physical education department. The word "coach" covered everything in those days, but Robinson had what all coaches would die for: unfailing support from the top. Jones loved athletics, and served as the school's baseball coach for 51 years.

"With 'Prez' as baseball coach, there was an emphasis on athletics," said Tellis Ellis, long-time Jackson State athletic director. "Also, they had a strong sports information director, so they got favorable recognition in the early years. They played all over the country, all because the administration was so supportive.

"Cast down your bucket where you are."—Booker T. Washington

Grambling, a pencilpoint speck on some maps, is sixty-five miles east of Shreveport, thirty-six miles west of Monroe and eight miles outside of Ruston, on Interstate 20. In 1901, the Grambling community's Farmer's Relief Association was looking for an educator and wrote to Booker T. Washington, Tuskegee Institute founder and president, requesting assistance.

Washington sent Charles P. Adams from Tuskegee to Allen Green, a town two miles west of Grambling, to create a school for farmer's called the Colored Industrial and Agricultural Institute of Lincoln Parish. In 1930, under the new name of Louisiana Negro normal and Industrial Institute, the school received a large appropriation and expanded its mission to the training of elementary teachers for black rural schools.

In 1926, Jones, a math teacher, came to the school from Southern University in Baton Rouge. Jones, the school's first football coach of record, would be a campus fixture for half a century. He became the school's president on July 1, 1936, when the school became state supported, but did not relinquish all of his coaching duties until 1977. When he took over as president, the student body numbered 120, the faculty 17. There were six buildings on campus, and the annual budget from the state was $54,000.

Jones was an optimist who taught self-reliance and was a builder of dreams. During his administration, the school experienced the most remarkable institutional growth and progress in Louisiana history. By the 1970s, Jones had implemented a $7 million campus construction program, increased the curriculum, and had seen the school's enrollment balloon to 4,000 students and 407 full-time faculty members, of which 56 held doctorate degrees.

He also supported a broad athletic program, and would symbolize the approach of spring by strolling from his office to the locker room, get into his baseball attire and head for the field. He was head football coach from 1926 to 1932, and was succeeded by Ira Smith, Joe Williams, Osiah Johnson, and Emory Hines before Robinson came on the scene in 1941 as football coach and athletic director.

Ironically, in running the athletic department, Robinson would have to approve Jones' baseball budget, but as school president, Jones had the final

These distinguished gentlemen were all present at the Alpha Phi Alpha Fraternity National Convention in New Orleans in 1993 when Coach Eddie Robinson received his Alpha Award of Merit. From left to right are Congressman Robert Scott, Virginia; Former U.S. Senator Edward W. Brooke, Massachusetts; Lionel B. Richie, Jr.; Milton C. Davis; Congressman Earl Hilliard, Alabama; and Coach Eddie Robinson. Courtesy of Alpha Phi Alpha Fraternity

In Robinson's second year with the Tigers, 1942, the team was a perfect 8-0-0 and unscored on. Colgate had done it ten years earlier, but no team has accomplished such a feat again. In 1942, the school had enrolled only 67 men, 33 were on this football squad. No. 18 (standing, first player on the left) is Fred Hobdy, current Grambling athletic director. Courtesy of Grambling

Robinson receives the inaugural Disneyland Pigskin Classic Heritage Award from Disneyland President Jack Lindquist in 1990 at Anaheim Stadium. Courtesy of David Hoply and Orange County Sports Association

"There is a legacy here at Grambling. You need to know about the legacy Coach Robinson has created through all these years. Be proud you are part of it. Coach used to tell us to aspire to come back to Grambling after our achievements. Then, he would stop practice for the player to address the team. Today, I ask you what coach once asked me: 'Someday, will you stop practice?'"
Buck Buchanan addresses the Grambling squad. Photo by Rich Clarkson

say on football expenditures requested by Robinson.

In 1974, Jones went before the Louisiana State legislature, seeking to change the name of the school to that of the town. Why? In part, Jones told the legislature: "Gentlemen, I should like to explain to you why we would like to change our name. Our team was playing a big game last season and the other team had the ball on our seven-yard line. Our student body began to appeal to our defense, 'Hold that line, Louisiana Negro Normal and Industrial Institute, hold that line! Hold that line, Louisiana Negro Normal and Industrial Institute, hold that line!' Gentlemen, before they could get that cheer out of their mouths, the other team had already scored."

Name changed approved.

"Coaching is a profession of love. You can't coach people unless you love them."—Eddie Robinson

Edward Gay Robinson was born February 13, 1919 in Jackson, Louisiana, a small, rural farming community, where three generations of his family had been sharecroppers and people of integrity, with strong religious faith. The family moved to Baton Rouge when he was six years old.

"My parents gave me a sense of pride and direction in life," said Robinson, an only child. "What I got from them was worth passing on to my players: 'There's no work too hard if it gets you what you need or where you want to go.'"

For that, Robinson used to tote blocks of ice off a mule-drawn wagon and into neighboring kitchens. His introduction to football came when he and his friends would play with a blown-up pig's bladder, or shredded, laminated bicycle tire.

"When we played a tough team across town, we used their real ball and got beat real bad," Robinson recalled. "Then a white player from the high school said he'd coach us, and he taught us blocking and tackling and real plays. The next time, we killed those (other) kids."

His inspiration to become a coach came as a third-grader when a Baton Rouge high school coach brought his team to Robinson's elementary school. The coach had his uniformed team in tow, all looking to sell $25 season tickets. Robinson's eyes were riveted on the coach.

"I liked him from the beginning," Robinson said. "I liked the way he talked to the team, the way he could make us all laugh. I saw the way the players all respected him."

Robinson spent his fall Saturday afternoons at Southern games. Saturday nights at Tiger Stadium for Louisiana State games. So to speak.

"Most of the time, I'd have to show up five to six hours early and find an odd job lining the field or something, to earn my admission," he said. "I couldn't help making a mental note as to how more elaborate the facilities, equipment and coaching methods were at LSU than they were at Southern. From that time on, I was interested in seeing black kids get the same opportunity as white players.

"I've always believed in the American system. I felt if I worked hard enough within the system, if I paid my dues, I could get the most out of life in America."

At Leland, Robinson was coached by I. S. Powell, a lawyer by trade, then Rueben S. Turner, the "preacher-coach," who, after attending a coaching clinic, came back and introduced Robinson to playbooks.

"That inspired me," Robinson. "We'd never had plays and books before. I'd always wanted to be a coach and he introduced me to a whole new world of football."

The summer he graduated from Leland, and after taking the job at Grambling, Robinson attended a coaching clinic in Chicago, where Michigan's Fritz Crisler and Lynn "Pappy" Waldorf of Cal were among the clinicians. Robinson asked Waldorf what advice he'd give a young coach.

"He said, 'Eddie, I'd tell him to get himself a system,'" Robinson said. "I asked him what a system was. He said, 'Take some of our plays, then put in some of your plays with them, and you've got yourself a system.' I took his advice, went home to Grambling and went to work on my system, the Grambling System, and I'm still using it today."

He learned about systems in Chicago, but Robinson had always been a leader. "Eddie was a leader at all times," said Albert "Startackle" Armour, a teammate of Robinson's in high school and at Leland. "He had enough personality to make you run through the line, when you knew you couldn't. You just wanted to do it for him."

While at Leland, Robinson majored in English. After school, he would promote boxing matches and manage fighters at the Temple Roof Garden in Baton

Robinson was a standout quarterback at now-defunct Leland College, of which teammate Daniel Nash said, "As small as this college was, it was the whole world."

Robinson with Los Angeles Mayor Tom Bradley and Grambling sports information director Collie Nicholson before the 1971 L.A. Classic.

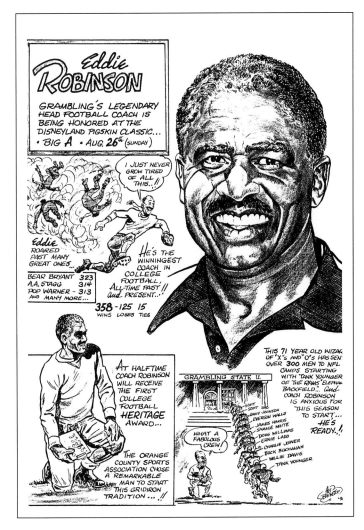

Richard Vargas portrait, commissioned in 1991 by Eddie Robinson Foundation, commemorating the coach's Fiftieth Anniversary of distinguished excellence as Grambling's head coach. Courtesy of Richard Vargas

Willie Brown. Courtesy of Grambling

Rouge. He also worked on a coal truck for twenty cents an hour, and was the campus barber.

He did it all.

As a coach, he's done it all.

"I took my inspiration from the great American coaches, Pop Warner and Amos Alonzo Stagg," Robinson said. "Man, I got to watch the'Bear' (late Alabama Coach Paul Bryant) work! I busted my butt. I always knew my part to play, and if my part ended up having something to do with history, then I'm happy. I never let anybody change my faith in this country. All I want is for my story to be an American story, not black or white. Just American.

"I want it to belong to everybody."

WILLIE BROWN
Defensive Back

Willie Brown arrived at Grambling with few thoughts of becoming a professional football player, but ended up another of the school's illustrious players to earn National Football League accolades. The Tigers have Willie Richardson, Jackson State's superb wide receiver, to thank for delivering Brown to Grambling.

The school has Ray Charles to thank for helping to keep him there.

Ray Charles?!

"Willie and I had really planned on going to Grambling together, because we had competed all through high school, in football, basketball, and track," said Brown, from Yazoo City, Mississippi. "So, I get to Grambling and I was looking for Willie and coach kept telling me, 'He'll be here next week.' I stuck around all summer waiting on Willie and he hasn't showed up yet!

"The next time I saw him was when we played against each other. We had a good reunion, and we beat them!"

Brown had been wavering on Grambling himself, considering Kentucky State. But his Grambling visit was the deciding factor.

"After I got there, during the summer, I saw all the pretty girls walking around campus and found me a little job," Brown said. "And Mrs. Robinson and the kids and the people in the community were so nice to me. So, I said, this was it for me."

Or was it? When it came time for summer drills, in preparation for the season, Brown got a wake-up call. The tune he heard was one thing, the message quite another.

"Coach wanted to make sure you learned good habits," Brown said. "So he'd come through the dormitory about 5:00 a.m. ringing that bell. Plus, he'd put on a lot of Ray Charles records, 'Hit the Road, Jack,' in particular. He'd put it on the stadium (loudspeakers) and you could hear it everywhere. He'd be right there and get you out of bed. At the time, as a kid, I'm thinking, the moon and stars were out and he's talking about getting up and playing football.

"You didn't think about it in terms of him and his pride and what he was trying to teach you. You thought, 'Damn! It's too early to be getting up.'"

The price of greatness. Brown got out of bed and worked hard enough to become a starter as a freshman and started all four of his seasons for Robinson. In Brown's senior year, 1962, the Tigers finished 6–2–2, but had the American Football League's top pick in defensive lineman Buck Buchanan.

"I hadn't even thought about the pros," Brown said. "My goal was to go to college and get my degree and go back home and start coaching in high school. But my senior year, we had twelve guys that signed pro contracts. I signed (with the AFL Houston Oilers) as a free agent. I just said I'll take a shot at it for a year and see what happens. There weren't that many blacks in the NFL at the time."

Brown became one of them via the AFL. Houston told Brown to hit the road, but he was picked up by the Denver Broncos and played there for four years before joining the Raiders for the remaining twelve years of his unexpected Hall of Fame career. He was inducted into Pro Football's Hall of Fame in 1984. Brown shares the Raiders career interception record (39) with Lester Hayes, was named to the All-Time AFL Team and the All-Time Black College Team. In Super Bowl XI, he set a Super Bowl record with a 75-yard interception return for touchdown against Minnesota.

ENSHRINED INTO THE FOOTBALL HALL OF FAME 1984

CORNERBACK WILLIE BROWN ALUMNUS GRAMBLING DENVER BRONCOS (AFL) 1963-66 OAKLAND RAIDERS 1967-1978

GOTCHA!

HE WAS ALL AFL/AFC SEVEN TIMES, NAMED TO ALL AFL IN 1969 HE PLAYED IN FIVE AFL ALL-STAR GAMES, FOUR AFC-NFC PRO BOWLS, NINE AFL/AFC TITLE GAMES AND TWO SUPER BOWL GAMES

YOU SHOULD BE TIRED

COACH

HE POSTED A CAREER TOTAL 54 INTERCEPTIONS, 472 YARDS. HE SCORED ON A 75 YARD INTERCEPTION IN SUPER BOWL XI

BY MORRIE TURNER

BUCK BUCHANAN

Defensive Tackle

When former Kansas Chiefs coach Hank Stram would hold his summer football camp upstate New York, one of the players he would bring with him to help conduct clinics was All-Pro Junious "Buck" Buchanan, the huge defensive lineman from Grambling.

"There would be about 150 kids there," Stram said. "I'd tell them we were going to coach them like we coach the Chiefs, and one thing we do with rookies is they all have to sing their school songs. All the black players knew their

The first player selected in the 1963 AFL draft. He had speed, size, determination, & durability. He missed only one game in 13 yrs. He was born in Gainesville, Alabama

LET ME IN THERE

FAME

ALUMINUS GRAMBLING

DEFENSIVE TACKLE

JUNIOUS (BUCK) BUCHANAN

KANSAS CITY CHIEFS 1963-75

ENSHRINED IN PRO-FOOTBALL HALL OF FAME IN 1990

I'M ON MY WAY TO ANOTHER POST SEASON GAME

SLAP!

HE EXCELLED AT INTIMIDATING PASSERS. HE BATTED DOWN 16 PASSES, 1967

BY MORRIE TURNER

HE WAS FOUR TIME ALL AFL, ALL AFC IN 1970. HE PLAYED IN SIX AFL ALL-STAR GAMES, AND TWO AFC/NFC PROBOWLS

school songs. Buck would get up there and halfway through his song, half the kids would be singing with him.

"His eyes would get watery as he sang, and everybody would be so impressed with his pride (for Grambling)."

Buchanan loved Grambling, but there were few people at Grambling or in Kansas City who did not love this giant of a man with an even bigger heart and incredible athletic skills. If you knew Buck Buchanan, if you knew of him, your eyes got watery on July 16, 1992 when he died at age fifty-one of lung cancer. He had been "All-Everything" as a football player, but was remembered more as "All-Human."

"Buck Buchanan was everything you'd want in a man," said Don Klosterman, former Kansas City Chiefs general manager who in 1963 made Buchanan the first overall pick in the AFL draft, and the first player from a black college taken in that slot, a choice Klosterman looks back on with great pride.

The choice was no where near disappointing. Buchanan would play in the first AFC-NFC Pro Bowl in 1970 and was a Pro Bowler again the next season. He was voted Chiefs MVP in 1965 and 1967, and All-AFL in 1967, 1968, and 1969. He was also integral in the Chiefs Super Bowl campaigns in 1966 (Super Bowl I) and 1969. Buchanan missed only one game in 13 pro seasons, all with the Chiefs, who have retired his No. 86. He was inducted into the Pro Football Hall of Fame in 1990.

At 6–7, 287 pounds, he was considered the prototype defensive lineman, combining size, speed, and strength. Yet, so gentle off the field. From 1972 to 1975, Buchanan served as director of the Kansas State Special Olympics.

"We build our sports heroes until they seem bigger than life," said Carl Peterson, current Chiefs president and general manager. "If anybody seemed to fit that description, it was Buck Buchanan. He was much more than the sum of his achievements. He was the personification of our sport—a hero in every way."

He had come to Grambling after Eddie Robinson had received a late night phone call from a fan in Birmingham, advising him, "There's a player here you need." Buchanan entered Grambling at 210 pounds.

"I didn't think Buck would be much of a player because he had his foot in a bucket," Robinson said. "It didn't look like he could move with lateral movement. Then, we'd start running our plays. If we went to the right, he'd tackle us. If we went to the left, he'd tackle us. If we went right at him, he'd tackle us.

"Boy, he was really tough."

Tough enough to be named All-American three times, and smart enough to make the SWAC's All-Academic team in 1961. In 1968, he was voted into the NAIA Hall of Fame.

Said Chiefs owner Lamar Hunt: "Buck was a fantastic person in so many ways, not just as a football player. He was always positive, a terrific leader."

WILLIE DAVIS

Defensive End

The Eddie Robinson "crying" stories always make the rounds when former Grambling players get together. The great coach has been known to shed some tears at halftime, exhorting his troops with a "You don't love Grambling" here and there. Motivational ploy or intense sincerity?

A bit of both, and the effect on his players, though they may chuckle about it, is lasting, especially once you look at the deeper meaning. Willie Davis did.

"He had that great emotion," recalled Davis, who left Texarkana, Arkansas, in 1952 to play for Grambling. "The first time I saw Eddie cry was before a game. It was the first time I had seen a man cry in a situation where he was in charge. He would get so caught up in the emotion of winning and participation until he would just become overwhelmed.

"It was a shock. I didn't know what was happening, but then I realized that things just meant that much to him. Sometimes, I'm sure, it was his struggle to get the players to understand what they were faced with and to be prepared to do it to the best of your ability. We joke about it now, from the standpoint that Eddie probably used it at some point to extract that sense of commitment out of us. He's probably faked a few cries over the years.

"The crying I saw as a freshman, was not quite the same I saw as a senior. But I didn't realize you could cry out of strength and that left an impression on me that if he can care that much, then, boy, I ought to at least feel something in this."

Willie Davis. Courtesy of Grambling

In 1964, muscular Henry Dyer, at 6-2, 230 pounds, led the NCAA College Division in scoring with points, then as a senior was an All-American. Said Robinson, "He could break off a score from anywhere on the field. He was a great blocker and an outstanding runner." On the suggestion of former Grambling and Rams great Tank Younger, Dyer was a fourth-round pick of the Rams in 1966. Courtesy of Grambling

Davis' emotion spilled onto the field, where he was an All-American, then went on to the Cleveland Browns, who drafted him seventeenth in 1956. He was traded to the Green Bay Packers in 1959. In ten years with Vince Lombardi's teams, Davis was named All-Pro five times, and made an equal number of appearances in the Pro Bowl. He played on five NFL title teams with Packers, including the first two Super Bowl-winning teams. He was inducted into the Pro Football Hall of Fame in 1981.

It was Lombardi who saw Davis' potential as a great pass rusher.

"In Willie Davis, we have a great one," Lombardi said. "You look for speed, agility, and size (in a great player). You may get two of these qualities in one man and when you have three, you have a great football player. For a big man (6–3, 245), he has excellent agility and he has great sincerity and determination."

Most of that, especially the latter two qualities, he'd picked up at Grambling. Lombardi would strengthen them.

"I saw the same experience with Lombardi that I did with Eddie," Davis said. "Lombardi would say, 'This is a game I would like to play. Because if I was playing this game, I would be very sure of the results.' But it was like, unfortunately, I have to leave it up to you."

Where Davis was concerned, things were in good hands. He graduated with a degree in industrial arts, then got his master's degree in business administration. Davis, who in his off seasons in Cleveland taught high school classes, has been honored for his community involvement. He was named the NAACP's Man of the Year in 1978. In 1967, he was awarded the Byron White Award, given to the athlete who contributes the most to his country, community, and team. Davis has had multi-business successes in Los Angeles.

"Eddie's whole credo for life stuck with me," Davis said. "From personal appearance, to how you conduct yourself, to just the simple things like being polite, understanding, and considerate of others. He was talking country and being a good citizen when it was a time you didn't hear that many people, especially blacks, talking about those things.

"At the time, I thought, 'Is Eddie for real?' But he truly believes in the things he says and that created positive expectations in you. I've been exposed to so many young people who have such negative attitudes and perceptions, images and everything else.

"I was determined to come out of professional football without someone having to do me a favor, with a job prospect that would give me some pride and a sense of achievement."

JAMES HARRIS
Quarterback

Eddie Robinson had sent Tank Younger off to the Los Angeles Rams in 1949 as the first black college player to make an NFL roster, and in 1965 he recruited quarterback James Harris out of Carroll High School in Monroe, Louisiana, with the express intent of grooming Harris to become the league's first impact black quarterback.

Michigan's Willie Thrower (1953 Chicago Bears) and Prairie View's Charlie "Choo-Choo" Brackins (Green Bay, 1955) had briefly taken NFL snaps, and Denver's Marlin Briscoe had thrown for 1,589 yards and 14 touchdowns in 1968. Minnesota's Sandy Stephens guided the Montreal Alouettes in the mid-Sixties, but Robinson had big plans for Harris, who would become the first black player drafted to play quarterback.

"We recruited James Harris to play quarterback in the National Football League," confirmed Robinson, who stressed to Harris, first, the importance of being a good student because, "the reasoning at the time was that a black didn't have it upstairs (to be a NFL quarterback). But he had the height (6–3) and the arm . . . and he could win. I told him, 'Work hard and you could be the first.' I don't think he could quite grasp the importance of what I was saying right then. That he might be a pioneer."

But he went about the business of doing just that. Harris led Grambling to four SWAC titles and a national championship in 1967 and, with Harris at quarterback, were 31–9–1. He threw for 4,705 yards and 53 touchdowns.

Henry Dyer, who would become a star fullback for the Rams, was a senior at Grambling in Harris' freshman season.

"James came in as a thrower," Dyer said. "He had scholarship offers from all over. Grambling was always noted as a running powerhouse. We didn't throw much. But James would change all that."

Which he did, and in 1969, the Buffalo Bills drafted Harris—in the eighth round.

Harris played little for the Bills and was waived in 1972 and sat out the season. In 1973 he signed with the Los Angeles Rams, where in 1974, Rams Coach Chuck Knox made Harris the starter. Harris led the Rams to NFC West titles in 1974 and 1975 and was named to the Pro Bowl following the 1974 season and won MVP honors in that game.

He finished his career with the San Diego Chargers. In 1993, he was named assistant general manager with the New York Jets.

James Harris. Courtesy of Grambling

CHARLIE JOINER

Wide Receiver

After 18 NFL seasons (1969–1986), Charlie Joiner retired at age thirty-nine as the oldest receiver who had ever played in the league. That was one of the least of his records. At the time of his retirement, Joiner was the league's all-time leader in receptions (750), and receiving yardage (12,146). Also, for his career, he had 65 touchdown catches, and his 586 receptions made him the Chargers all-time leader.

His 239 games were also the most in NFL history for a wide receiver. He played in three Pro Bowls (1976, 1979, and 1980), and was also named All-Pro in 1980. Twice, the City of San Diego honored him with a "Charlie Joiner Day." He was inducted into the Louisiana Sports Hall of Fame (1990) and served, from 1980 to 1986 as U.S. Sports Ambassador and official spokesperson for the United Nations Children's Fund (UNICEF).

At Grambling, teaming with quarterback James Harris, Joiner caught 78 passes from 1965 to 1968, as the Tigers went 23–6–1. Joiner was originally a fourth-round pick of the Houston Oilers, and was traded to Cincinnati in 1972, to San Diego in 1976.

"Charlie is the most intelligent, the smartest, the most calculating receiver the game has ever known," said Stanford's Bill Walsh, who formerly was head coach of the San Francisco 49ers, but as offensive coordinator with the Bengals and then Chargers, coached Joiner.

"The more I played, the more I enjoyed it," Joiner said. "I don't know about being intelligent and perceptive, but I know when I came into the league everything was man-to-man coverage. It never changed. Now, it's so sophisticated. Everything's computerized and every team has a different defense. I tried to stay on top of that, recognizing defenses. To play for a long time in this league, you have to read defenses."

With the Chargers, Joiner was on the receiving end of many passes from Hall of Fame quarterback Dan Fouts, who said of Joiner: "One of the highlights of my career, is that I played with the greatest receiver that ever played the game."

COLLIE NICHOLSON
Sports Information Director

In 1946, after serving in the U.S. Marines as a combat correspondent during World War II, Collie Nicholson returned to Grambling to complete the final two years for his education degree. He had no idea he would begin a public relations assault which would make the school and its athletic programs household names.

"The school had no money and no sports information director," said Nicholson, who would become the first full-time SID at a black college. "I thought that any improvement would have been far ahead of what we had. Once I started to work, my long-range goal was to move Grambling to another level and be supportive of (Head Football Coach) Eddie (Robinson). I had no goals beyond that.

"It didn't dawn on me that it would be a job I'd want for the rest of my life."

Nicholson stayed on the job for over thirty-one years leaving in 1978, after teaming with Robinson and Dr. Ralph Waldo Emerson Jones, "Prez," the school's president who was devoted to building the school and the athletic program into national prominence. Nicholson would flood the media, especially the Associated Press-Negro Press and black newspapers (which had numbered 250 nationwide, at one point), with Grambling press releases, photos, or game stories.

He helped put together a nationally-syndicated Grambling Football television show which aired on 135 stations nationwide from 1970 to 1974, and coordinated a national radio network on the now-defunct Mutual Black Network. His media guides won NCAA and NAIA awards.

"[Jones] wanted an innovative approach," said Nicholson, a native of Winnfield, Louisiana. The SID did his homework, and delivered, making Grambling "The Notre Dame of Black Colleges."

Little wonder.

"I got ideas from Notre Dame and Tuskegee," Nicholson said. "Tuskegee, under Cleve Abbott was playing throughout the Deep South and in Chicago. We'd mimic them. Notre Dame would play in New York one week, (Chicago's) Soldier Field one week, and the (Los Angeles) Coliseum one week. Our theory was that Notre Dame was the national Catholic school. We had an opportunity to be the national black institution.

"If we could demonstrate that we had merit equal to programs elsewhere, we could take the program anywhere and make money."

They had equal merit, made money, and the roadshow began. At the 1968 NCAA Convention in New York City, Nicholson took a stroll over to Madison Avenue to see if there was interest in the team playing in that city. His meetings there started the ball rolling for the Grambling-Morgan State games in Yankee Stadium.

"After that, we started criss-crossing the country," he said. And, then, the globe.

When Nicholson heard Muhammad Ali was going to fight a wrestler in Japan in 1976, Nicholson told Robinson, the team should play there.

"He laughed," Nicholson said. "He said, 'That's just another of your crazy ideas.' Prez laughed, too. I said, sounds good to me. Prez called me back, and said maybe it was a good idea. We had already played in Hawaii three times."

So Nicholson headed to Hawaii and took a crash course in Japanese.

"If you can't pronounce names, you lose face and no one will do business with you," he said. "By the third day, no one would talk to me and I was ready to come home. By the fourth day, they had quit laughing. It was 50 percent bold, 50 percent stupidity. But there are always ways to make things work. You have to have a plan and operate it.

"Black schools have a plan, but no operation. It takes innovation, perseverance, and hard work 365 days a year. We also sold baseball, basketball and track. It doesn't mean he's (Robinson) the best coach ever, but he had the best marketing support. None of the other black schools had marketing."

Sammie White, was only 5–11, 189 pounds but was a big time player for the Tigers from 1972 to 1975. He was a two-time All-American, and three-time All-SWAC wide receiver, who set school records for career receiving yardage (2,169) and career receptions (100). White was a second-round pick of the Minnesota Vikings and was named NFL's Rookie of the year in 1976. Courtesy of Grambling

Nicholson currently writes for *Sports View* magazine, a publication devoted to black college football and basketball.

"You have to believe that almost anything is possible," he said. "At the black level we accept the fact that a special level has been carved out for us and we can never achieve above that. We didn't believe that at Grambling. It was great fun. The camaraderie, spirit, between the athletes and coaches exceeds anything you have today. We were all one family.

"Today, there's no feeling of support. They taught us well in slavery. No esprit de corps. It's only about beating each other. But 2,370,000 people attended black college games in 1992, more than the combined total for black attendance of the NBA, Major League Baseball, and the NFL. The economic impact was $200 million.

"So, the marketing possibilities are there."

Now, who'd like to lead the assault?

ERNIE LADD

Defensive Lineman

Eddie Robinson dispatched a recruiter to Orange, Texas, in 1957 to bring 6–9, 210-pound Ernie Ladd up to Grambling for a visit. On their way back, the recruiter, Dr. Charles D. Henry, stopped to call the Grambling coach with this advice: "Hold the dining hall open. I don't known if I have enough money to feed him." Ladd had already eaten breakfast—twice, and added a huge

Ernie Ladd. Courtesy of Grambling

dinner. Upon arriving at the Grambling dining hall, he loaded his tray and announced to Robinson: "I like the way you feed here." Four years later, Ladd, a defensive tackle, went off to chow down on professional football, and weighed-in at 290 pounds, when he joined the San Diego Chargers. During his career, he played at 315 pounds, easy, but his size—extraordinary by professional football standards at the time—was dwarfed by his ability. He played eight seasons in the AFL without missing a game and retired at age 30, and took up a wrestling career. Former league executive Don Klosterman said of Ladd: "He was not a fluke. He had a great mind. He was smart." And good. "He told me how good he was," Robinson said, "and I'd say, 'Sure.' Then, he hurt everybody. Sometimes, I'd feel sorry for the people he was tackling." There was little escape for them, for Ladd, dubbed, "The Big Cat," played two seasons at Grambling with Buck Buchanan, 6–7, 285.

DOUG WILLIAMS

Quarterback

Doug Williams became a starter five games into his redshirt freshman season at Grambling in 1974, and went on to become a three-time All-American and Heisman Trophy candidate and a first-round draft pick of the Tampa Bay Buccaneers in 1978. Grambling was 37–5 with Williams at quarterback.

The Zachary, Louisiana, native threw for 38 TD's as a senior, a school-record 93 for his four year career (seven in a game against Langston). His 8,411 career passing yards are also records at Grambling. At Tampa Bay, Williams guided the Bucs to their first-ever NFC Central title (1978) before joining the Washington Redskins after a brief stint in the USFL. He guided the Redskins to Super Bowl XXII, where he was the game's most valuable player, in Washington's 42–10 win over Denver.

"He had a timing that only comes from God and parents," said Eddie Robinson, Grambling head coach. "When he was drafted in the first round, as a quarterback, an old ache was healed. It was just something you waited for. Doug had all the tools, the desire. The physical and mental tools, patience, and perseverance. James Harris had disspelled the belief that blacks couldn't play quarterback. My feeling was football was football, whether at Notre Dame or Grambling. We told Doug he had the potential to be a good quarterback.

"He worked at it. He worked at it hard."

But there was more involved. In October 1992, Williams wrote this story about the effect Robinson has had on Williams' career. The story appeared in *USA Today*:

"Attempting to explain what Eddie Robinson has meant to me and other athletes might be the toughest task I've faced, probably tougher than going against former black college defensive players such as Ed 'Too Tall' Jones, Harry Carson, Richard Dent, and L. C. Greenwood.

"If I were writing this in 1973, I might not have felt the way I do now about Coach Robinson. When Coach Rob redshirted me my freshman year at Grambling State, I thought that was the worst thing that could have happened to me. I thought I was as good, if not better, than the other quarterbacks who were there. I guess father does know best, and when you think of Coach Rob he is a father-type. He had to be a father figure to many of the athletes. After being around Coach Rob for a while, I realized how fortunate I was to have an opportunity to earn a degree and play for the greatest college coach of all time.

"Try to imagine the number of opportunities he has given young men across this country. Black college football is 100 years old, and one man has been coaching at one university for half that time.

"Two of the greatest tributes he paid to me were in 1977 and 1988.

Doug Williams. Courtesy of Grambling

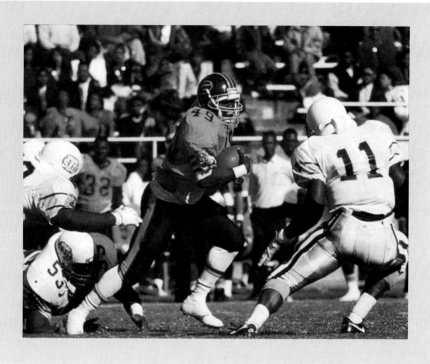

Running back Eric Gant was a first team All-SWAC performer in 1991. Courtesy of Sports View

When I finished fourth in the 1977 Heisman Trophy balloting, he told the team, after a come-from-behind 35–32 victory against Temple, that he felt the Heisman Trophy winner was right in our locker room. I'll never forget how that made me feel.

"In 1988, when I started Super Bowl XXII for the Washington Redskins and we won, he said that was the proudest moment in his professional career."

TANK YOUNGER

Running Back

Like any other college student, Paul Younger left Grambling looking for work in his chosen profession. Generally, maybe the student would find something, maybe not, and his favorite professor sent him off with a "good-luck-write-if-you-get-work" farewell.

All of which would have been fine, except Younger was not like other college students, especially at black colleges, in 1949. His profession was football, his nickname was "Tank," his professor was Eddie Robinson, and, if he got work in the National Football League it would indeed be something worth writing home about. At the time, the NFL had yet to get into the habit of employing players from black colleges. So, after Younger, at age 20, signed a free agent contract worth $6,000 with the Los Angeles Rams, he departed for Los Angeles with a rather weighty farewell from Robinson.

"Coach Robinson said to me, 'Listen, Tank, this is a great opportunity for black college football. You're the outstanding player in black college football. If you fail, it's no telling when another player will get an opportunity. They'll say we took the best you had and he failed.' "

The only failure involved, however, was the Rams, or any NFL team's, neglect in actually drafting Younger, who had already been picked by the Brooklyn Dodgers of the All-American Football League. The Detroit Lions had also expressed interest. Yet, despite the odds, he was the NFL's first-ever can't-miss free agent. The future of black college players rested on his sturdy shoulders, steadied by his very capable hands.

Several black college players had NFL opportunities before him. Younger was the first to stick, two years after Jackie Robinson broke into Major League Baseball and was Rookie of the Year.

"After talking to Eddie, I knew I would make it,' said Younger, who not only made it, but made it big, going on to become a five-time Pro Bowl selection as both a fullback and linebacker, and who now serves as the Rams' director of player relations. "I felt it was something I had to do. In today's language, I was focused. But I'm not so naive as to think I was the first to come along that was good enough.

"I was the first because I had an opportunity, a chance to prove black college athletes could excel at the highest level."

Previously, that level, for blacks, peaked in college, with many of the best and brightest players concluding their careers, then heading back to their hometown to, perhaps, become high school coaches and/or teachers. Some eventually went back to their colleges to coach and/or teach. Younger also had thoughts of coaching, however, after dominating black college football, he seemed destined for a higher calling which cannot be overstated.

Said another former Grambling great, Willie Davis: "For all of us who followed, the identity and awareness of players (from black colleges) was well established basically by the Tank Younger performance."

As a 6-3, 216-pound freshman Younger led the nation in touchdowns (25) and would score 35 more during his career at Grambling, though he started his career as an offensive tackle, as a freshman, compiling all those touchdowns primarily on a trick play in which he was moved to end and the Tigers would use him for an end-around play. His 60 career scores were, at the time, a collegiate record.

(Note: NCAA records—through 1991—list 16 players with 60 or more career TDs, led by Joe Dudek's 79 for Plymouth State between 1982–1985. Younger is 18th on the scoring list with 369 points, however, only he and Army's Glenn Davis (354 points, 59 TDs, 1943–1946), are among the top 25 listed who competed prior to 1954.)

Even at that, it took a while before Robinson finally moved Younger to halfback, after he had also shown in practice that he was pretty good at returning kicks.

He could dash 100 yards in 10.0 seconds.

"You know, I've got to be the dumbest fool in the world," Younger recalled Robinson saying. "Here's this guy trying to tell me where he should be playing, and I won't listen."

Yet, the message was loud and clear. That freshman season, Grambling beat a Selma Field Air Force all-star team, 25–0, with Younger scoring all of Grambling's points. As a junior, he rushed for 1,207 yards and scored 18 touchdowns. In four years for Grambling, Younger also completed 43 of 73 pass attempts, 11 for TDs. He also played linebacker for the Tigers. He was named an All-American following his junior and senior seasons. After his senior season, he was named black college football's Player of the Year.

He was nicknamed "Tank" by former Grambling publicist Collie Nicholson, a war veteran with the Marines.

"It was just after World War II and I was watching him run over everybody he couldn't run around," Nicholson said. "I'd been in the South Pacific, and it reminded me of what I saw those tanks doing there."

Tank Younger signed as a free agent with the Rams in 1949 and became a starter as a rookie, at both fullback and linebacker. He was the first player from a black college to make an NFL roster. Courtesy of Grambling

Nicholson had also described Younger as combining the "outstanding qualities of elephant and antelope." Ironically, with the Rams, Younger, bulked to 235 pounds, was a member of what became known as the "Bull Elephant" backfield, along with Deacon Dan Towler and Dick Hoerner. Each player topped 200 pounds. As a rookie, Younger started at fullback and linebacker for the Rams, but his making the team was the first of several "firsts" for him.

He would become the first black to play in the NFL All-Star game, and in 1975, the Rams would make him the league's first black assistant general manager, a job he also held for 12 seasons with the San Diego Chargers. Still, he awaits a call from the Pro Football Hall of Fame.

His Rams' teammates included Norm Van Brocklin, Bob Waterfield, Elroy "Crazy Legs" Hirsch, and Tom Fears—all Hall of Famers.

"His heroics have never been properly recognized," said sportscaster Howard Cosell. "He opened the door to a new talent source and gave pro football a new dimension. Tank Younger was a great player. No matter what criteria they use in the selection process, the NFL has diluted its Hall of Fame in bypassing Younger."

Don Paul, former Rams linebacker, embellished that sentiment: "Tank

Younger should be in the Hall of Fame for either offense or defense. He and Waterfield were a team all by themselves."

Said Younger: "It doesn't bother me. I think the average fan who knows Tank Younger feels I should be there and I appreciate that. It seems to bother a lot of other people, but I don't worry about it. Whenever I see a player from a black school achieve greatness, it makes me feel good to know I had something to do with it. I've been really lucky. The game's been good to me."

Good, but early on, somewhat cruel.

As a rookie, he and Willie Steele (an Olympic broad jump champion from San Diego State) almost missed a preseason game in San Antonio because a white stadium security officer didn't believe they played for the Rams.

"He wanted to know, 'Where did you niggers steal these passes?' " Younger recalled.

A Rams assistant coach, George Grafton, was nearly arrested trying to help the players get in. The game promoter finally came down and convinced the security officer they were indeed who they said they were.

Too, during one game, Younger was booed by white fans for a bone-jarring hit on New York Bulldogs quarterback Bobby Layne (whose helmet was knocked off—and he lost the ball!). Asked by Rams head coach Clark Shaughnessy if the booing was bothering him, Younger replied: "I don't hear none of that. I want to make the club. I want to play. I told him the only thing I could hear was the offensive and defensive calls. I like to think from that time on, the old man gained a lot of confidence in me.

"I don't know if I felt like a trailblazer, but I experienced some of the same things as Jackie Robinson. But, I guess I was willing to do a lot of things to achieve my goal and my goal was to be a football player in the NFL. So, if this is what I had to put up with, I put up with it.

"But it's been fourth-and-goal all my life. The first thing I can remember in my life, I was three-years-old and our house was on fire and I was in it. I made it through that, and I've faced quite a few challenging situations."

Dear, coach: Got work, and they're still hiring.

Need more players.

Tell 'em Tank sent you.

Alpha Phi Alpha Fraternity General President Milton Davis presents Coach Eddie Robinson with the Alpha Phi Alpha Award of Merit, their highest honor, for his contributions on and off the football field. Courtesy of Alpha Phi Alpha Fraternity

Florida A&M's "Marching 100" stakes its claim to No. 1 fame. Courtesy of Keith Pope

CHAPTER FIVE

Halftime
"The Band Be Kickin'!"

By Michael Hurd and Stan C. Spence

"It is my proud privilege to warn you that, eyes have not seen, ears have not heard, the spectacle that awaits you now. Introducing the "International Institution of Sound," the irresistible musical force, the CIAA Marching Machine. The unbloodied, unbound, unbeaten band of excellence. This(!), is the Johnson C. Smith University Marching Golden Bulls Band, under the Direction of Mr. Duncan C. Gray.

"Band(!), this is your field, do with it as you will."
— Gerald Jackson's halftime introduction of the JCSU band

Popcorn, and nature, can wait. It's halftime, the fun is about to begin, and you've been warned.

Man, you *gotta* see this!

Think the folks who have gotten out of their seats are headed for the concession stands? No way, they got up to get down. You can't sit in your seat, not for this, whether you need to stretch your legs or not. Better flex your toes and get to tappin'.

Halftime used to be musical filler in the name of John Phillip Sousa. The teams headed for the locker rooms to regroup, the bands marched rigidly onto the field to the tune of the school fight song, went through a few formations, threw in a rendition of "Stars and Stripes, Forever," played the fight song, again, and headed back to the stands amid polite applause from the fans.

Borrrrrrrring.

At black college football games it's debatable whether halftime is fill for the game, or vice-versa. Here, you have it all—pomp and circumstance, rhythm and blues, marching and dancing. They call it pageantry, but that's a pretty stuffy description for what goes on here. Halftime is "showtime," nothing less, and when the curtain goes up, anything goes. Pump it up and hang on.

It's halftime with attitude, and you are compelled to pay attention! Drum majors and musicians contorting their bodies in ways accomplished gymnasts

Southern's band members sing. . .
Courtesy of Sports View

. . . and dance, as well as they want to . . .

would envy. The bands quick-step, 180 to 360 steps a minute, to a heavy drum beat, and perform precision drills, or maybe the entire band sings *a capalla*, or maybe they have a celebrity artist sit in. (Though Dr. Isaac Greggs, director of Southern University's band—"The Human Juke Box"—eschews that tactic, saying: "We don't use that. We don't need it.")

A learned explanation of what black college bands are noted for, would be: "Musical fanfares, dramatic exits, quality symbolic literature, variety of pulsating percussion cadences . . . animated maneuvers . . . intricate dance steps emphasizing mass movement . . . fancy arm, leg and instrument movements, deceptive facing movements, four-dimensional figured formations, quick-change or "neon-flash" formations, precision drill, Kaleidoscopic patterns and dance steps interwoven into one concise routine, arranging and scoring to yield a spectrum of sound comparable to that of a symphonic band, and a full percussion ensemble as opposed to the usual snare drum-cymbal combinations."

Got that?

That rather weighty description is in reference to the innovations produced by Dr. William Foster, director of the famed Florida A&M "Marching 100," which now actually numbers "280." Foster and the Rattlers' band began introducing the above-mentioned maneuvers in 1946 and most of what you see black college bands doing today stem from Foster's creativity. And his success with the world-reknowned Rattlers have given that band the reputation as the best in the land, maybe the world.

But, don't tell that to the folks at Southern, or Grambling, or South Carolina State, or Tennessee State, et al. For black college bands, the distinc-

. . . and they're good-looking, as well.
Courtesy of Southern University

tion of which band is best is not clear cut and they work hard to keep it that way. Some schools now use computers to choreograph halftime routines. The football teams compete, the bands compete harder. A lot of fans know Grambling football, a lot more know the Grambling band. Guaranteed.

The bands, whose members may practice three or four hours a day, are in just as great physical shape as the football players, with competition for positions just as keen with private lessons, twirling and band camps now almost the rule for band membership.

Football teams hold secret practices, so do the bands. Tempers flare during the game, tempers flare at halftime. (At an Alabama St.-Alabama A&M game, the A&M band went on first and played well past its allotted time. A fight ensued between the two bands as the A&M group tried to hurry their counterparts off the field! The Texas Southern ("Ocean of Soul") and Grambling bands had such a fierce rivalry, it was nothing to find the bands rehearsing well before dawn, and again well into the night, in preparing for their showdown.)

And, inevitably, after most black college games, someone will say: "We might have lost the game, but we won halftime!" Or, worse, "We lost the game *and* the halftime!"

Leonard Pitts, Jr. of *Sports View* magazine, asked Greggs what makes his band so great. His response?: "Me. And hard work. When people talk about the 'Jaguar Romp,' you know it's something special. All bands will march and play, especially black bands. So, we try to give something special."

Greggs notes that his only competition is from the many bands that rip off his ideas. "Florida (A&M) does not imitate me," he said. "That's why I don't worry about 'em."

As for kids who come up to him at games and tell him they want to be in his band, he says: "I understand. If I was sittin' up there in high school, I'd want to be in this band, too. Sounds like I'm braggin', don't it.?"

Well, yes, but that's okay. Gregg and his juke box heroes are indeed as much a favorite at halftime as the "Marching 100." In his twenty-three years with the Jaguar band, Greggs has led the group to performances at four Sugar Bowls, five Super Bowls, several television specials, the official opening of the Louisiana Superdome, and for shows in most of the nation's major cities, plus trips abroad to Costa Rica and Russia.

Who dat talkin' 'bout beatin' them Jags?

Them Rattlers.

Foster and his group are heavily decorated and, in the battle of the bands, you have to like the Rattlers chances. And, why not? They have been called, "The Lena Horne of Bands." Silky smooth, beautiful to watch—and hear.

Johnson C. Smith, "unbound" Courtesy of Johnson C. Smith

William Foster, FAMU band director, accepts the 1985 Sudler Trophy, the Heisman Trophy for bands. Left to right: Frederick Humphries, FAMU president, then Florida Governor Bob Graham, Foster, and officials from the John Philip Sousa Corp,, sponsors of the award. Courtesy of Florida A&M University

South Carolina State's "Marching 101" Band takes to the air. Courtesy of South Carolina State

A South Carolina State dancer. Courtesy of Sports View

Alabama A&M's "Marching Maroon and White" dancers have been described as "nothing short of spectacular." Courtesy of Alabama A&M

Says Foster: "The FAMU marching band stands alone as the premier band in the country, and I think our record speaks for itself." Sounds like he's braggin', too, don't it? For the record, FAMU's accomplishments include:

Thirty-four nationally-televised halftime appearances, beginning with the 1963 Orange Bowl.

Three films, four national television shows (including ABC-TV's *20/20*, and CBS' *60 Minutes*), and three television commercials.

The 1985 John Philip Sousa Foundation's Sudler Trophy, the marching band equivalent of the Heisman Trophy.

Marching in France's Bicentennial Celebration (Bastille Day) parade in Paris.

A performance at the 1984 Summer Olympic Games in Los Angeles.

As for Foster, he was director of the McDonald's All-American High School Band for eleven years (1980–1991), taking the band to appearances at the Macy's Thanksgiving Day Parade in New York City and the Tournament of Roses Parade in Pasadena. His book, *Band Pageantry*, has become a must-read in marching band circles.

"I seize upon every opportunity for improvement," Foster said. "Creativity and innovation are the keys. We take things here one note at a time."

His first notes came in Kansas City, at age three, when—using a twig and standing on a tree stump—he envisioned conducting a high-stepping band. He bought this first instrument—a outdated, second-hand saxophone—at age twelve, but he would eventually take up the clarinet. He attended the University of Kansas, but despite what he felt was a good audition, he was not allowed to play in the band because of his race. As a senior in 1941, the school's Dean of Fine Arts tried to discourage Foster from pursuing a career as a musical conductor, citing, "There are no opportunities for a Colored person as a conductor." From those events, Foster decided to pursue his

career at a black institution and to develop "a black band as fine or finer than any white band in the country."

He landed in Tallahassee after short stops at Fort Valley State and Tuskegee.

The first Florida A&M band was organized in 1892. The band was popular statewide pre-World War II, but the start of that war saw the band's number dwindle to only sixteen members by early 1946, prior to Foster's arrival in the fall of that year, but ballooned to forty-five for Foster's first year. To build the program, he persuaded the administration to reconstruct Army barracks for use as a band hall, which included classrooms and practice rooms. He would also develop a curriculum which offered a baccalaureate degree in instrumental music and prepared students to become band directors.

During summer rehearsals, heading into the fall football season, Foster would integrate basic and new marching techniques, but he would also experiment. He theorized that an outstanding marching band would also lead to more interest in the school's symphonic concert band. It was during one pre-fall practice that the band's double- and triple-time marching steps began, as "rehearsal horseplay."

From that, also came the "death march" cadence (24–80 steps per minute), then, during the 1950s, the instrument arc (180 degrees) and high knee lift were incorporated, with instruments swinging across the body.

The band was in such demand, some opposing teams, to boost game attendance, would finance the band's travel expenses. Foster estimates over 5 billion people have seen the band (live or via television).

Texas Southern's "Ocean of Soul" is one of the most entertaining groups in the nation, shown here performing at lunchtime in downtown Houston. Photographs by Dan Hardy, courtesy of the Houston Post

Above, Conrad Hutchinson, former Grambling band director. Facing page: The Grambling band, which "embodies the spirit of Sousa and the soul of Ray Charles," has appeared. The first Grambling band was formed in 1926 by Ralph Waldo Emerson Jones, who would become the school's president. Jones could play all instruments, and bought the first band's instruments using Sears Roebuck credit. Courtesy of Grambling

A FAMU "Dance Routine Committee" (much like other schools) allows five students to spend much of May and June "researching" the most popular dance steps among young black Americans, reporting back to faculty members to work out steps and music for the fall performances.

"Bands have changed immensely over the years," Foster said. "There's certainly more variety in things bands do today, and the format of their shows is based primarily on relevancy, relating to the audience."

Despite that, despite the format's popularity, there are detractors. Some musicologists have addressed the question of "black music" being played on the field. The primary concern of these researchers is that music education is being replaced by music entertainment. Greggs obviously disagrees, and addresses the larger issue of reaching the young people that the traditional collegiate football game was intended to reach.

"It would take me ten years to get as many people to come to a concert as we get at a football game," he said. "We reach many youngsters through halftime. Which one do you think is more important?"

The bands can also motivate its football team.

"Right before the game, you look up into the stands, see those friendly faces, hear their good music and it makes you feel good," said the late Howard Gentry, former Tennessee State head coach. "It does something to make you want to go a little harder. Sometimes, if a player hears his band while the game is in progress, you're in trouble."

Stand up and get down. At one game, after halftime, a father turns to his young son and asks, "How you like the band?"

Replied the son: "The band be kickin', huh?"

Oh, yeah.

South Carolina State high-steps into a precision formation. Courtesy of South Carolina State

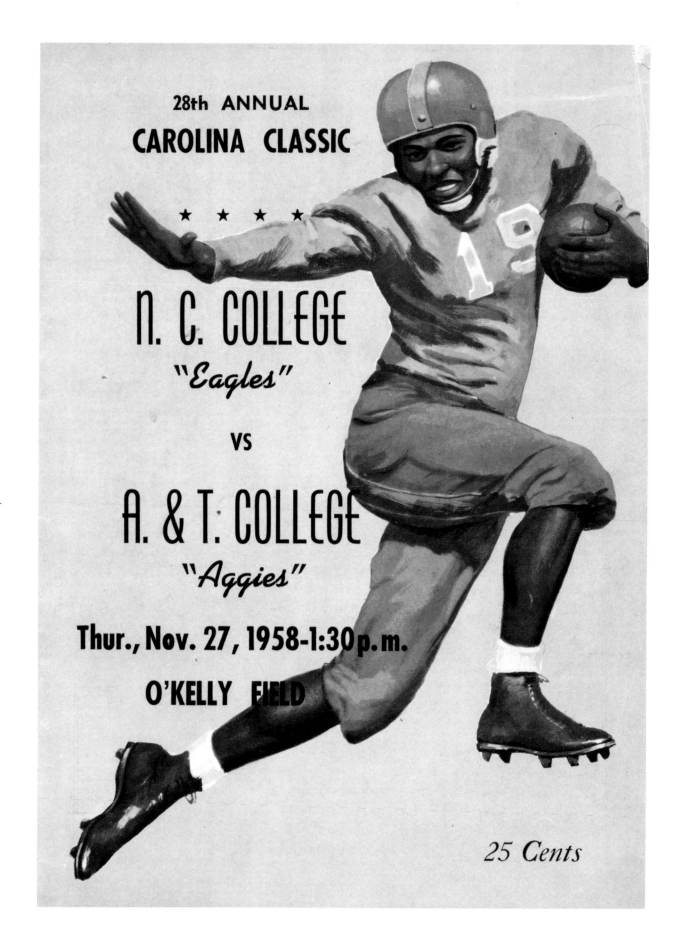

28th ANNUAL
CAROLINA CLASSIC

★ ★ ★ ★

N. C. COLLEGE
"Eagles"

VS

A. & T. COLLEGE
"Aggies"

Thur., Nov. 27, 1958-1:30 p.m.

O'KELLY FIELD

25 Cents

CHAPTER SIX

Rivalries and Classics

If you're at an historically black college and you haven't played in a "Classic" football game, you'd better check the school's charter.

In black college football, "Classics" are *de rigueur*, and there were thirty-seven such games in 1991, played in such divergent sites as Dallas (State Fair Classic) and the Meadowlands (Whitney Young Classic) and Indianapolis (Circle City Classic).

Classic, Classic, who's got a Classic?

Everybody, or so it seems.

Therein, the problem. The basic concept is great: small colleges getting exposure in big-city markets, or corporate sponsorship for games featuring local teams. In the best of intentions, the out of state "Classics" are an opportunity to deliver a piece of home to displaced Southern Blacks. The local events are nothing more than the continuation of annual intrastate or intracity rivalries, or homecoming games, flying corporate banners. Regular season bowl games, if you will.

On the down side, there is a growing disenchantment with the concept, with many school administrators feeling used, and that the product is being abused by promoters looking for a quick buck, doing little to market the games properly.

Said Chuck Prophet, athletic director for Mississippi Valley State, whose team (which included Jerry Rice and Willie Totten) played in the inaugural Circle City Classic, "They're a good thing, but athletic directors and promoters need to take a long look at them. They need to cut down on the number, look at the cities they put them in and the amount of money they're going to put into promoting them."

Hardly anyone knew about the 1991 Capital Classic, when Jackson State played Delaware State in 55,683-seat RFK Stadium in Washington, D.C. The game drew a dismal 5,231 fans. The Motor City Classic, played at the Pontiac Silverdome, drew only 7,114 for its game, Alcorn State and Hampton. Silverdome capacity is 80,500.

"There were some very good classics," said W. C. Gorden, Jackson State's

Texas Southern vs. Prairie View

20,000 AWAIT ANNUAL NEW YEAR'S BOWL GAME

Tiger Men—Here's the starting lineup for the Texas Southern University Tigers which will meet Prairie View A. and M. College in Houston, Tex., in the annual New Year's Day bowl game. The Tigers, clad in maroon and gray, have been installed as 6-point favorites to repeat their early 13-6 win over PVSC. Over 20,000 Texas fans are expected to be on hand for the clash in the Public High School Stadium.

The Prairie View Bowl was always a huge attraction, and one of several non-NCAA-sanctioned New Year's Day games played by black college teams. Courtesy of the Pittsburgh *Courier*

athletic director. "The Circle City Classic is one. It is well-organized, well-planned and the community is involved. The impression I get is they're not so much interested in making money as they are in providing social experiences and outlets for blacks. As a result, it's first-class.

"But, these fly-by-night deals where the promoter gets funding on the premise that they're doing something for historically black schools is a bad situation for the schools and the citizenry as a whole. They're poorly planned. They're put on for one purpose—to make some money for the promoters. They come off as bad ventures that many people charge to black institutions because we're participants."

However, game promoters must now present letters of credit, guaranteeing the game, 180 days in advance, and schools must be given a minimum of $100,000 per team.

The Circle City game's success (they've sold out the last three games) is peculiar in that Indianapolis does not have a large black population, there is no black college in the state (the nearest such schools are Kentucky State in Frankfort (northern Kentucky) and Central State and Wilberforce, both in Wilberforce, Ohio, in the western part of that state.

"We have a central location," said Steve Bassett, the Circle City Classic's general coordinator. "We get quite a few people from Detroit, Milwaukee, and we're building on the Chicago market. A lot of people were surprised at the game's success. This was the first annual game planned in the north and a lot of people, unfamiliar with black college football, didn't think it would get off the ground."

Texas Southern and Prairie View square off in their annual battle. At times, this rivalry was so intense, it was played before standing room only crowds, with many fans forced to stand around the field. Courtesy of Texas Southern University

The "Classics" trend took off in the 1920s when Lincoln University would travel to Washington, D.C. to play Howard on Thanksgiving Day. That game, for many years, was one of the major events of the season for Washington's black social elite. The first game in that series was hastily organized between Armistice Day (November 11) and Thanksgiving Day, November 21, 1918.

Tuskegee and Morehouse have been playing for eighty years, dating to 1912, in the longest series in black college football, with the last fifty-seven games played as a "Classic." The game has been played as the Tuskegee-Morehouse Classic at Columbus, Georgia, since 1936, when it was organized by E. E. Farley, Dr. Thomas Brewer, Dr. Kid Terry, C. L. Abbott (Tuskegee football coach), and Dr. Frank L. Forbes.

Alabama A&M and Alabama State drew 70,200 for their game in Birmingham in 1991, the largest attendance for classic games in 1991. That event, for fifty years, has been called the Magic City Classic.

The Turkey Day Classic is the oldest of the black college football "Classics," dating to Thanksgiving Day 1924, and is played primarily between Alabama State and Tuskegee. The first game drew eight thousand spectators, but has since drawn crowds as large as 30,000.

Ironically, the two people most responsible for that game's inception were white Montgomery businessmen, Cliff Green (who owned an athletic equipment store) and Fred Cramton, a home builder and lumber-yard owner.

The Orange Blossom Classic, as it is affectionately known, was organized in 1933 by Florida A&M business manager J. R. E. Lee, Jr., and for years served as the unofficial black college national championship game, primarily because of the powerful Rattler teams, headed by Jake Gaither.

Lee's idea was derived from watching the Howard-Lincoln Classic. Howard was the Rattlers' first opponent for the OBC. The Howard team boarded a train, after playing the Thanksgiving Day game against Lincoln, and traveled to Jacksonville to meet Florida A&M at Myrtle Field on December 2.

Florida A&M won that game, 9–6, and is 37–20–2 in the OBC, which has lost a bit of its luster. However, during its heyday, the game was always played in the early weeks of December and attracted huge crowds to Miami's Orange Bowl Stadium. In 1961, a series-record 47,191 fans watched as Florida A&M capped a 10–0 season by beating Jackson State, 14–8.

The game has now become merely a designated game on the Rattlers regular season schedule, but in 1984, the Pro Football Hall of Fame honored the game for its contributions to the NFL by serving as a showcase for the top black college talent during the 1950s and 1960s.

However, the "Classic" that has gained the most exposure for black colleges is, by far, the 19-year-old Bayou Classic, the annual "cat" bout in the Louisiana Superdome, where Grambling's Tigers and Southern's Jaguars renew acquaintances in full view of a national television audience, the only black college game with network TV exposure. The game has grossed over $1 million

Southern and Grambling play now in the Bayou Classic, the showcase game for black college football. Their annual match is played in New Orleans and televised nationally by NBC. Courtesy of Sports View

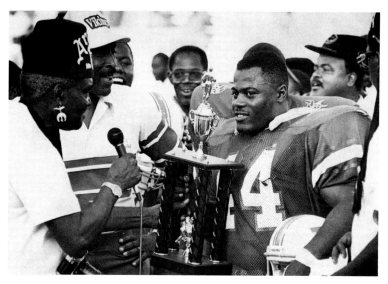

Elizabeth City State running back Alvin Smith accepts Most Valuable Player award at the 1986 Fish Bowl, played in Norfolk, Virginia. Courtesy of Elizabeth City State University

annually for the last twelve years, with an annual economic impact of $16 million on the city of New Orleans, whose hotels are generally sold out for that weekend. The city's taxi drivers reported after the 1992 game (played on the first Saturday after Thanksgiving) their biggest weekend since Mardi Gras, and reservation lists at local restaurants were booked from Thanksgiving Day until the Sunday after the game.

It is the largest minority athletic event in the country.

"For three days, it's the place to be for Grambling and Southern fans," said Marino Casem, athletic director and former head football coach at Southern. "A fan who doesn't show up is probably sick or out of the country. But he's probably got two tickets in his pocket, wherever he is."

Former Grambling sports information director, Collie Nicholson, is the game's founder. He is the same man whose innovative marketing approach put the Tigers on the map as "America's College Team—and Band," as Grambling played in games from coast to coast and became the icon for black college football.

Now, the Bayou Classic carries such national exposure and financial importance, both teams have in the past declined NCAA Division 1-AA playoff berths to play in this event, which coincides with the beginning of the playoffs.

"I think the sky's the limit for this game," said Eddie Robinson, Grambling's head football coach. "You get a major network like NBC involved, and they're going to promote it and let people everywhere know what we've got going down here. It means a lot not only to Grambling and Southern, but to all smaller schools throughout the nation. It's their day in the sun, too."

THE ORANGE BLOSSOM CLASSIC

(Note: All games played at Miami's Orange Bowl, except where noted.)

*1933—FAMU 9, Howard 6	*1943—Hampton 39, FAMU 0	1953—Prairie View 33, FAMU 27
*1934—FAMU 13, Virginia State 12	*1944—Virginia State 19, FAMU 6	1954—FAMU 67, Maryland State 19
*1935—Kentucky State 19, FAMU 10	*1945—Wiley 32, FAMU 6	1955—Grambling 28, FAMU 21
*1936—Prairie View 25, FAMU 10	*1946—Lincoln (Mo.) 20, FAMU 6	1956—Tennessee State 41, FAMU 39
@1937—FAMU 25, Hampton 20	1947—FAMU 7, Hampton 0	1957—FAMU 27, Maryland State 21
@1938—FAMU 9, Kentucky St. 7	1948—Virginia Union 10, FAMU 6	1958—Prairie View 26, FAMU 8
@1939—FAMU 42, Wiley 0	1949—North Carolina A&T 20, FAMU 14	1959—FAMU 28, Prairie View 7
@1940—FAMU 15, Wilberforce 0	1950—Central State (Ohio) 13, FAMU 6	1960—FAMU 40, Langston 6
@1941—FAMU 15, Tuskegee 7	1951—FAMU 67, North Carolina College 6	1961—FAMU 14, Jackson State 8
*1942—FAMU 12, Texas College 6	1952—FAMU 29, Virginia State 7	1962—Jackson State 22, FAMU 6

1963—FAMU 30, Morgan State 7
1964—FAMU 42, Grambling 15
1965—Morgan State 36, FAMU 7
1966—FAMU 43, Alabama A&M 26
1967—Grambling 28, FAMU 9
1968—Alcorn 36, FAMU 9
1969—FAMU 23, Grambling 19
1970—Jacksonville St. (Ala.) 21, FAMU 7
1971—FAMU 27, Kentucky St. 9
1972—FAMU 41, Maryland-Eastern Shore 21
1973—FAMU 23, South Carolina State 12
1974—FAMU 17, Howard 14

1975—FAMU 40, Kentucky St. 3
1976—FAMU 26, Central State (Ohio) 21
1977—FAMU 37, Delaware State 15
1978—FAMU 31, Grambling 7
1979—FAMU 18, Southern 6
+1980—FAMU 57, Delaware State 9
1981—South Carolina State 16, FAMU 15
1982—FAMU 35, North Carolina A&T 7
#1983—FAMU 31, Southern 14
#1984—Alcorn 51, FAMU 14
1985—FAMU 10, Morris Brown 0
1986—FAMU 33, Alcorn State 0

1987—FAMU 10, Central State (Ohio) 10
1988—FAMU 58, North Carolina A&T 7
1989—FAMU 31, Morgan State 13
1990—FAMU 31, Morgan State 15
1991—FAMU 24, Southern 20
1992—Miami 34, FAMU 0

*—Jacksonville
@—Orlando
#—Tampa
+—Tallahassee

THE BAYOU CLASSIC (Louisiana Superdome, New Orleans)

(Note: All games played in the Superdome, except inaugural game in 1974, played at Tulane Stadium.)

1974—Grambling 21, Southern 0 (76,753)
1975—Grambling 33, Southern 17 (73,214)
1976—Grambling 10, Southern 2 (76,188)
1977—Grambling 55, Southern 20 (68,518)
1978—Grambling 28, Southern 15 (72,000)
1979—Southern 14, Grambling 7 (75,000)
1980—Grambling 43, Southern 6 (75,000)

1981—Southern 50, Grambling 20 (67,500)
1982—Southern 22, Grambling 17 (71,555)
1983—Grambling 24, Southern 10 (58,199)
1984—Grambling 31, Southern 29 (51,752)
1985—Grambling 29, Southern 12 (50,742)
1986—Grambling 30, Southern 3 (58,960)
1987—Southern 27, Grambling 21 (55,783)

1988—Southern 10, Grambling 3 (55,450)
1989—Grambling 44, Southern 30 (64,333)
1990—Grambling 25, Southern 13 (70,600)
1991—Southern 31, Grambling 30 (62,891)
1992—Grambling 30, Southern 27 (71,283)

THE CIRCLE CITY CLASSIC (Indianapolis Hoosierdome)

1984—Mississippi Valley State 48, Grambling 36
1985—Mississippi Valley State 28, Tennessee State 13
1986—Central State 41, Florida A&M 3

1987—Central State 31, Tennessee State 28
1988 - Florida A&M 10, Jackson State 10
1989—Jackson State 27, Bethune-Cookman 7

1990—Grambling State 27, Alabama A&M 20
1991—Alcorn State 46, Howard 27
1992—Central State 34, Alabama State 13

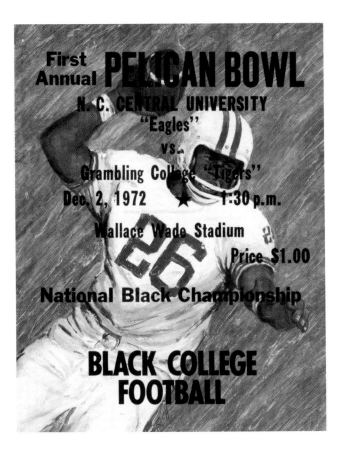

CHAPTER SEVEN

The Pros and "SBCs" (Small Black Colleges)

Paul "Tank" Younger opened the door to the National Football League for black college players. Or did he just leave it ajar? For despite Younger's entrance to the league, which had ignored black college players and had an unspoken quota system for all black players, there was no immediate blitz to allow more black players into the fold.

The door was open, yes, but the only views most black players still got of the NFL were through the keyhole, and there was a long line of players waiting to take a peek.

Then in 1960, along came the American Football League, and the spirited new kids on the football block were a wild and crazy, try anything bunch. Off the field, they were throwing around big bucks in player signing wars with the curmudgeons from the NFL. On the field they were pass-happy, just plain throwing, throwing, throwing the ball. They lived for the pass, for speed. The NFL was still basically a bunch of plodders and bruisers.

Ah, the Sixties, what a fun time. The smell of change was in the air and nowhere, athletically, would it smell as sweet as at black colleges, whose athlete's futures were suddenly about to come up roses, in bunches. If ever there was a match made in heaven, or on Madison Avenue, it was the AFL and players from historically black college football programs. Both were seeking exposure and an opportunity to prove themselves at the highest level.

"The desire to prove they were worthy of playing in the NFL was always very impressive," said Hank Stram, who was head coach of the Dallas Texans/ Kansas City Chiefs, and whose early rosters were loaded with players from black colleges. "There was great pride in the schools they represented. I'd go to Grambling and be so impressed with the overall pride at the school. Everyone was so close, involved and proud of what they were doing. Eddie (Robinson) was so eager to learn (about how the pro teams operated and played). It was a fun thing, great rapport.

"We were the underdog and they were too. It was a good mix." Prior to 1960, before Younger's breakthrough in 1949, if you played football at a black college, your next step after graduation was to return to your home town and

Rayfield Wright was a two-sport star at Fort Valley State. He was drafted by the Dallas Cowboys, but also pursued by the Cincinnati Royals in the National Basketball Association. Here, he leads the way for Robert Newhouse. Courtesy of the Dallas Cowboys

become a coach and/or teacher. But now, they could look to educating in a much bolder, public arena. Their students? The fans, coaches, teammates, et al. who knew little to nothing about the wealth of uncovered football talent at "SBC's" (Small Black Colleges), as some black college players referred to themselves, mimicking the media, which attached that label to a player's school, as in: "Jimmy Kearney, from Prairie View, a small black college outside of Houston."

"It was an untapped market," said Don Klosterman, former general manager of the Kansas City Chiefs. "And there was something about a black college campus. It was really nice. No tensions. The AFL could give those players a chance to play right away. They hadn't had exposure, and we could give that, too."

What a trade-off. Everybody won. And by the time the Kansas City Chiefs made Grambling tackle Buck Buchanan the first overall pick in the 1963 AFL draft (the first of only two black college players so honored in either league's history, with Tennessee State defensive end Ed Jones—Dallas, 1974, the other), the raids were really on. In 1965, the Chiefs drafted wide receivers Otis Taylor (Prairie View), Frank Pitts (Southern), and Gloster Richardson (Jackson State), all major contributors to the Chiefs success in the late Sixties.

"You take the Raiders and San Diego, those two teams predominantly had more blacks than any team in the AFL," said former cornerback Willie Brown, who went to the Houston Oilers in 1960 from Grambling as a free agent, then signed on with the Denver Broncos, before finishing his sixteen-year career with a Hall of Fame stint with the Raiders. "The NFL had only one or two guys sprinkled throughout the whole league. After Tank made it, then you kind of found one or two NFL teams starting to look around for guys at black colleges.

"But there weren't that many blacks in the NFL at the time. Blacks didn't really start going into pro football (in large numbers) until 1960–1962, in that

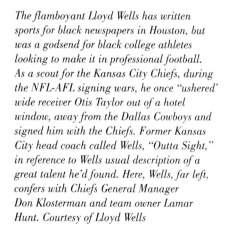

The flamboyant Lloyd Wells has written sports for black newspapers in Houston, but was a godsend for black college athletes looking to make it in professional football. As a scout for the Kansas City Chiefs, during the NFL-AFL signing wars, he once "ushered" wide receiver Otis Taylor out of a hotel window, away from the Dallas Cowboys and signed him with the Chiefs. Former Kansas City head coach called Wells, "Outta Sight," in reference to Wells usual description of a great talent he'd found. Here, Wells, far left, confers with Chiefs General Manager Don Klosterman and team owner Lamar Hunt. Courtesy of Lloyd Wells

Tennessee State quarterback "Jefferson Street" Joe Gilliam's star-crossed career had him, at one time, starting for the Pittsburgh Steelers (in 1974, ahead of Terry Bradshaw)—for six games before getting benched. From there, personal problems plagued him. His last stop was with the Washington Federals of the USFL. Many had felt Gilliam was one of the most talented players ever. "Sometimes, my heart would bleed when I took a fall," he said. "I let some people down, and I hurt them. I was responsible, and I paid for it. No one was as sorry or as hurt as I was." Courtesy of Lloyd Wells

area, and that happened more or less because of the AFL. The AFL came in, and that's when the majority of black football players got the opportunity to play professional football."

In 1971, Grambling had a record 43 players in NFL training camps, but pro scouts had gotten out their road maps and begun seeking out black college talent at other previously unheard of institutions. It was a get-acquainted period.

Once, Klosterman visited Richmond, Virginia to take a look at Virginia Union running back Hezikiah Braxton. Klosterman talked with a coach about Braxton's ability:

Klosterman: "What kind of runner is he?"

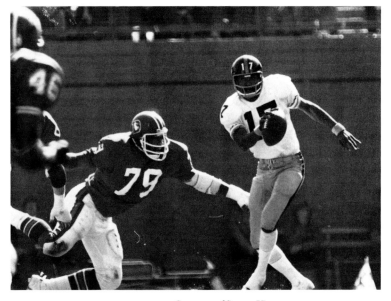

Courtesy of Sports View

Coach: "He's a quick runner, and when he separates the line, you should see the defensive backs scatter for the sidelines."

Klosterman: "Is he a good blocker?"

Coach: "Blocker? You mean he's not carrying the ball? Shoot, you done made your first mistake."

In 1960, a scout was talking with Georgia Tech's coach Bobby Dodd in Atlanta, asking if he had any players or knew of any players worth a look. Dodd suggested the scout take a trip to nearby Morris Brown College. Once there, the scout talked to the football coach, who said he didn't have anybody but he'd seen "the baddest guy God ever gave ten toes." The scout asks, "Is he tough?" The coach added, "He's personally responsible for eleven stretcher cases, seven limp-offs, and four positively refused to return to the games. And

Otis Taylor was outstanding all-around prep athlete and went to Prairie View as a quarterback. Once there, he took one look at Jimmy Kearney, and decided his future would be at wide receiver. The two became an exciting passing combination for Billy Nicks stellar Panther teams of the Sixties. In Super Bowl IV, Taylor capped the Chiefs 23–7 win over Minnesota with a 46-yard scoring pass from Len Dawson. Courtesy of Lloyd Wells

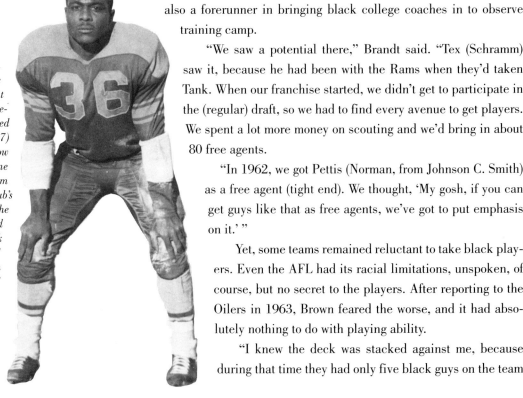

Clemon Daniels, shown here as a back for Prairie View, is still prominent among Oakland/Los Angeles Raiders records. He played seven seasons (1961–1967) with the Raiders, and is now that club's third all-time leading rusher (5,103). From 1962 to 1967, he was the club's leading rusher. In 1963, he rushed for two hundred yards against the New York Jets. Only Bo Jackson's 221 yards against Seattle in 1987 is better in Raiders' history. Courtesy of Lloyd Wells

you ask me if he's tough!"

The player in question was Grambling's massive defensive tackle Ernie Ladd (who once touted college teammate Buck Buchanan this way: "He can run a 22.5 220 with a goat under each arm!).

On one of Gil Brandt's scouting trips for the Dallas Cowboys, he ate chitlin's with Bob Hayes mother in Jacksonville. On another trip, he arrived on a campus to watch a player practice. There was plenty of time to chit-chat, because the available game film was out with the weekend's opponent and, as the coach explained, "We don't practice on Thursday. It's ROTC day." Brandt: Well, how good is he?"

Coach: "He may be the second-best player in the world. Maybe better than Jim Brown. But I'm personally familiar with your team, and it'll take him two days to make your team."

Brandt: "Two days?"

Coach: "Yeah. The first day is picture day, ain't it?"

Brandt and the Cowboys scouted black colleges heavily, and had one scout (Chuck Chatfield) whose only duty was to scout black colleges. The Cowboys would also throw a party for Central Intercollegiate Athletic Association football coaches at the conference's basketball tournament. The team was also a forerunner in bringing black college coaches in to observe training camp.

"We saw a potential there," Brandt said. "Tex (Schramm) saw it, because he had been with the Rams when they'd taken Tank. When our franchise started, we didn't get to participate in the (regular) draft, so we had to find every avenue to get players. We spent a lot more money on scouting and we'd bring in about 80 free agents.

"In 1962, we got Pettis (Norman, from Johnson C. Smith) as a free agent (tight end). We thought, 'My gosh, if you can get guys like that as free agents, we've got to put emphasis on it.' "

Yet, some teams remained reluctant to take black players. Even the AFL had its racial limitations, unspoken, of course, but no secret to the players. After reporting to the Oilers in 1963, Brown feared the worse, and it had absolutely nothing to do with playing ability.

"I knew the deck was stacked against me, because during that time they had only five black guys on the team in camp and speculation was they were only going to keep two, and those two were the guys who had been there the year before," Brown recalled. "So, I knew my chances were going to be slim, because, at that time, they wanted to have blacks so each other would have a roommate. So they were only supposed to keep two on the team. I knew that going through training camp and preseason.

"I only had one ball caught on me all preseason. I thought I should make the team. But, then again, Houston had three guys in the secondary who had made All-Pro and I knew that they probably wouldn't cut those guys. Fortunately for me, Denver saw the things I had done during the preseason and picked me up. There was a quota during that time. With some teams, not all teams, just certain teams."

Tom Williams grew up in the Watts section of Los Angeles, but was an assistant football coach and head track coach at Prairie View, then Grambling. He later was a scout for the Houston Oilers. During the signing wars, he helped Klosterman find and sign players from black colleges, but many of his efforts to bring in players were fruitless.

"I was working in a prejudiced situation," Williams said. "So, I called Rob (Eddie Robinson) and said, 'These people don't know talent. Send me the 1960 and 1961 film on Grambling-Jackson State.' Of the guys in those games, 27 were in the NFL. Willie Richardson, Verlon Biggs, Ben McGee, Buck Buchanan, Ernie Ladd, and Willie Brown were some of them. I showed that film, and said (to Head Coach Wally) Lemm, 'See that big number 70, that's Ernie Ladd. Number 53? That's Garland Boyette.' Wally got to shaking, and said, 'Well, I'll be damned.'

"After the 1966 draft, the Oilers went from 4–10 to 11–4 (in 1967)." He realized if you're looking at a kid at say, University of Houston, then a kid at Texas Southern, you have to do some projecting. There's so much difference in the facilities, but that didn't mean he was not a better football player."

And an opportunity to show that was all that had been asked. Said Art Shell, Los Angeles Raiders head coach, and a graduate of Maryland State of the early black college players in the pro leagues: "It said we were here, we'd made it. We just had to perform."

They did.

"Contact," Willie Lanier, was the pros first black middle linebacker. A Pro Football Hall of Famer, Lanier played for Earl Banks at Morgan State. Courtesy of Lloyd Wells

Left: "Outrageous" barely begins to describe the career of Thomas Henderson, the two-time All-American from Langston who talked and partied his way through a seven-year career. But, the man who nicknamed himself "Hollywood" was quite a show on the football field. Henderson played defensive end at Langston, but was moved to linebacker by the Dallas Cowboys, who made him a first-round pick in 1975, though, as a senior at Langston, his team won only one game. At 6–2, 220, Henderson had great speed, and once returned a kickoff (after a reverse hand-off) 97 yards. He finished the play by "dunking" the ball over the crossbar. Henderson played in the Pro Bowl following the 1978 season. He had a team-best 7 tackles in the Cowboy's 27–10 win over Denver in Super Bowl XII. He also played in San Francisco and Houston, before a neck injury ended his career in 1981 with the Miami Dolphins. His autobiographical book was aptly titled, "Out of Control." "If I was a mute, I couldn't play this game," he once said as a Cowboy. "I love publicity. I love credit for the great playing I do at linebacker. It's been a long way from Langston, from the Dirt Bowl, to the Super Bowl." Henderson, who struggled with substance abuse problems, now lives in Austin, Texas, and is an anti-drug speaker.

Lem Barney had a Pro Football Hall of Fame career for the Detroit Lions. He was a second-round pick out of Jackson State, and played in seven Pro Bowls in his eleven years. Courtesy of the Detroit Lions

Above right and right: Ernie Barnes grew up a shy, sensitive kid in Durham, North Carolina. He went on to play for North Carolina Central, and a career with the San Diego Chargers and Denver Broncos as an offensive lineman. He was named to the All-time Black College Football Team, but his fame these days is as an artist. Barnes recently finished a mural for Seton Hall University. Courtesy of the Company of Art

Alcorn fullback Jack Spinks was the first player from Mississippi drafted to the NFL (1953, Pittsburgh). Courtesy of Alcorn State

Pittsburgh cornerback Mel Blount popularized the bump-and-run, forcing the NFL to change its rules about downfield contact. A Hall of Famer, the former Southern Jaguar's toughness and durability saw him play in all but two of a possible 219 games in his career, in which he became the Steelers all-time interception leader. Courtesy of the Pittsburgh Steelers

Art Shell was a devastating offensive tackle for the Oakland Raiders. He became the NFL's first modern day black head coach since Fritz Pollard in the 1920s. As a player (all 15 seasons with the Raiders), the former Maryland State star was on two Super Bowl teams, teaming with guard Gene Upshaw for a formidable blocking tandem. Courtesy of NFL Properties

Mississippi Valley wide receiver Jerry Rice is unquestionably the best receiver in the game today. At MVSU, he set 18 NCAA Division I-AA records and left with 4,693 receiving yards. San Francisco took Rice in the first round pick. Courtesy of NFL Properties

All SIAC offensive tackle Johnathan Borden. Courtesy of Sports View

CHAPTER EIGHT

The Conferences

CENTRAL INTERCOLLEGIATE ATHLETIC ASSOCIATION (CIAA)

Conference Headquarters: Hampton, Virginia

Commissioner: Leon G. Kerry

Public Relations Director: Wallace Dooley, Jr.

NCAA Affiliation: NCAA Division II

Member Schools: Northern Division: Bowie State, Elizabeth City State, Hampton, Norfolk State, Saint Paul's College, Virginia State, and Virginia Union. Southern Division: Fayetteville State, Johnson C. Smith, Livingstone, North Carolina Central, Saint Augustine's College, Shaw, and Winston-Salem State.

The fourteen-member CIAA is the oldest black athletic conference, having been formed in 1912, and boasts of having two of its teams—Livingstone and Biddle (now Johnson C. Smith)—play in the first-ever college football game involving black colleges in 1892.

Of the fourteen conference members, only eleven are currently participating in football—excluding Shaw, Saint Paul's, and Saint Augustine's.

CIAA Commissioner Kerry.
Courtesy of the CIAA

CIAA CHAMPIONS
(with overall and conference records)

1912	Howard (50, 3–0)	1927	North Carolina A&T (7–0, 6–0)	1942	Morgan State (6–1–1, 5–1–1)
1913	Hampton (6–0, 4–0)	1928	Hampton (8–1, 8–0)	1943	Morgan State (5–0, 2–0)
1914	Hampton (3–1, 2–1)	1929	Virginia State (8–1, 7–0)	1944	Morgan State (6–0–1, 4–0)
1915	Hampton (4–0, 3–0)	1930	Morgan State (8–1, 7–1)	1945	Virginia State (7–0–2, 6–0–1)
1916	Hampton (4–0, 3–0)	1931	Hampton (7–0–1, 6–0–1)	1946	Morgan State (8–0, 7–0)
1917	Virginia Union (4–0, 2–0)	1932	Morgan State (7–0–1, 6–0–1)]	1947	Shaw (10–0, 6–0)
1918	Lincoln (Pa.) (5–0, 2–0)	1933	Morgan State (9–0, 8–0)	1948	West Virginia State (5–2–2, 5–1)
1919	Lincoln (2–0–1, 2–0–1)	1934	Morgan State (5–0–3, 5–0–2)	1949	Morgan State (8–0, 7–0)
1920	Howard (7–0, 4–0)	1935	Morgan State (8–0, 7–0)	1950	North Carolina A&T (6–2–1, 5–0–1)
1921	Virginia (6–0–2, 3–0)	1936	Virginia State (6–0–2, 6–0–2)	1951	West Virginia State (6–2–1, 5–0–1)
1922	Hampton (5–1, 4–1)	1937	Morgan State (7–0, 6–0)	1952	Virginia State (8–1, 7–0)
1923	Virginia Union (6–0–1, 5–0)	1938	Virginia State (7–0–1, 6–0–1)	1953	North Carolina College (5–3, 5–1)
1924	Lincoln (6–0–1, 5–0–1)	1939	Virginia State (7–1–1, 7–0–1)	1954	North Carolina College (7–1–1, 6–0–1)
1925	Hampton (4–1–1, 4–1–1)	1940	Morgan State (7–0–1, 6–0–1)	1955	Maryland State (9–0, 7–0)
1926	Hampton (7–0–1, 6–0–1)	1941	Morgan State (6–1, 6–1)	1956	North Carolina College (5–2–2, 5–0–2)

1957	Maryland State (6–1–1, 6–0–1)		Southern, Winston-Salem State (6–4, 6–3)	1983	Northern, Virginia Union (10–2, 6–1)
1958	North Carolina A&T (7–2, 6–0)	1972	Northern, Virginia State (8–3, 5–0)		Southern, Winston-Salem State
1959	North Carolina A&T (6–2, 5–0)		Southern, J. C. Smith (6–5, 4–0)		(8–2–1, 6–0–1)
1960	Maryland State (5–1–1, 5–0–1)	1973	Virginia Union (9–1, 9–0)	1984	Northern, Norfolk State (10–2, 6–1)
1961	North Carolina College (7–0–2, 5–0–2)	1974	Norfolk State (8–2, 8–0)		Southern, Winston-Salem (9–2, 7–0)
1962	Morgan State (8–2, 8–1)	1975	Norfolk State (8–3, 7–1)	1985	Northern, Hampton (10–2, 6–1)
1963	North Carolina College (8–1, 6–1)	1976	Norfolk State (8–3, 7–1)		Southern, Winston-Salem (9–2, 6–1)
1964	North Carolina A&T (6–3–1, 6–0–1)	1977	Winston-Salem (10–1, 8–0)	1986	Northern, Virginia Union (10–0, 7–0)
1965	Morgan State (9–0, 8–0)	1978	Winston-Salem (11–1, 8–0)		Southern, Winston-Salem (7–3, 7–0)
1966	Morgan State (9–0, 8–0)	1979	Virginia Union (10–2, 8–0)	1987	Northern, Hampton (9–3, 6–2)
1967	Morgan State (8–0, 8–0)	1980	North Carolina Central (7–5, 7–0)		Southern, Winston-Salem (9–2, 8–0)
1968	Morgan State (8–1, 7–1)	1981	Northern, Virginia Union (11–1, 7–0)	1988	Northern, Virginia State (7–4, 5–1)
1969	J.C. Smith (8–1, 6–1)		Southern, North Carolina Central		Southern, Winston-Salem (5–1, 10–2)
1970	Northern Division, Morgan State (8–2, 5–0)		(7–4, 6–1)		
	Southern Division, J.C. Smith (8–2, 6–1)	1982	Northern, Virginia Union (8–3, 6–1)		
1971	Northern, Elizabeth City State (7–3, 7–2)		Southern, North Carolina Central (7–4, 6–1)		

THE SOUTHWESTERN ATHLETIC CONFERENCE (SWAC)

Conference Headquarters: Louisiana Superdome, New Orleans, Louisiana

Commissioner: James Frank (Tenth year)

Director of Publicity: Lonza Hardy, Jr.

NCAA Affiliation: Division 1-AA

Member Schools: Alabama State, Alcorn State, Grambling State, Jackson State, Mississippi Valley State, Prairie View A&M, Southern University, Texas Southern.

The Southwestern Athletic Conference was formed in 1920 with a tightly-grouped "Super Six" line-up of Texas teams, most church-supported, and all located within a somewhat ragged central-to-east Texas corridor. The teams were: Bishop and Wiley colleges in Marshall, Paul Quinn College in Waco, Sam Houston College in Austin, Prairie View College (just west of Houston), and Texas College in Tyler.

The founding fathers were C. H. Fuller of Bishop, E. B. Evans, H. J. Evans, H. J. Mason, and Willie Stams of Prairie View, Red Randolph and C. H. Patterson of Paul Quinn, G. Whitte Jordan of Wiley, and D. C. Fuller of Texas College.

Paul Quinn, having won two conference titles (1922, 1924), left the group in 1929, with Langston University in Oklahoma being admitted in 1931 as the first of the league's state-supported schools. Langston would exit the SWAC in 1957, taking nine conference championship trophies with them (though only one — 1939 — was won outright). Langston won, or shared, five consecutive titles from 1936 to 1940.

Southern's Jaguars (Baton Rouge) joined the conference in 1934, followed by Arkansas AM&N (Pine Bluff) in 1936 and Texas Southern in 1954. The Jags wasted little time dominating play, winning their first conference title in 1937. They won eight SWAC championships in their first sixteen years in the league, including five consecutive from 1946 to 1950 under legendary Head Coach Arnett "Ace" Mumford.

As enrollment at state-supported schools grew rapidly, the SWAC's church-

SWAC Commissioner Frank.
Courtesy of the SWAC

supported members begin to stumble, unable to adequately finance their programs and keep pace. They were slowly pushed aside by the incoming tide of bigger, better-supported state schools such as Grambling College and Jackson State. Those two schools came aboard in 1958, but Bishop (in 1956) and Langston (1957) had already departed. Sam Houston dropped out in 1959.

Grambling, guided by coach Eddie Robinson, strongly challenged Southern's superiority. In a sixteen year stretch (1965–1980) Grambling won or shared twelve titles, though it should be noted that Mumford retired in 1961, and Grambling did not win its first outright title until 1965. Their first-ever title was shared with Southern and Prairie View in 1960.

In 1961, Texas College withdrew from the ranks, but Alcorn A&M was admitted the following season. Wiley became the fifth of the original six charter schools to exit in 1968, with Mississippi Valley State College being added that same year. Arkansas AM&N left in 1970 and it would be twelve years before the next and final addition—Alabama State University—leaving Prairie View A&M the lone charter member among the current "Super Eight."

The Panthers have gotten little respect in recent years. They've had only one season (6–5, 1976 under Hoover Wright) finishing better than .500 since 1964, the next to last season for head coach Billy Nicks. However, in Nicks' sixteen seasons, Prairie View was one of the premier football programs in the country. He guided the Panthers to five black national titles and eight of Prairie View's ten SWAC championships.

James Frank, of Aliquippa, Pennsylvania, is only the conference's second full-time commissioner. From 1981 to 1983, Frank was president of the NCAA. He is a 1953 graduate of Lincoln University.

Winston-Salem State quaterback Mitch Nicholson led the nation (Division II) in passing in 1990 with 22 TD's, only 6 interceptions. Courtesy of Sports View

SWAC CHAMPIONS (1921–1991)

Note: Conference and overall records prior to 1944 unavailable

1921	Wiley College	1941	No Champion (Prairie View declared ineligible)	1957	Wiley College (6–0, 10–0–1)
1922	Paul Quinn College			1958	Prairie View (5–0, 8–0–1)
1923	Wiley College	1942	Texas College	1959	Southern (7–0, 8–2–1)
1924	Paul Quinn College	1943	No Champion (War)	1960	Southern (6–1, 9–1), Prairie View (6–1, 9–1), Grambling State (6–1, 9–1)
1925	Bishop College	1944	Texas College (5–1, 8–1), Wiley (5–1, 8–1), Langston (5–1, 6–2–1)		
1926	Sam Houston College				
1927	Wiley College			1961	Jackson State (6–1, 9–1)
1928	Wiley College	1945	Wiley College (6–0, 10–0)	1962	Jackson State (6–1, 9–1)
1929	Wiley College	1946	Southern (5–1, 8–2–1)	1963	Prairie View (7–0, 9–0)
1930	Wiley College	1947	Southern (7–0, 10–2)	1964	Prairie View (7–0, 10–1)
1931	Prairie View	1948	Southern (7–0, 11–0)	1965	Grambling State (6–1, 8–2)
1932	Wiley College	1949	Southern (6–0–1, 10–0–1), Langston (6–0–1, 8–1–1)	1966	Southern (4–2–1, 7–2–1), Grambling (4–2–1, 6–2–1), Texas Southern (4–2–1, 5–4–1), Arkansas AM&N (4–2–1, 4–5–1)
1933	Langston, Prairie View, Wiley College				
		1950	Southern (7–0, 10–0–1)		
1934	Texas College	1951	Prairie View (6–1, 8–1)		
1935	Texas College	1952	Prairie View (6–0, 7–1)	1967	Grambling State (6–1, 8–1)
1936	Texas College, Langston	1953	Prairie View (6–0, 10–0)	1968	Alcorn State (6–1, 8–1), Grambling State (6–1, 8–2), Texas Southern (6–1, 8–1)
1937	Southern, Langston	1954	Prairie View (6–0, 9–1)		
1938	Southern, Langston	1955	Southern (6–1, 7–2–1)		
1939	Langston	1956	Texas Southern (5–1, 9–1), Wiley (5–1, 6–3–1)	1969	Alcorn State (6–1, 8–0–1)
1940	Southern, Langston			1970	Alcorn State (6–0, 8–1)

1971	Grambling State (5–1, 9–2)	1976	Alcorn State (5–1, 8–2)	1984	Alcorn State (7–0, 9–1)
1972	Grambling State (5–1, 10–2), Jackson State (5–1, 8–3)	1977	Grambling State (6–0, 10–1)	1985	Grambling State (6–1, 9–3), Jackson State (6–1, 8–3)
1973	Grambling State (5–1, 9–2), Jackson State (5–1, 9–2)	1978	Grambling State (5–0–1, 9–1–1)	1986	Jackson State (7–0, 9–3)
1974	Grambling State (5–1, 11–1), Alcorn State (5–1, 9–2)	1979	Alcorn State (5–1, 8–2), Grambling State (5–1, 8–3)	1987	Jackson State (7–0, 8–3–1)
		1980	Grambling State (5–1, 10–2), Jackson State (5–1, 8–3)	1988	Jackson State (7–0, 8–1–2)
1975	Grambling State (4–2, 10–2), Jackson State (4–2, 7–3), Southern (4–2, 7–3)	1981	Jackson State (5–1, 9–2–1)	1989	Grambling State (7–0, 9–3)
		1982	Jackson State (6–0, 9–2)	1990	Jackson State (5–1, 8–4)
		1983	Grambling State (6–0–1, 8–1–2)	1991	Alabama State (6–0–1, 11–0–1)

OFFENSIVE PLAYERS OF THE YEAR

1984	Willie Totten,	QB	Mississippi Valley State	1988	Lewis Tillman	RB	Jackson State
1985	Willie Totten	QB	Mississippi Valley State	1989	Clemente Gordon	QB	Grambling State
1986	Brad Baxter	FB	Alabama State	1990	Walter Dean	FB	Grambling State
1987	Lewis Tillman	RB	Jackson State	1991	Steve McNair	QB	Alcorn State

DEFENSIVE PLAYERS OF THE YEAR

1984	Bruce Green	LB	Texas Southern	1988	Kevin Dent	DB	Jackson State
1985	Jackie Walker	LB	Jackson State	1989	Darion Conner	LB	Jackson State
1986	Kevin Dent	DB	Jackson State	1990	Eddie Robinson, Jr.		Alabama State
1987	Andre Lloyd	LB	Jackson State	1991	Eddie Robinson, Jr.		Alabama State

COACHES OF THE YEAR

1984	Marino Casem	Alcorn State	1988	W. C. Gorden	Jackson State
1985	W. C. Gorden	Jackson State	1989	Eddie Robinson	Grambling State
1986	W. C. Gorden	Jackson State	1990	Houston Markham	Alabama State
1987	W. C. Gorden	Jackson State	1991	Houston Markham	Alabama State

FOOTBALL PLAYERS IN THE SWAC HALL OF FAME

(inaugural inductees, May 23, 1992)

Lem Barney	Jackson State (DB)	Severne Frazier	Alabama State
Buck Buchanan	Grambling (DL)	Ken Houston	Prairie View (DB)
Marino Casem	Alcorn (coach)	U.S. McPherson Jr.	Mississippi Valley (coach)
Parnell Dickinson	Mississippi Valley (QB)	Arnett W.	Mumford, Southern (coach)
Alexander Durley	Texas Southern (coach)	William J. Nicks	Prairie View (coach)
Edward B. Evans	Prairie View (former school president and founding father of the conference)	Eddie Robinson	Grambling (coach)
Audrey Ford	Texas Southern (QB)	Johnny Spinks	Alcorn

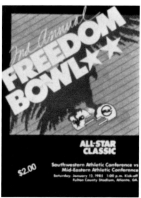

The MEAC and SWAC faced-off in four all-star games, from 1984–1986, called the "Freedom Bowl." The first three were played at Atlanta's Fulton County Stadium, the final game in RFK Stadium, Washintton, D.C. Courtesy of Russell Stockard

SOUTHERN INTERCOLLEGIATE ATHLETIC CONFERENCE (SIAC)

Conference Headquarters: Atlantic, Georgia

Commissioner: Wallace Jackson

Public Relations Director: Gary Abernathy

NCAA Affiliation: NCAA Division II

Member school: Alabama A&M University, Albany State College, Clark Atlanta University, Fort Valley State College, LeMoyne Owen College, Miles College, Morehouse College, Morris Brown College, Paine College, Savannah State College and Tuskegee University. (Note: LeMoyne Owen and Paine do not field football teams.)

The SIAC initially came together on December 30, 1913, when representatives from eleven black colleges and universities assembled at Morehouse College in Atlanta. The officials came from these colleges: Alabama State University, Atlanta University, Clark College, Fisk University, Florida A&M University, Jackson College, Knoxville College, host Morehouse College, Morris Brown College, Talladega College, and Tuskegee Institute. The representatives agreed to name their league the Southeastern Intercollegiate Athletic Conference.

The present name was adopted in 1929, after several charter members first dropped from the conference then rejoined. Talladega, Fisk, Morehouse, Knoxville, and Atlanta withdrew to form the Collegiate Athletic Conference. However, at year's end the two conferences merged to form the SIAC.

Clark, Morris Brown, and Tuskegee are the only schools to hold continuous membership in the league. Other schools have also held SIAC membership, including: Allen University, Benedict College, Edward Waters College, Lane College, South Carolina State College, Stillman College, Tennessee State University, Rust College and Xavier University.

Eight of the current eleven schools are located in Georgia.

SIAC Commissioner Jackson.
Courtesy of the SEAC

SIAC CHAMPIONS

1920	Morehouse	1939	Florida A&M	1958	Florida A&M	1977	Florida A&M
1921	Morehouse	1940	Morris Brown	1959	Florida A&M	1978	Florida A&M
1922	Morehouse	1941	Morris Brown	1960	Florida A&M	1979	Alabama A&M
1923	Morehouse, Fisk	1942	Florida A&M	1961	Florida A&M	1980	Alabama A&M
1924	Tuskegee	1943	Florida A&M	1962	Florida A&M, Alabama A&M	1981	Alabama A&M
1925	Tuskegee	1944	Tuskegee	1963	Florida A&M	1982	Fort Valley State
1926	Tuskegee	1945	Florida A&M	1964	Florida A&M	1983	Fort Valley State
1927	Tuskegee	1946	Florida A&M	1965	Florida A&M	1984	Albany State
1928	Tuskegee, Clark	1947	Florida A&M	1966	Alabama A&M	1985	Albany State, Fort Valley State
1929	Tuskegee	1948	Florida A&M	1967	Florida A&M		
1930	Tuskegee	1949	Florida A&M	1968	Florida A&M	1986	Albany State
1931	Tuskegee	1950	Florida A&M	1969	Florida A&M	1987	Tuskegee
1932	Tuskegee	1951	Morris Brown	1970	Florida A&M	1988	Albany State
1933	Tuskegee	1952	Bethune-Cookman	1971	Florida A&M	1989	Alabama A&M
1934	Tuskegee, Morris Brown	1953	Florida A&M	1972	Alabama A&M	1990	Alabama A&M
1935	Morris Brown	1954	Florida A&M	1973	Bethune-Cookman	1991	Alabama A&M, Clark Atlanta, Fort Valley State, Morehouse, Tuskegee
1936	Alabama State	1955	Florida A&M	1974	Tuskegee		
1937	Tuskegee	1956	Florida A&M	1975	Bethune-Cookman		
1938	Florida A&M	1957	Florida A&M	1976	Bethune-Cookman	1992	Fort Valley State

MEAC Commissioner Free.
Courtesy of the MEAC

MID-EASTERN ATHLETIC CONFERENCE (MEAC)

Conference Headquarters: Greensboro, North Carolina

Commissioner: Ken Free (seventeenth year)

Information Director: Larry Barber

NCAA Affiliation: NCAA Division 1-AA

Member Schools: Bethune-Cookman College, Coppin State College, Delaware State College, Florida A&M University, Howard University, Maryland Eastern Shore University, Morgan State University, North Carolina A&T State University, South Carolina State University.

The MEAC, the newest of the four historically black college football conferences, got its inception in 1969, after several intercollegiate athletics veterans met to discuss the feasibility of organizing a new conference along the Atlantic coastline. The resulting steering and planning committee reported to interested schools and representatives from the institutions convened to adopt a program. The result was the MEAC, their pact confirmed in 1970 with these seven charter members: Delaware State, Howard University, Maryland Eastern Shore, Morgan State University, North Carolina A&T State, North Carolina Central, and South Carolina State College.

The league's first additions came in 1979 when Bethune-Cookman and Florida A&M were voted in. However, that same year, Morgan State, North Carolina Central, and Maryland Eastern Shore withdrew from the conference. Maryland was re-admitted in 1981, and Morgan State rejoined the fold in 1984. Florida A&M also took a hiatus, dropping out in 1984, but returning in 1986. Coppin State had been added bringing the conference to its current make-up.

The conference was granted Division I status by the NCAA in 1980 and has had representatives in the Division 1-AA playoffs in 1981, 1982, 1986. South Carolina State has been the conference's dominant team, winning or sharing nine of the twenty championships, and placing 120 players on the All-MEAC team, easily out-distancing Delaware State's 75, second in that department. From 1977 to 1983, State's Bulldogs won six of the seven titles, with a 29–1–1 conference record. In 1981 and 1982, South Carolina State advanced to second round play in the NCAA's I-AA Championships.

Among the conference's top players who have gone on to success in the National Football League include: LB Harry Carson (South Carolina State/New York Giants), DL Barney Chavous (South Carolina State/Denver Broncos—including entrance to the team's "Ring of Honor"), DE Carl Hairston (Maryland Eastern Shore/Philadelphia Eagles), DB Donnie Shell (South Carolina State/Pittsburgh Steelers), WR Steve Wilson (Howard/Denver Broncos—as a defensive back), OL Edwin Baily (South Carolina State/Seattle Seahawks), DL Nate Newton (Florida A&M/Dallas Cowboys—as offensive lineman), and WR John Taylor (Delaware State/San Francisco 49ers).

Free is the league's first and only full-time commissioner. He is a graduate of. North Carolina A&T. A former baseball player, Free once caught legendary pitcher Satchel Paige during a barnstorming tour.

N. C. Central quarterback Earl Harvey set thirteen Division II records in his four-year career (1985–1988). Courtesy of Sports View

YEARLY CHAMPIONS

(overall and conference record)

1971	Morgan State (6–4–1, 5–0–1)	1978	South Carolina State (8–2–1, 5–0–1)	1985	Delaware State (9–2, 4–0)
1972	North Carolina Central (9–2, 5–1)	1979	Morgan State (9–2, 5–0)	1986	North Carolina A&T (9–3, 4–1)
1973	North Carolina Central (7–4, 5–1)	1980	South Carolina State (10–1, 5–0)	1987	Howard (9–1, 5–0)
1974	South Carolina State (8–4, 5–1)	1981	South Carolina State (10–3, 5–0)	1988	Bethune-Cookman (5–6, 4–2)
1975	South Carolina State (8–2–1, 5–1)	1982	South Carolina State (9–3, 4–1)	1989	Delaware State (7–4, 5–1)
1976	South Carolina State (10–1, 5–1)	1983	South Carolina State (7–3, 4–0)	1990	Florida A&M (7–4, 6–0)
1977	South Carolina State (9–1–1, 6–0)	1984	Bethune-Cookman (7–3, 4–0)	1991	Delaware State (9–2, 5–1)

COACHES OF THE YEAR

1971	George Quiett,	North Carolina Central	1980	Jim McKinley,	North Carolina A&T
1972	Tillman Sease,	Howard	1981	Bill Davis,	South Carolina State
1973	Willie Jeffries,	South Carolina State	1982	Bill Davis,	South Carolina State
1974	Willie Jeffries,	South Carolina State	1983	Joe Purzycki,	Delaware State
	Hornsby Howell,	North Carolina A&T	1984	Larry Little,	Bethune-Cookman
	Douglas Porter,	Howard	1985	William Collick,	Delaware State
1975	Hornsby Howell,	North Carolina A&T	1986	Mo Forte,	North Carolina A&T
1976	Willie Jeffries,	South Carolina State	1987	N/A	
	Henry Lattimore,	Morgan State	1988	Ken Riley,	Florida A&M
1977	Edmund Wyche,	Delaware State	1989	Steve Wilson,	Howard
1978	Willie Jeffries,	South Carolina State	1990	Ken Riley,	Florida A&M
1979	Clarence Thomas,	Morgan State	1991	Bill Hayes,	North Carolina A&T

OFFENSIVE PLAYERS OF THE YEAR

1971	Willie Wright,	SE,	North Carolina A&T	1982	Tracy Singleton,	WR,	Howard
1972	Jefferson Inman,	RB,	North Carolina Central	1983	Ray Alexander,	WR,	Florida A&M
1973	Eddie Richardson,	SE,	Howard	1984	Gene Lake,	RB,	Delaware State
1974	Michael Banks,	QB,	Howard	1985	John Taylor,	WR,	Delaware State
1975	George Ragsdale,	RB,	North Carolina A&T	1986	Alan Hooker,	QB,	North Carolina A&T
1976	Elsworth Turner,	QB,	North Carolina A&T	1987	Harvey Reed,	RB,	Howard
1977	Ricky Anderson,	RB,	South Carolina State	1988	Lee DeBose,	QB,	Howard
1978	Nate Rivers,	QB,	South Carolina State	1989	Amir Rasul,	RB,	Florida A&M
1979	Darrell Coulter,	QB,	Morgan State	1990	Connell Maynor,	QB,	North Carolina A&T
1980	Ron Wilson,	QB,	Howard	1991	Connell Mayner,	QB,	North Carolina A&T
1981	Tracy Singleton,	WR,	Howard				

DEFENSIVE PLAYERS OF THE YEAR

1971	Ben Blacknall,	LB,	North Carolina A&T	1982	John Courtney,	DL,	South Carolina State
1972	Alexander Jones,	LB,	North Carolina Central	1983	Barney Bussey,	DB,	South Carolina State
1973	Eugene Sims,	LB,	Morgan State	1984	John Bostic,	DB,	Bethune-Cookman
1974	Harry Carson,	DE,	South Carolina State	1985	Dan Candeloro,	DL,	Delaware State
1975	Harry Carson,	DE,	South Carolina State	1986	Joe Burton,	DB,	Delaware State
1976	Robert Sims,	DT,	South Carolina State	1987	Robert Presbury,	DL,	Delaware State
1977	Dwaine Board,	DE,	North Carolina State	1988	Demetrius Harrison,	LB,	North Carolina A&T
1978	Bobby Moore,	DE,	South Carolina State	1989	Demetrius Harrison,	LB,	North Carolina A&T
1979	Phillip Murphy,	DT,	South Carolina State	1990	James Dozier,	DL,	Morgan State
1980	John Alford,	DL,	South Carolina State	1991	Robert Porcher,	DL,	South Carolina State
1981	Booker Reese,	DL,	Bethune-Cookman				

Morgan State's All-MEAC safety Robert Johnson. Courtesy of Sports View

CHAPTER NINE

The Schools

ALABAMA A&M

Location: Normal, Alabama

Founded: 1875 (enrollment 4,500)

Stadium: Milton Frank (10,000)

Nickname: Bulldogs

Colors: Maroon and White

All-time Record: 249–223–25

Conference: SIAC

Year To Remember: 1979, earned first-ever trip to NCAA Division II playoffs.

Coach To Remember: Louis Crews, 95–51–3 (1960–1975; undefeated, 8–0, in 1963)

Players To Remember: WR John Stallworth, RB Ronnie Coleman, OL Howard Ballard.

Band: The Marching Maroon and White (W.C. Handy "Father of the Blues" was the band's director from 1900–1903).

ALABAMA STATE

Location: Montgomery, Alabama

Founded: 1874 (enrollment 4,500)

Stadium: Cramton Bowl (24,600)

Nickname: Hornets

Colors: Old Gold and Black

All-time Record: 349–323–40

Conference: SWAC

Year To Remember: 1991, 11–0–1 (first SWAC title; first undefeated season in school history; played in inaugural Heritage Bowl—first NCAA-sanctioned postseason game for black colleges).

Coach To Remember: Houston Markham, Jr. ("The Quiet Storm"), has had only one losing season in six years with Hornets (44–19–3).

Players To Remember: LB Eddie Robinson, Jr., Brad Baxter, Curtis Green, Terry Greer, DB Ricky Jones, G William Coger.

Band: Marching Hornets

ALBANY STATE

Location: Albany, Georgia

Founded: 1903 (enrollment 2,400)

Stadium: Hugh Mills (12,000)

Nickname: Golden Rams

Colors: Blue and Gold

All-time Record: 210–203–21

Conference: SIAC

Year To Remember: 1960, Rams finished 7–0–2 and did not give up a score. (Ninety-five percent of that team's players received their diplomas.) 1984, won SIAC Championship.

Coach To Remember: Obie O'Neill (80–112–10; 1951–1967, one undefeated season).

Player To Remember: Dan Land, record for single season rushing yards (1,311 yards, 1986).

Band: The Show Band of Southwest Georgia (dancers, "Passionettes")

Eddie Robinson, Jr. (No. 57) is not related to the legendary Grambling coach, but they do have something in common: both are winners. Robinson was an All-American and SWAC Defensive Player of the Year in 1990. He's currently with the Houston Oilers. Courtesy of Sports View

ALCORN STATE

Location: Lorman, Mississippi

Founded: 1830 (enrollment 3,300)

Stadium: Henderson (10,000)

Nickname: Braves

Colors: Purple and Gold

All-time Record: 336–217–37

Conference: SWAC

Year To Remember: 1968, 1969 (combined 17–1–1, back-to-back National Black Champions)

Coach To Remember: Marino "The Godfather" Casem (132–65–8 (.644), 1964–1985; only 3 losing seasons, seven SWAC titles, seven times SWAC Coach of the Year, 4 national titles).

Players To Remember: DB Roynell Young, FB Jack Spinks, LB/C Rayford Jenkins, DB Willie Alexander, DE Lawrence Pillars, TE Jimmy Giles, DB Ike Holt.

Band: "Sounds of Dyn-o-mite" with dancers, "Golden Girls"

ALLEN UNIVERSITY

Location: Columbia, South Carolina

Founded: 1870 (1990 enrollment, 233)

Year To Remember: 1981, last year of program.

ARKANSAS-PINE BLUFF

Location: Pine Bluff, Arkansas

Founded: 1873 (enrollment 3,672)

Stadium: Pumphrey

Nickname: Golden Lions

Colors: Black and Gold

All-time Record:

Year To Remember: 1971, last time played Grambling.

Conference: (NAIA)

Players To Remember: DL L. C. Greenwood, Ivory Lee Brown, RB Charles Williams, DL Ronald Bryant, WR Robert Marshall.

Band: Marching Musical Machine of the Mid-South

BENEDICT COLLEGE

Location: Columbia, South Carolina

Founded: 1870 (enrollment 1,500)

Year To Remember: 1967, program dropped.

BETHUNE-COOKMAN COLLEGE

Location: Daytona Beach, Florida

Founded: 1904 (enrollment 2,300)

Stadium: Municipal (10,000)

Nickname: Wildcats

Colors: Maroon and Gold

All-time Record: 292–186–22

Conference: MEAC

Coach To Remember: Larry Little (1983–1991), won two MEAC titles 1984,

1988 (tri-champs); MEAC 1984 Coach of the Year.

Players To Remember: OL Larry Little, DL Lee Williams, DL Booker Reese, QB Bernard Hawk, DB John Bostic.

Band: Marching Wildcats

BISHOP COLLEGE

Location: Marshall/Dallas, Texas

Founded: 1881

Year To Remember: 1920, one of founding schools in SWAC, withdrew in 1956. Program dropped in 1987, school closed in 1988.

Players To Remember: G Reedy Spignor, G Epius Von Rettig, RB Nat Pendleton.

BLUEFIELD STATE COLLEGE

Location: Bluefield, West Virginia

Founded: 1895 (enrollment 2,700)

Nickname: Big Blue

Years To Remember: 1921, 1928 National Championships; 1981, program dropped.

Coach To Remember: Harry Jefferson (coached both national championship teams)

Players To Remember: T Ted Gallion, QB "Bad News" Buford, FB Artis Graves, T Earl Cunningham, QB Herb Cain

BOWIE STATE UNIVERSITY

Location: Bowie, Maryland

Founded: 1865 (enrollment 4,400)

Stadium: Bulldog (6,000)

Nickname: Bulldogs

Colors: Black and Gold

All-time Record: 69–127–5

Conference: CIAA

Year To Remember: 1975, 9–1, 1988, 9–2–1, best seasons in school history.

Coach To Remember: Clarence Thomas (1975), Dave Dolch (1988).

Players To Remember: LB David Swann, RB Ergie Smith, QB Thomas Harris. Marco Tongue, DB, Victor Jackson, DB

Band: The Bowie State Marching Band

CENTRAL STATE UNIVERSITY

Location: Wilberforce, Ohio

Founded: 1887 (enrollment 2,900)

Stadium: McPherson (7,000)

Nickname: Marauders

Colors: Maroon and Gold

All-time Record: NA

Conference: NAIA Division I Independent

Year To Remember: 1986–1990 Black College National Champions; 1990 NAIA National Champions.

Coach To Remember: Gaston "Country" Lewis, 1940–1963; Billy Joe,

1981–Present.

Players To Remember: DE Melvin Lunsford, OG Early Lawhorn, DB Vince Buck, Eric Williams, Roosevelt Nix, DL Harold Hogue

CHENEY STATE

Location: Cheney, Pennsylvania
Founded: 1937 (enrollment 1,800)
All-time Record: 79–258–4

CLAFLIN COLLEGE

Location: Orangeburg, South Carolina
Founded: 1869 (enrollment 900)
Year To Remember: 1965, last year of program.
Players To Remember: FB Claude Willis

CLARK ATLANTA UNIVERSITY

Location: Atlanta, Georgia
Founded: Clark College and Atlanta University in 1989 (enrollment 3,500)
Coach To Remember: In 1928, Samuel Taylor led Clark College's "Black Battalion of Death" to a 13–9 upset of Cleve Abbott's powerful Tuskegee team, snapping their 46-game win streak.
Tuskegee had led 9–0.
All-time Record: 172–252–23

DELAWARE STATE COLLEGE

Location: Dover, Delaware
Founded: 1891 (enrollment 2,600)
Stadium: Alumni (5,000)
Nickname: Hornets
Colors: Columbia Blue and Red
All-time Record: 206–228–8
Conference: MEAC
Year To Remember: 1985, 9–0
Coach To Remember: Bill Collick, led Hornets to first-ever MEAC title in 1985, and was also MEAC 1985 Coach of the Year.
Players To Remember: WR John Taylor, RB Walter Tullis, RB Gene Lake, P David Parkinson, RB Clarence Weathers.
Band: The Marching Masters

DILLARD UNIVERSITY

Location: New Orleans, Louisiana
Founded: 1869 (enrollment 2,000)
Year To Remember: 1965, last year of program.

EDWARD WATERS COLLEGE

Location: Jacksonville, Florida
Founded: 1866 (enrollment 600)
Year To Remember: 1968, last year of program.

ELIZABETH CITY STATE UNIVERSITY

Location: Elizabeth City, North Carolina
Founded: 1891 (enrollment 1,800)
Stadium: Roebuck Field (10,000)
Nickname: Vikings
Colors: Royal Blue and White
All-time Record: 222–216–18
Conference: CIAA
Year To Remember: 1971, first and only CIAA title, guided by coach Tom Caldwell.
Coach To Remember: Donald G. Brandon, 1934–1944, coaching football and basketball, member ECSU Hall of Fame, one of founders of Eastern Intercollegiate Athletic Association in 1939. Tom "Tricky" Caldwell, 86–66, created "Flex-T" offense, one of first coaches to use nickel and dime defenses. Was named CIAA Coach of the Year for 1967.
Players To Remember: QB John Walton, DL Jethro Pugh, RB Alex Haley, RB Ernelle White, RB James McClease, QB Adolphus Woodhouse, DE Everette "Big Mac" McIiver, C Thurlis Little, WR Reggie Langhorne, DB Bobby Futrell, OL Tracy Boyd.
Band: The Sound of Class

FAYETTEVILLE STATE UNIVERSITY

Location: Fayetteville, North Carolina
Founded: 1867 (enrollment 3,300)
Stadium: Bronco (6,000)
Nickname: Broncos
Colors: White and Royal Blue
Conference: CIAA
All-time Record: 156–252–23
Year To Remember: 1992, finished 5–4–1 record, third in CIAA after being picked to finish last.
Coach To Remember: Ray McDougal, 55–69–3
Player To Remember: DT Blenda Gay
Band: The FSU Marching Band

FISK UNIVERSITY

Location: Nashville, Tennessee
Founded: 1867 (enrollment 911)
Nickname: Bulldogs
Year To Remember: 1893, first team organized, calling themselves, "The Sons of Milo," after school president Erastus Milo Cravath; 1907, coached by John W. Work, leader of the Jubilee Singers, took the team on two-week tour, playing four games and singing a dozen concerts; 1984, last year of program.
Coach To Remember: Charles Snyder, who organized first team; Warren G. Waterman, of Yale, first official coach (1899). Players To Remember: Booker T. Washington, Jr., QB Charles Wesley; RB "Jack Rabbit" Poole, RB Henderson A. "Tubby" Johnson, RB Joseph Wiggins, T Booker Pierce.

FLORIDA A&M UNIVERSITY

Location: Tallahassee, Florida

Founded: 1887 (enrollment 8,200)

Stadium: Bragg Memorial (25,500)

Nickname: Rattlers

Colors: Orange and Green

All-time Record: 415–162–18

Conference: MEAC

Years To Remember: Jake Gaither era, 1945–1969; 1977 and 1978 back-to-back National Championships

Coach To Remember: Alonzo S. "Jake" Gaither, 25 seasons (203–36–4, .844—best winning percentage of any coach with 200 or more wins—1945–1969; six National Championships; three undefeated seasons; no losing seasons); Bill Bell, 45–9–6 (1936–1942); Rudy Hubbard, 1974–1985, 83–48–3 (11–0 and 12–1 in 1977–1978, back-to-back national championships).

Players To Remember: RB Willie Galimore, WR Nathaniel "Traz" Powell, WR Bob Hayes, DB Ken Riley, RB Hewritt Dixon, OL Curtis Miranda, RB Eugene Bragg, RB Aldolphus Frazier, L Tyron McGriff, RB Clarence Childs, RB Robert Paremore.

Band: "Marching 100," "America's Band"

FORT VALLEY STATE COLLEGE

Location: Fort Valley, Georgia

Founded: 1895 (enrollment 2,500)

Stadium: Wildcat (7,500)

Nickname: Wildcats

Colors: Royal Blue and Gold

Conference: SIAC

All-time Record: 259–165–20

Year To Remember: 1982, posted most wins (10) in a single season and made first appearance in Division II playoffs.

Coach To Remember: Douglas T. Porter, winningest coach in school history, 92–44–2.

Players To Remember: A. C. Jenkins, first Wildcat player ever drafted by the NFL (1954), OL Rayfield Wright, Eugene Hunter, DB Willie Canady, DB Eddie Anderson.

Game to Remember: Nov. 1972, beat Fisk, 13–7, in national televised game.

Band: Marching Blue Machine

Fort Valley State has won or shared 10 SIAC championships (1970, 1971, 1972, 1976, 1980, 1982, 1983, 1984, 1985, 1991) and played in Division II playoffs twice (1982, 1985).

HAMPTON UNIVERSITY

Location: Hampton, Virginia

Founded: 1868 (enrollment 5,700)

Stadium: Armstrong Field (11,000)

Nickname: Pirates

Colors: Royal Blue and White

All-time Record: 385–316–34

Conference: CIAA

Years To Remember: 1985. The Pirates finished 10–2, won the CIAA Championship and received their first NCAA playoff bid. In 1992, they were 9–2–1 and once again won the championship and their second playoff bid.

Coach To Remember: Gideon Smith, 1921–1940, five CIAA titles, 97–46–12; C. H. Williams, 1914–1920 (15–2), three consecutive CIAA titles, 1914–1915–1916; Joe Taylor, 9–2–1, CIAA and Division II playoffs.

Players To Remember: HB, Tom Casey (HU's first player to play professionally), DE Reggie Doss, RB Dennis "The Franchise" Mahan, DB Don Rose, OL Lucias Reeburg, RB Carl Painter, WR Johnnie Barnes.

Band: Marching Force

HUSTON-TILLOTSON

Location: Austin, Texas

Founded: 1952, with merger of Sam Huston and Tillotson Colleges

Years To Remember: 1951, last year of program for Tillotson, and 1952, last year of program for Huston, which was one of founding teams in SWAC.

HOWARD UNIVERSITY

Location: Washington, D.C.

Founded: 1867 (enrollment 12,500)

Stadium: Green Memorial (8,000)

Nickname: Bison

Colors: Navy Blue and White

All-time Record: 378–307–42

Year To Remember: National Championship in 1920, with team called "The Thundering Herd." 1920 team was co-National Champion (with Talledega) for first Pittsburgh *Courier* poll, Edward Morrison was coach. Favored to repeat as CIAA champ in 1921 and got off to 6–0, outscoring opponents 139–3, but was upset in Philadelphia by Lincoln, 13–7. Morrison's career record was 25–5–3. Howard has played 96 consecutive seasons, since 1897.

Coach To Remember: Doug Porter 1974 MEAC Co-Coach of the Year; Steve Wilson, 1989 MEAC Coach of the Year; Willie Jeffries.

Players To Remember: RB Floyd Wellman "Terrible" Terry, RB Harvey Reed, DB Robert Sowell, DB Steve Wilson, WR Derrick Faison, WR Tracy Singleton, QB Michael Banks, WR Eddie Richardson.

JACKSON STATE UNIVERSITY

Location: Jackson, Mississippi

Founded: 1877 (enrollment 6,800)

Stadium: Mississippi Veterans Memorial (62,512)

Nickname: Tigers

Colors: Blue and White

All-time Record: 299–163–12

Conference: SWAC

Years To Remember: 1962, 1985 national titles; 1961 and 1962, for the first time, the Tigers were SWAC Champions (9–1 and 5–3–1).

Coach To Remember: John Merritt, 48–37–6, won national title in 1962 (10–1); W.C. Gorden (1976–1991, winningest coach in school history,

Tellis Ellis, the guiding force for Jackson State's rise to prominence. His first major hire was football coach John Merritt. Ellis began his run at State in 1947 when the school's football field was "dusty and had no bleachers." He coached basketball, football, and taught five classes. "I was jest about everything. I could have left a number of times, but I had a belief the school would grow, and I wanted to be a part of it." Courtesy of Jackson State

only one losing season, SWAC-record 28 consecutive victories 1985–1989, nine Division 1-AA playoff appearances, won or shared SWAC title 8 times, conference Coach of the Year 6 times.

Players To Remember: DB Lem Barney, RB Walter Payton, LB Robert Brazile, WR Willie Richardson, WR Jerome Barkum, OL Jackie Slater, OL Leon Gray, OL Houston Hoover, DL Leon Seals, LB Darion Conner, DL Verlon Biggs, DE Coy Bacon, WR Richard Caster, RB Perry Harrington, QB Roy Curry, DL Robert Hardy, WR Harold Jackson, DE Ben McGee.

Band: Sonic Boom of the South and the "Prancing J'Settes"

JARVIS CHRISTIAN COLLEGE

Location: Hawkins, Texas

Founded: 1912 (enrollment 600)

Year To Remember: 1967, last year of program. First team was organized in 1916 by Dean C.W. Smith. The first game was played against Texas College at Tyler (Tex.) in 1917, with Texas College winning, 6–0. Among coaches in the school's history was Arnett "Ace" Mumford.

JOHNSON C. SMITH UNIVERSITY

Location: Charlotte, North Carolina

Founded: 1867 (enrollment 1,300)

Stadium: Memorial (24,000)

Nickname: Golden Bulls

Colors: Blue ad Gold

All-time Record: 263–282–34

Conference: CIAA

Year To Remember: 1892, played in first black college football game, vs. Livingstone.

Coach To Remember: Eddie C. McGirt 1958–1977

Players To Remember: TE Pettis Norman, QB Luther Carter, RB Tim Newman, RB William Dusenberry, QB Elroy Duncan, DL Daniel Beauford, WR Jack Brayboy.

Band: The Marching Golden Bulls, "The Institution of Sound"

KENTUCKY STATE UNIVERSITY

Location: Frankfort, Kentucky

Founded: 1886 (enrollment 2,500)

Stadium: Alumni

Nickname: Thorobreds

Colors: Green and Gold

Conference: Great Lakes Conference

All-time Record: 272–315–25

Year To Remember: 1934, 8–0, and outscored opponents 189–2. KSU has played in 6 black college bowl games (four in the Orange Blossom Classic), Prairie View Bowl (a 19–13 win over PV), and the 1948 Vulcan Bowl, beating N.C. A&T, 23–13.

Coach To Remember: Henry A. Kean, 13 years (1930–1943), 74–3–6. Produced 13 All-Americans, won national titles in 1934, 1935, and 1937.

Players To Remember: T William Coleman, HB George "Big Bertha" Edwards, QB Joe "Tarzan" Kendall, D'Artagnan Martin, Wiley Epps, Frank Oliver, DB Henry Ross, DL Mike Johnson, Alvin Hanley, WR William Reed, RB William Bass, G Herbert Trawick

Band: Kentucky State University Marching Band

KNOXVILLE COLLEGE

Location: Knoxville, Tennessee

Founded: 1875 (enrollment 1,300)

Coaches To Remember: Iris Brown, Julian Bell, Joseph Cornelius

Players To Remember: A. S. "Jake" Gaither, Paul Brown, Searl Henderson, Michael House, Kevin Campbell, Leroy Dobbins, Eric Carter, T. T. Johnson, Toney Hall, Andre Williams, C. H. Moore.

LANGSTON

Location: Langston, Oklahoma

Founded: 1897 (enrollment 2,800)

Stadium: W.E. Anderson Field

Nickname: Lions

Colors: Orange and Navy Blue

All-time Record: 259–274–28

Conference: Oklahoma Intercollegiate Conference, NAIA Division I

Year To Remember: 1939, 9–0, national champions

Coach To Remember: Felton "Zip" Gayles (1930–1957), 146–78–18, NAIA Hall of Fame; Tobe Crisp (1958–1969), 53–53–2.

Players To Remember: Thomas Henderson, Booker T. Robinson, E John T. Williams, Jake Diggs, QB Don Smith, QB Prinson Poindexter, E Kenneth Payne.

Band: The Marching Pride

LEMOYNE-OWEN COLLEGE

Located: Memphis, Tennessee

Founded: 1862, when LeMoyne and Owen Colleges merged (enrollment 1,000)

Year To Remember: 1951, last year of program.

Player To Remember: E Charles Spearman

LINCOLN UNIVERSITY

Location: Jefferson City, Missouri

Founded: 1866 (enrollment 3,600)

Stadium: Dwight T. Reed (5,600)

Nickname: Tigers

Colors: Navy Blue and White

Conference: Mid-America Intercollegiate Athletic Association

All-time Record: 209–217–19

Years To Remember: 1952, '53, '64 undefeated; co-National Champions 1952.

Coach To Remember: Dwight T. Reed 1949–1972 (152–82–7)

Players To Remember: RB Leo Lewis, RB John Bradley, RB Louis Hefner, RB Lemar Parrish, WR Ricky King, WR John McDaniel, DB Zeke Moore, DB Jim Tolbert, LB Demetrice Jackson, WR Robert Waters.

LINCOLN UNIVERSITY

Location: Lincoln, Pennsylvania

Founded: 1854 (enrollment 1,400)

Nickname: Lions

Year To Remember: 1918–1919 CIAA champions; 1961, last year of program.

Players To Remember: RB Franz "Jazz" Byrd, RB Robert Scott, E Richard J. "Eph" Morris, E Livingstone Mzimba, E Ulysses Young, QB Henry Collins, E Byrd Crudup, T Wayman Coston, RB Walter Johnson, RB Jimmy Law.

LIVINGSTONE COLLEGE

Location: Salisbury, North Carolina

Founded: 1879 (enrollment 700)

Stadium: Alumni Field (5,000)

Nickname: Fighting Blue Bears

Colors: Black and Blue

All-time Record: 170–220–14

Conference: CIAA

Year To Remember: 1892, played Biddle (John C. Smith) in first black college football game.

Coaches To Remember: William Trent, Sr., coached first team; Ben B. Church, in 11 years six titles (1912, 1914, 1915, 1921, 1922, 1923) in North Carolina Interscholastic Athletic Association.

Players To Remember: QB "Alfred the Great" Tyler, Johnny Miller, Jojo White, Sylvester Sutton, Horace Ballard, John Farrar, Larry Lee, Ben Coates, Norris Wiggins, James Simpson, Roy Hudson.

MARYLAND EASTERN SHORE (MARYLAND STATE)

Location: Princess Anne, Maryland

Founded: 1886

Stadium: Hawk

Nickname: Hawks

Colors: Maroon and Gray

All-time Record: N/A

Conference: MEAC

Year To Remember: 1980, last year of football program.

Coach To Remember: Vernon "Skip" McCain. In 14 years at Maryland

State, 84–13–4. Inducted into CIAA Hall of Fame in 1981.

Players To Remember: DE Carl Hairston, RB Johnny Sample, OL Art Shell, WR Mack Alston, WR Marshall Cropper, RB Emerson Boozer, DL Roger Brown, DB Curtis Gentry, DB Bill Thompson, RB Moses Denson

MEHARRY MEDICAL SCHOOL

Location: Nashville, Tennessee

Founded: 1876 (enrollment 623)

Year To Remember: 1899, first year of program; 1911, last year of program

Coach To Remember: J. M. T. Baskette, who coached first team.

Players To Remember: (Note: Most Meharry players were graduate students who had played at other schools.) John L. McGriff, Tom Zuber, C L. N. Bass, DB A. J. "Big Chief" Cochrane, T H. D. Cannady.

MILES COLLEGE

Location: Birmingham, Alabama

Founded: 1905 (enrollment 680)

Stadium: Rickwood (10,000)

Nickname: Golden Bears

Colors: Purple and Gold

All-time Record: 43–155–6

Conference: SIAC

Program shut down in 1989, resumed in 1990. No further information available.

MISSISSIPPI VALLEY STATE UNIVERSITY

Location: Itta Bena, Mississippi

Founded: 1950 (enrollment 2,200)

Stadium: Magnolia (10,000)

Nickname: Delta Devils

Colors: Green and White

All-time Record: 166–199–9

Conference: SWAC

Year To Remember: 1984, Willie Totten, Jerry Rice and RB Carl Byrum set 14 school records as team finishes 9–2.

Coach To Remember: Ulysses S. McPherson, Jr., 28–8–1 (1954–1958); Archie Cooley 42–27–2 (1980–1986)

Players To Remember: WR Jerry Rice, QB Willie Totten, QB Parnell Dickinson, RB Carl Byrum.

Band: The "Mack of the SWAC" Music Machine

MOREHOUSE COLLEGE

Location: Atlanta, Georgia

Founded: 1867 (enrollment 2,400)

Stadium: Burwell T. Harvey

Nickname: Maroon Tigers

Colors: Maroon and White

All-time Record: 320–330–49. Program began in 1908, the same year school changed its name from Atlanta Baptist College to Morehouse.

Conference: SIAC

Years To Remember: 1920–1923, won consecutive SIAC titles.

Coach To Remember: Samuel Archer was undefeated from 1905–1908; Burwell T. Harvey, 59–22–8 in 13 years.

Players To Remember: T A. Louis Irving, James Nabrit, QB W. A. Scott, WR George D. Brock

MORGAN STATE UNIVERSITY

Location: Baltimore, Maryland

Founded: 1867 (enrollment 4,700)

Stadium: Hughes (10,000)

Nickname: Golden Bears

Colors: Blue and Orange

Conference: MEAC

All-time Record: 350–241–30

Year To Remember: 1932–1938, longest non-losing streak in the nation—57 games without a loss; 32-game winning streak, 1964–1968.

Coaches To Remember: Eddie P. Hurt, 173–51–19 (1929–1959; 11 undefeated seasons, 6 consecutive—1932–1937); Earl C. Banks, 94–30–2 (1960–1973; three consecutive undefeated seasons—1965–1967, 24–0), one of only two black college coaches inducted into the College Football Hall of Fame.

Players To Remember: OL Roosevelt Brown, LB Willie Lanier, Clarence "Big House" Gaines, WR Raymond Chester, RB Leroy Kelly, RB John "Frenchy" Fuqua, DB Mark Washington, RB George Nock, TE Greg Latta, RB Bobby Hammond, OL James Phillips.

Band: The Magnificent Marching Machine of the North

MORRIS BROWN COLLEGE

Location: Atlanta, Georgia

Founded: 1881 (enrollment 2,000)

Stadium: Herndon (13,000)

Nickname: Wolverines

Colors: Purple, Black and White

All-time Record: 302–270–37

Conference: SIAC

Year To Remember: 1940–1941, back-to-back national championships; also 1951 national champs.

Coach To Remember: Billy Nicks, Edward "Ox" Clemons, Artis Graves.

Players To Remember: RB John "Big Train" Moody, DB Steve Calhoun, DL Tony Robinson, LB Royal Reed, WR "Tiny" Smith, T Jim Reid, QB Shag Jones, G Charlie Parker, G Alvin Neeson.

NORFOLK STATE UNIVERSITY

Location: Norfolk, Virginia

Founded: 1935 (enrollment 8,300)

Stadium: Foreman Field (26,000)

Nickname: Spartans

Colors: Green and Gold

All-time Record: 158–142–6

Conference: CIAA

Year To Remember: 1974, '75, '76, consecutive CIAA titles.

Coach To Remember: Dick Price, coached championship teams in the Seventies.

Players To Remember: WR "Sticky" Bob Smith, T Moses Trotter, DB Leroy Haynesworth, OL Rod Daniels.

NORTH CAROLINA A&T STATE UNIVERSITY

Location: Greensboro, North Carolina

Founded: 1891 (enrollment 7,100)

Stadium: Aggie (17,500)

Nickname: Aggies

Colors: Royal Blue and Gold

All-time Record: 333–275–39

Coaches To Remember: B. Piggot, 57–40–4 (1957–1967, 3 CIAA titles); H. Howell, 55–34–4 (1968–1976, one National Championship); W. Bell, 51–35–7 (1946–1956, I CIAA title); Bill Hayes 1988–Present (34–23), 1990 Sheridan National Coach of the Year 1990, MEAC Coach of the Year 1991, back-to-back MEAC titles in 1991 and 1992.

Players To Remember: RB Stoney Polite, LB Demetrius Harrison, DL Dwaine Board, DL Elvin Bethea, FB J.D. Smith, T Tommy Day, DB Merl Code, QB Cornell Gordon, FB Robert "Stonewall" Jackson, RB Richard Westmoreland, RB George Ragsdale, RB Mel Phillips.

NORTH CAROLINA CENTRAL UNIVERSITY

Location: Durham, North Carolina

Founded: 1910 (enrollment 5,000)

Stadium: O'Kelly-Riddick (11,500)

Nickname: Eagles

Colors: Maroon and Gray

All-time Record: 311–236–4

Conference: CIAA

Years To Remember: 1953–1954, back-to-back CIAA titles.

Coach To Remember: Herman Riddick (coached the Eagles for 20 years, beginning in 1945 and totalled a 113–57 record. His teams won CIAA titles in 1953, 1954, 1961, and 1963. Riddick was CIAA Coach of the Year five times (1945, 1953, 1954, 1961, and 1963, and, in 1967, was awarded the conference's CIAA Football Coaches Award for outstanding service); Henry Lattimore, won CIAA in 1980, 1981, 1982.

Players To Remember: L Ernie Barnes, QB Earl Harvey, QB Gerald Fraylon, WR Robert Clark.

PAUL QUINN COLLEGE

Location: Dallas, Texas

Founded: 1872 (enrollment 1,000)

Years To Remember: 1922, '24 SWAC champions; 1961, last year of program.

PHILANDER SMITH

Location: Little Rock, Arkansas

Founded: 1877 (enrollment 600)

Year To Remember: 1965, last year of program.

PRAIRIE VIEW A&M

Location: Prairie View, Texas

Founded: 1876 (enrollment 5,000)

Stadium: Blackshear Field (6,600)

Nickname: Panthers

All-time Record: 327–296–31

Conference: SWAC

Year To Remember: 1958, victory over FAMU in the National Championship game 28–6.

Coaches To Remember: William J. "Billy" Nicks Winningest coach in Prairie View history (1951–1965).

Players To Remember: WR Otis Taylor, DB Ken Houston, WR John "Bo" Farrington, QB Jimmy Kearney, RB Clemon Daniels, Bivian Lee, OL Harold Norfleet, TE Alvin Reed, DB C.L. Whittington.

Band: Prairie View Marching Band featuring "Black Foxes"

RUST COLLEGE

Location: Holly Spring, Mississippi

Founded: 1866 (enrollment 1,000)

Year to Remember: 1965, last year of program.

Player to Remember: RB Eddie Smith

SAINT AUGUSTINE'S COLLEGE

Location: Raleigh, North Carolina

Founded: 1867 (enrollment 1,900)

Year to Remember: 1966, last year of program.

SAINT PAUL'S COLLEGE

Location: Lawrenceville, Virginia

Founded: 1888 (enrollment 600)

Year to Remember: 1988, last year of program.

SAVANNAH STATE COLLEGE

Location: Savannah, Georgia

Founded: 1890 (enrollment 2,100)

Stadium: Theodore A. Wright

Nickname: Tigers

Colors: Orange and Blue

All-time Record: 150–204–13

Conference: SIAC

Year to Remember: 1989, 8–1.

Coach to Remember: Bill Davis, school record for wins and winning pecentage.

Player to Remember: WR Shannon Sharpe, DB Robert Slocum, WR Doug Grant.

SHAW UNIVERSITY

Location: Raleigh, North Carolina

Founded: 1865 (enrollment 1,900)

Years to Remember: 1947, 10–0, co-National Champions, CIAA champi-

ons; 1979, last year of program.

Coach to Remember: Brutus Wilson, coached 1947 team.

Players to Remember: FB John H. Love, QB Manuel Taylor, T Zenas Tantsi, G Island Johns, FB Joseph Brown.

SOUTH CAROLINA STATE

Location: Orangeburg, South Carolina

Founded: 1896 (enrollment 5,200)

Stadium: Oliver C. Dawson Bulldog (14,000)

Nickname: Bulldogs

Colors: Garnet and Blue

All-time Record: 352–210–27

Conference: MEAC

Years to Remember: 1976—National Championship, 10–1 record (6 shutouts). 1977, co-National Champions, outright national title in 1981.

Coach to Remember: Willie Jeffries, 73–20–4 (10 years, 1973–1978, 1989–Present; guided team to five consecutive MEAC titles (1974–1978); Bill Davis, coached 1981 National Champions (9–0).

Players to Remember: FB Marion Motley; DE David "Deacon" Jones; WR John Gilliam; DE Robert Porcher (first MEAC player drafted in the first round), DB Donnie Shell, DL Barney Chavous, LB Harry Carson, OL Edwin Bailey.

Game to Remember: 1981 Division 1-AA playoffs (first round) win over Tennessee State, 26–25 in overtime.

Band: The Marching 101

SOUTHERN UNIVERSITY-BATON ROUGE

Location: Baton Rouge, Louisiana

Founded: 1880 (enrollment 9,000)

Stadium: A.W. Mumford (24,000)

Nickname: Jaguars

Colors: Columbia Blue and Gold

All-time Record: 403–247–25

Conference: SWAC

Year To Remember: 1948 Jaguars, 12–0 and National Championship.

In 1991, Savannah State's Lucious Cole was the first Tiger running back to go over the 1,000-yard mark in eight years. Courtesy of Sports View

Coach to Remember: Arnett W. "Ace" Mumford,178–60–15 (1936–1961)
235–82–25 (overall), with 11 SWAC titles, four national championships, in one 45-game span, his teams were 42–0–3, with four
consecutive undefeated seasons.

Players to Remember: LB Rufus Porter, LB Isiah Robertson, WR Frank
Pitts, WR Harold Carmichael, RB Odie Posey, RB Ray Hill, C Ulysses
Jones, RB Leonard Barnes, DL Ken Times, G Robert Holder, G
Herman Hadley, RB Warren Braden, T Normell Keller, E Leslie
Greathouse.

Band: "The Human Jukebox"

TALLEDEGA COLLEGE

Location: Talledega, Alabama

Founded: 1867 (enrollment 700)

Years to Remember: 1920, '21 National Champions; 1918 SIAC champs;
1901, played Atlanta University in first game in program's history.

Coaches to Remember: Jubie Bragg, William Decatur

Player to Remember: RB Floyd Wellman Terry, T Andrew Savage, C
Samuel Coles, Charleston B. Cox, E Napoleon Rivers, E Porter James,
QB Eugene Bragg.

TENNESSEE STATE UNIVERSITY

Location: Nashville, Tennessee

Founded: 1912 (enrollment 7,400)

Stadium: William Jasper Hale (16,500)

Nickname: Tigers

Colors: Blue and White

All-time Record: 419–144–30

Conference: Ohio Valley

Year To Remember: In 1956, National Champions (10–0), defeated FAMU
in Orange Blossom Classic.

Coaches to Remember: John Merritt, 172–33–7 (1963–1983, five
undefeated seasons); Henry Kean, 93–14–3 (1944–1954, three
undefeated seasons)

Players to Remember: QBs Eldridge Dickey, Joe Gilliam, Jr., Joe "747"
Adams, Brian Ransom, DLs Claude Humphrey, Ed "Too Tall" Jones,
Richard Dent, DB Jim Marsalis, PR Nolan "Super Gnat" Smith, C
Forrest Strange, LB Waymond Bryant, DE Cleveland Elam, OL Vernon
Holland.

Band: The Aristocrat of Bands

TEXAS SOUTHERN UNIVERSITY

Location: Houston, Texas

Founded: 1947 (enrollment 8,250)

Stadium: Robertson (22,000)

Nickname: Tigers

Colors: Maroon and Gray

All-time Record: 277–232–27

Conference: SWAC

Year to Remember: 1952 when team went undefeated 10–0–1, under coach
Alexander Durley, and tied for National Championship.

Coach to Remember: Alexander Durley, who became TSU's second head
coach in 1948. In 16 years, he was 101–55–7.

Players to Remember: WR Warren Wells, DL Ernie Holmes, DL Julius
Adams, WR Homer Jones, QB David Mayes, LB Michael Strahan, QB
Audrey Ford, WR Charles Wright, RB Willie Ellison, OL Winston
Hill, DB W. K. Hicks, WR William Glosson, WR Ken Burrough, DB
Mike Holmes, DL Charles Philyaw.

Band: "The Ocean of Soul"

TOUGALOO COLLEGE

Location: Tougaloo, Mississippi

Founded: 1869 (enrollement 1,000)

Years to Remember: 1930, won SCAC title; 1961, last year of program.

TUSKEGEE UNIVERSITY

Location: Tuskegee, Alabama

Founded: 1881 (enrollment 3,600)

Stadium: Alumni Bowl (10,000)

Nickname: Golden Tigers

Colors: Old Gold and Crimson

All-time Record: 477–286–50 (95 years), 17 SIAC titles, 6 national

*Dr. Walter S. Davis was the force behind the growth of Tennessee
State's athletic programs, especially football. He envisioned the
Tigers someday competing against teams in the Southeastern
Conference. Said former Tennessee State coach Howard Gentry:
"President Davis said he wanted his teams to be able to play in the
biggest stadiums all over the United States to crowds of 40,000,
50,000, or 60,000 people. That was out of the realm of the imagina-
tion." Courtesy of Tennessee State*

championships (1924, '25, '26, '27, '29, '30); nation's winningest black college football program, and second all-time among NCAA Division II schools.

Conference: SIAC

Years To Remember: 1974, Bobby Shaw kicks field goal with 15 seconds to play to defeat Norfolk State, 15–14, in first Gate City Bowl in Atlanta Stadium; 1980, Korda Joseph's 45-yard field goal, with no time on clock, gives TU a 22–20 win over Alabama A&M.

Coach to Remember: Cleve Abbott, 203–96–29 (1923–1954, won 6 National Championships, 11 SIAC titles, 6 undefeated seasons; guided teams to 46 consecutive wins (five ties) from 1923–1928, and 79 wins (1 loss and 8 ties) from 1923–1931.

Players to Remember: RB Benjamin Stevenson, LB Ken Woodward, DB Cecil Leonard, QB Authur Hendley, E Owen Duncan, C Oscar Tadlock, QB Paul Smith, QB William Mobley, FB Ernest Bailey, T Ben McKinney.

Band: Marching Crimson Pipers

UNIVERSITY OF DISTRICT COLUMBIA

Location: Washington, D.C.

Founded: 1851 (enrollment 12,000)

Year To Remember: 1974, last year of program.

VIRGINIA STATE UNIVERSITY

Location: Petersburg, Virginia

Founded: 1882 (enrollment 3,500)

Stadium: Rogers (13,500)

Nickname: Trojans

Colors: Orange and Blue

All-time Record: 398–259–48

Conference: CIAA

Years To Remember: 1936, 1952 co-National Champions

Players To Remember: James Mitchell, OL Larry Brooks, OL James Brown, G Davis Battle, WR Floyd Keene.

Coach To Remember: Harry Jefferson, Sylvester "Sal" Hall

Band: The Marching Trojan Explosion

VIRGINIA UNION UNIVERSITY

Location: Richmond, Virginia

Founded: 1865 (enrollment 1,300)

Stadium: Hovey Field (10,000)

Nickname: Panthers

Colors: Maroon and Steel

All-time Record: 426–253–44; 21 consecutive winning seasons.

Conference: CIAA

Years To Remember: 1923, 6–0–1, National Championship; 1973, 9–0 under Willard Bailey; 1990, 10–0 (regular season), under Joe Taylor.

Coach To Remember: Harold Martin, coached 1923 team; Thomas "Tricky" Harris, 1950–1983.

Players To Remember: OL Herb Scott, Anthony Leonard, RB Hezekiah Braxton, Frank Dark, G Andrew Rodez.

WEST VIRGINIA STATE

Location: Institute, West Virginia

Founded: 1891 (enrollment 4,800)

Stadium: Lakin Field (10,000)

Nickname: Yellowjackets

Colors: Gold and Black

Conference: Division 1 (NAIA) West Virginia Intercollegiate Athletic Conference

Year To Remember: 1936 National Champions, 8–0.

Coach To Remember: Adolph Hamblin, 1936 team.

Players To Remember: RB Floyd Meadows, G James Ware, C Chris Morgan, RB Mark Cardwell, E Sam Holland.

WILBERFORCE UNIVERSITY

Location: Wilberforce, Ohio

Founded: 1856 (enrollment 800)

Year To Remember: 1931, National Champions

Coach To Remember: Harry Graves, coached 1931 team.

Players To Remember: FB Elmer Moore, RB Harry "Wu Fang" Ward, QB Ed Ritchie, C William Buchanan.

WILEY COLLEGE

Location: Marshall, Texas

Founded: 1873 (enrollment 500)

Years To Remember: 1920, founding member of SWAC, also first black college in southwest to introduce football; National Champions in 1921, 1924, 1928, 1932, 1945; 1969, last year of program.

Coach To Remember: Fred "Pop" Long

Players To Remember: RB Andrew Patterson, FB Elza Odell, QB Jimmy Webster.

WINSTON-SALEM STATE

Location: Winston-Salem, North Carolina

Founded: 1892 (enrollment 2,500)

Stadium: Bowman Gray Stadium (18,000)

Nickname: Rams

Colors: Scarlet and White

All-time Record: 253–199–19

Years To Remember: 1977, 1978, 1990–1991 CIAA titles.

Coach To Remember: Bill Hayes, 21–0 combined record for 1977, 1978.

Players To Remember: RB Tim Newsome, Kermit Blount, Arrington Jones, Cornelius Washington.

XAVIER UNIVERSITY

Location: New Orleans, Louisiana

Founded: 1915 (enrollment 3,000)

Year To Remember: 1960, last year of program.

Player To Remember: G John Hurse

Players To Remember: L Marino Casem, C Summers, G William Bloxton, G E. Campbell.

CHAPTER TEN

Significant Events

DECEMBER 27, 1892: Biddle (now Johnson C. Smith) defeats Livingstone, 4–0, in Salisbury, North Carolina, in the first game between black colleges.

FEBRUARY 2, 1912: Officials of Hampton, Shaw, Virginia Union, Lincoln (Pa.), form the first athletic conference for black colleges, the Colored Intercollegiate Athletic Conference (now Central Intercollegiate Athletic Conference).

SEPTEMBER 23, 1949: Paul Younger, a fullback-linebacker from Grambling, starts for the Los Angeles Rams as a free agent, becoming the first athlete from a black college to play in the National Football League.

JANUARY 22, 1950: North Carolina A&T running back Robert "Stonewall" Jackson is the first player from a black college drafted by a NFL team when he is selected in the eleventh round by the New York Giants.

DECEMBER 1, 1962: The Kansas City Chiefs make Grambling defensive tackle Junious "Buck" Buchanan their No. 1 pick, the first player from a black college to attain that status in professional football.

JANUARY 30, 1968: The first black college quarterback drafted in the first round is Tennessee State's Eldridge Dickey, taken by the Oakland Raiders.

AUGUST 3, 1968: Marion Motley, who played at South Carolina State and then Nevada, is the first player with black college experience inducted in the Pro Football Hall of Fame.

SEPTEMBER 11, 1971: Morgan State beats Grambling, 9–7, at Yankee Stadium, in the first nationally televised (ABC) college division game.

DECEMBER 3, 1974: Jackson State running back Walter Payton becomes the first black college player to garner Heisman Trophy votes, finishing fourteenth.

SEPTEMBER 25, 1976: In Tokyo, Grambling and Morgan State play in the first regular season college game outside the United States. Grambling wins, 42–16.

NOVEMBER 29, 1977: Grambling quarterback Doug Williams is the first black college player named to the Associated Press All-America First Team.

DECEMBER 9, 1978: Florida A&M, coached by Rudy Hubbard, beats Massachusetts, 35–28, to win the first-ever NCAA Division 1-AA national championship. It is also the first NCAA title for a black college.

OCTOBER 5, 1985: Eddie Robinson, Grambling's head coach, gains his 324th victory when the Tigers beat Prairie View, 27–7, in Dallas. The win makes Robinson the winningest coach in college football history.

JANUARY 26, 1986: Tennessee State's Richard Dent, defensive end, becomes the first player from a black college to be named Most Valuable Player in the Super Bowl, as the Chicago Bears defeat the New England Patriots.

JANUARY 31, 1988: Williams makes history again when he starts for the Washington Redskins in Super Bowl XXII against the Denver Broncos. He is the first black college quarterback to start in that game, and also is named the game's Most Valuable Player.

DECEMBER 21, 1991: Alabama State (SWAC) beats North Carolina A&T (MEAC), 36–13, in the first NCAA-sanctioned postseason game between black colleges.

TOP TWENTY ALL-TIME WINS

1. Tuskegee	(95 years)	477–286–50 (.617)	
2. Virginia Union	(92)	426–253–44 (.620)	
3. Tennessee State	(65)	419–144–30 (.732)	
4. Florida A&M	(60)	415–162–18 (.713)	
5. Southern-Baton Rouge	(71)	403–247–25 (.616)	
6. Virginia State	(81)	398–259–48 (.584)	
7. Hampton	(91)	385–316–34 (.547)	
8. Grambling	(50)	381–136–15 (.730)	
9. Howard	(96)	378–307–42 (.549)	
10. Morgan State	(72)	350–241–30 (.588)	
11. South Carolina State	(66)	352–210–27 (.621)	
12. Alabama State	(87)	349–332–41 (.512)	
13. Alcorn State	(69)	336–217–37 (.601)	
14. Prairie View A&M	(66)	327–296–31 (.524)	
15. North Carolina A&T	(69)	333–275–39 (.545)	
16. Morehouse	(93)	320–330–49 (.493)	
17. North Carolina Central	(62)	311–236–24 (.566)	
18. Morris Brown	(67)	302–270–37 (.526)	
19. Jackson State	(47)	299–163–12 (.643)	
20. Bethune-Cookman	(54)	292–186–22 (.606)	

(Source: NCAA)

WINNINGEST BLACK COLLEGE COACHES

1. Eddie Robinson, Grambling: 381–136–15 (.716)
2. Arnett Mumford, Jarvis Christian/Bishop/Texas College/Southern: 233–85–23 (.717)
3. John Merritt, Jackson State/Tennessee State: 232–65–11 (.771)
4. Fred Long, Paul Quinn/Wiley/Prairie View/Texas College/Wiley: 227–151–31 (.593)
5. Jake Gaither, Florida A&M: 203–36–4 (.844)

(Source: *Sports View*)

BLACK COLLEGE NATIONAL CHAMPIONS

(Year, Team, Record, Coach)

Year	Team	Record	Coach	Year	Team	Record	Coach
1920	Howard	7–0–0	Edward Morrison	1945	Wiley	10–0–0	Fred Long
	Talladega	5–0–1	Jubie Bragg	1946	Tennessee State	10–1–0	Henry Kean
1921	Talladega	6–0–1	Jubie Bragg		Morgan State	8–0–0	Edward Hurt
	Wiley	7–0–1	Jason Grant	1947	Tennessee State	10–0–0	Henry Kean
1922	Hampton	6–1–0	Gideon Smith	1948	Southern	12–0–0	Arnett "Ace" Mumford
1923	Virginia Union	6–0–1	Harold Martin	1949	Southern	10–0–1	Arnett "Ace" Mumford
1924	Tuskegee	9–0–1	Cleve Abbott		Morgan State	8–0–0	Edward Hurt
	Wiley	8–0–1	Fred Long	1950	Southern	10–0–1	Arnett "Ace" Mumford
1925	Tuskegee	8–0–1	Cleve Abbott		Florida A&M	8–1–1	Alonzo "Jake" Gaither
	Howard	6–0–2	Louis Watson	1951	Morris Brown	10–1–0	Edward "Ox" Clemons
1926	Tuskegee	10–0–0	Cleve Abbott	1952	Florida A&M	8–2–0	Alonzo "Jake" Gaither
	Howard	7–0–0	Louis Watson		Texas Southern	10–1–0	Alexander Durley
1927	Tuskegee	9–0–1	Cleve Abbott		Lincoln (Mo)	8–1–0	Dwight Reed
	Bluefield State	8–0–1	Harry Jefferson		Virginia State	8–1–0	Sylvester "Sal" Hall
1928	Bluefield State	8–0–1	Harry Jefferson	1953	Prairie View	12–0–0	William "Billy" Nicks
	Wiley	8–0–1	Fred Long	1954	Tennessee State	10–1–0	Henry Kean
1929	Tuskegee	10–0–0	Cleve Abbott		Southern	10–1–0	Arnett "Ace" Mumford
1930	Tuskegee	11–0–1	Cleve Abbott		Florida A&M	8–1–0	Alonzo "Jake" Gaither
1931	Wilberforce	9–0–0	Harry Graves		Prairie View	10–1–0	William "Billy" Nicks
1932	Wiley	9–0–0	Fred Long	1955	Grambling	10–0–0	Eddie Robinson
1933	Morgan State	9–0–0	Edward Hurt	1956	Tennessee State	10–0–0	Howard Gentry
1934	Kentucky State	9–0–0	Henry Kean	1957	Florida A&M	9–0–0	Alonzo "Jake" Gaither
1935	Texas College	9–0–0	Arnett "Ace" Mumford	1958	Prairie View	10–0–1	William "Billy" Nicks
1936	West Virginia State	8–0–0	Adolph Hamblin	1959	Florida A&M	10–0–0	Alonzo "Jake" Gaither
	Virginia State	7–0–2	Harry Jefferson	1960	Southern	9–1–0	Arnett "Ace" Mumford
1937	Morgan State	7–0–0	Edward Hurt	1961	Florida A&M	10–0–0	Alonzo "Jake" Gaither
1938	Florida A&M	8–0–0	Bill Bell	1962	Jackson State	10–1–0	John Merritt
1939	Langston	9–0–0	Felton "Zip" Gayles	1963	Prairie View	10–1–0	William "Billy" Nicks
1940	Morris Brown	9–1–0	Artis Graves	1964	Prairie View	9–0–0	William "Billy" Nicks
1941	Morris Brown	8–1–0	William "Billy" Nicks	1965	Tennessee State	9–0–0	John Merritt
1942	Florida A&M	9–0–0	Bill Bell	1966	Tennessee State	10–0–0	John Merritt
1943	Morgan State	5–0–0	Edward Hurt	1967	Morgan State	8–0–0	Earl Banks
1944	Morgan State	6–1–0	Edward Hurt		Grambling	9–1–0	Eddie Robinson

1968	Alcorn State	9–1–0	Marino Casem		1981	South Carolina State	10–3–0	Bill Davis
	N.C. A&T	8–1–0	Hornsby Howell		1982	Tennessee State	9–0–1	John Merritt
1969	Alcorn State	8–0–1	Marino Casem		1983	Grambling	8–1–2	Eddie Robinson
1970	Tennessee State	11–0–0	John Merritt		1984	Alcorn State	9–1–0	Marino Casem
1971	Tennessee State	9–1–0	John Merritt		1985	Jackson State Oh	8–3–0	W. C. Gorden
1972	Grambling	11–1–0	Eddie Robinson		1986	Central State Oh	10–1–1	Billy Joe
1973	Tennessee State	10–0–0	John Merritt		1987	Central State Oh	10–1–1	Billy Joe
1974	Grambling	11–1–0	Eddie Robinson		1988	Central State Oh	11–2–0	Billy Joe
1975	Grambling	10–2–0	Eddie Robinson		1989	Central State Oh	10–2–0	Billy Joe
1976	South Carolina State	10–1–0	Willie Jefferies		1990	Central State Oh	11–1–0	Billy Joe
1977	South Carolina State	9–1–1	Willie Jefferies			(Also NAIA Division 1 National Champion)		
	Grambling	10–1–0	Eddie Robinson		1991	Alabama State	11–0–1	Houston Markham
	Florida A&M	11–0–0	Rudy Hubbard		1992	Grambling	10–2–0	Eddie Robinson
1978	Florida A&M	12–1–0	Rudy Hubbard					
1979	Tennessee State	8–3–0	John Merritt					
1980	Grambling	10–2–0	Eddie Robinson					

(Source: Pittsburgh *Courier*, 1920–1980; Sheridan Broadcasting Network 1981–Present) (Black College National Championship Trophy is named after W. A. Scott, founder of the Atlanta *Daily World* newspaper)

NATIONAL FOOTBALL LEAGUE FIRST ROUND DRAFT PICKS FROM BLACK COLLEGES

—1963: Buck Buchanan, DT, Grambling, Kansas City

—1967: Willie Ellison, RB, Texas Southern, Los Angeles Rams

—1968: Eldridge Dickey, QB, Tennessee State, Oakland

—1968: Claude Humphrey, DE, Tennessee State, Atlanta Falcons

—1969: Jim Marsalis, DB, Tennessee State, Kansas City

—1969: John Shinners, G, Xavier, New Orleans

—1970: Ken Burrough, WR, Texas Southern, New Orleans

—1970: Raymond Chester, TE, Morgan State, Oakland

—1970: Doug Wilkerson, G, North Carolina Central, Houston

—1971: Richard Harris, DE, Grambling, Philadelphia

—1971: Vernon Holland, Tennessee State, T, Cincinnati

—1971: Frank Lewis, WR, Grambling, Pittsburgh

—1971: Isiah Robertson, Southern, LB, Los Angeles Rams

—1972: Jerome Barkum, WR, Jackson State, New York Jets

—1972: Moses Denson, RB, Maryland State, Washington

—1973: Mike Holmes, DB, Texas Southern, San Francisco

—1974: Waymond Bryand, LB, Tennessee State, Chicago

—1974: Billy Corbett, T, Johnston C. Smith, Cleveland

—1974: Ed "Too Tall" Jones, DE, Tennessee State, Dallas

—1974: Henry Lawrence, T, Florida A&M, Oakland

—1974: Donald Reese, DE, Jackson State, Miami

—1975: Robert Brazile, LB, Jackson State, Houston

—1975: Thomas Henderson, LB, Langston, Dallas

—1975: Gary Johnson, DT, Grambling, San Diego

—1975: Walter Payton, RB, Jackson State, Chicago Bears

—1976: James Hunter, DB, Grambling, Detroit

—1976: Charles Philyaw, DT, Texas Southern, Oakland

—1978: Doug Williams, QB, Grambling, Tampa Bay

—1981: Michael Holston, WR, Morgan State, Houston

—1982: Rod Hill, DB, Kentucky State, Dallas

—1985: Jerry Rice, WR, Mississippi Valley State, San Francisco

—1992: Robert Porcher, DL, South Carolina State, Detroit

—1993: Lester Holmes, T, Jackson State, Philadelphia

PITTSBURGH *COURIER* BLACK COLLEGE ALL-AMERICA TEAMS

(Note: Bill Nunn, Sr., Chester Washington, Wendell Smith, and Bill Nunn, Jr., have selected the teams through the years, collaborating with black college coaches and black NFL scouts. For the following listings, some editions of the *Courier* were not available including the first few years of the poll, which began in the early twenties, but several of the later editions were also missing.

Too, many of the early players were listed by last name only. Original *Courier* style is used for most position designations, with only slight variance for modern style to lessen some confusion. Only eleven players were chosen for many of the early teams because most of the players played both offense and defense. Included on the 1942 team is Ralph Oves, a center from Lincoln (Pa.) University. He is the only white player even named to the *Courier* teams, and was described as a "brilliant" player.

1927

E	Tyson, Howard	HB	Coleman, North Carolina A&T	C	Patterson, North Carolina A&T
E	Williams, Langson	FB	Graves, Bluefield	QB	Baker, Clark
T	Lee, Hampton			HB	Marshall, Howard
T	Gallion, Bluefield	**1928**		HB	Stevenson, Tuskegee
G	Miller, North Carolina A&T	E	Jeffries, Bluefield	FB	Cavill, Wiley
G	Redd, Wiley	E	Mendenhall, Wilberforce	Utility back	Marks, Prairie View
C	Tadlock, Tuskegee	T	Stevens, West Virginia	Utility line	Redd, Wiley
QB	Cain, Bluefield	T	Gallion, Bluefield	Utility end	Henderson, Virginia Seminary
HB	Stevenson, Tuskegee	G	Cogar, Alabama State		
		G	Slaughter, Atlanta University		

1930

E   Jeffries, Bluefield
E   Fowler, Wilberforce
T   Kane, Lincoln
T   Pierce, Fisk
G   Franklin, Wiley
G   Kane, Lincoln
C   Smith, Morehouse
QB McCain, Langston
HB Wiggins, Fisk
HB Stevenson, Tuskegee
FB Moore, Wilberforce

1931

E   Wells, Knoxville
E   Robinson, Wilberforce
T   Scott, West Virginia State
T   Gaines, Hampton
G   Franklin, Wiley
G   Hockett, Tuskegee
C   Robinson, Clark
QB Johnson, Virginia State
HB Jones, Morris Brown
HB Conrad, Morgan
FB Terry, Wilberforce

1932

E   "Tiny" Smith, Morris Brown
E   Winesberry, Langston
T   Lash, Alabama State
T   Coleman, Kentucky State
G   Wares, West Virginia State
G   Rettig, Wilberforce
C   Lewis, Virginia State
QB Moberly, Tuskegee
HB Conrad, Morgan
HB Banks, Bluefield
FB O'Dell, Wiley

1933

E   Charles Smith, Tuskegee
E   "Tiny" Smith, Morris Brown
T   Jim Reid, Morris Brown
T   B. McKinney, Tuskegee
G   DuBignon, S.C. St.
G   L. Williams, Morris Brown
C   Ulysses Williams, Alabama State
QB "Shag" Jones, Morris Brown
HB William "Bill" Porter, South Carolina State
HB Silvey, Tuskegee
FB Edward Adams, Tuskegee

1934

E   Hardin, Kentucky State
E   Spearman, Lemoyne
T   Robinson, Wilberforce
T   Calhoun, Florida A&M
G   Perry, Langston
G   Drake, Morgan
C   Stevens, Bluefield
QB Smith, Morris Brown
HB Kendall, Kentucky State
HB Banks, Bluefield
FB Edwards, Kentucky State

1935

E   Reid, Kentucky State
E   Henderson, Wilberforce
T   Wingo, Tuskegee
T   Martin, Alabama State
G   Hines, Texas College
G   Hibbler, Wiley College
C   DeVault, Florida A&M
QB Morris, Alabama State
HB Kendall, Kentucky State

HB Price, West Virginia State
FB Troupe, Morgan

1936

E   Pinkston Rettig, Texas College
E   Charles "Bo" Spearman, Lemoyne
T   Edward "Wimpy" Taylor
T   Herbert Wheeler, Alabama State
G   Roscoe "Bro" Johnson, Morehouse
G   Cushionberry, Tuskegee
C   Jackson, ———
QB Meadows, ———
HB Kendall, Kentucky State
HB Briscoe, ———
FB Simpson, ———

1938

E   John Anderson, Benedict
E   Percy Slaughter, Alcorn
T   Arthur C. Walls, Bethune-Cookman
T   Charles Simon, Jarvis Christian
G   John H. Figgers, Tougaloo
G   Clarence Watson, Jackson
C   Andrew Jackson, Shorter
HB Eddie Smith, Rust
HB Allen "Runt" Smith, Jarvis Christian
HB Leroy T. Walker, Benedict
HB John Gravely, Edward Waters

1939

E   James Brewer, Virginia State
E   John Brewer, Virginia State
T   Herschel Schnebly, Wilberforce
T   John Montgomery, Prairie View
G   Timothy Evans, Xavier
G   Herbert Norris, Lincoln (Pa.)

C   Leroy Perry, Bluefield
B   Chaney Umphrey, Tennessee A&I
B   Bill Gayles, Langston
B   G. Stanley Strachan, Florida A&M
B   John "Big Train" Moody, Morris Brown

1940

E   Horton, Florida A&M
E   Brayboy, Johnson C. Smith
T   Schnebly, Wilberforce
T   Milton, Bluefield
G   Griffin, Morris Brown
G   Trawick, Kentucky State
C   Summers, Xavier
QB Kee, Morgan College
HB Price, Wilberforce
HB Hill, Southern
FB Moody, Morris Brown

1941

E   Roger Pierce, Langston
E   Jack Brayboy, J.C. Smith
T   George Washington, Langston
T   William Wysinger, Morris Brown
G   Herbert Trawick, Kentucky State
G   Roy Gant, Florida A&M
C   George Mack, North Carolina A&T
B   Wallace Mosby, Morgan College
B   Leonard Barnes, Southern
B   Andrew Hopkins, Prairie View
B   John "Big Train" Moody, Morris Brown

1942

E   Jack Brayboy, J.C. Smith
E   Warren Cyrus, Kentucky State
T   Herbert Trawick, Kentucky State

T   Heywood Settles, Morris Brown
G   Arthur Farrell, Clark College
G   Gus Gaines, North Carolina A&T
C   Ralph Oves, Lincoln (Pa.)
B   James Wilson, West Virginia State
B   Macon Williams, Florida
B   Ralph Allen, Texas College
B   Oscar Givens, Morgan

1944

E   Clarence Harkins, Langston
E   James Fisher, J.C. Smith
T   Clarence Gaines, Morgan State
T   Everett Loch, Wiley
G   David Battle, Virginia State
G   Will Lee Gipson, Prairie View
C   Willie M. Green, Texas College
QB Alva Tabor, Tuskegee
HB Terry P. Day, Morgan State
HB Karl Baylor, Wilberforce
FB John L. Williams, Texas College

1945

E   Clarence Harkins, Langston
E   Talmadge Owen, Clark
T   James Moore, Wilberforce
T   Wilfred Rawl, West Virginia State
G   Richard Bolton, Clark
G   Willie Moses, Wiley
C   Isaiah Wilson, West Virginia State
B   Leroy Cromartie, Florida
B   William Bass, Tennessee
B   Shelly Ross, Wiley
B   Bernard Ingraham, Florida

1946

E   Nathaniel "Traz" Powell, Florida A&M
E   Roger Pierce, Langston
T   Robert Drummond, Tennessee
T   Robert Smith, Southern
G   French Nickens, Virginia State
G   Herman Mabrie, Tuskegee
C   John Brown, North Carolina Central
B   Nathaniel Taylor, Tennessee
B   Whitney Van Cleve, Tuskegee
B   Raymond Von Lewis, Texas College
B   James Turpin, Morgan

1948

E   Albert Gillyard, Wilberforce
E   Clarence Clark, West Virginia State
T   Benjamin Whaley, Virginia State
T   Joseph Williams, North Carolina A&T
G   Adam McCullough, Wilberforce

G   Herman Hadley, Southern
C   Clyde Dillard, West Virginia State
B   Warren Braden, Southern
B   Clyde Galbreath, North Carolina State
B   Ulysses Curtis, Florida A&M
B   Paul "Tank" Younger, Grambling

1949

E   Clarence Clark, West Virginia State
E   Marvin Whaley, Morgan
T   Verdese Carter, Wilberforce
T   George Gilchrist, Tennessee
G   Herman DeVaughan, Texas College
G   Robert Holder, Southern
C   Clyde Dillard, West Virginia State
B   Warren Braden, Southern
B   Sylvester "Swifty" Polk, Maryland State
B   Ulysses Curtis, Florida A&M
B   George Rooks, Morgan

1950

Offense:

E   Harold Turner, Tennessee State
E   Ernest Warlick, North Carolina College
T   Bill Boyers, North Carolina A&T
T   Normell Keller, Southern
G   Charles Robinson, Morgan State
G   Robert Holder, Southern
C   Walter Gillespie, Tennessee State
B   William "Red" Jackson, North Carolina A&T
B   Sylvester "Swifty" Polk, Maryland State
B   Roland Miles, St. Augustine
B   George Rooks, Morgan State

Courier's 23rd All America Team Has Power

Leo Lewis Leads Talented Squad

FIRST TEAM

SECOND TEAM

Defense:

E	Leslie Greathouse, Southern
E	Costa Kittles, Florida A&M
T	Ray Newman, Wilberforce
T	Charles Maloney, Florida A&M
G	Charlie Parker, Morris Brown
G	William Bloxton, Xavier
C	Gene Rouse, Wilberforce
B	Cal Martin, Maryland State
B	Oliver Ellis, West Virginia State
B	Ray Dillon, Prairie View
B	Johnny Spinks, Alcorn

1951

Offense:

E	Ernest Warlick, North Carolina
E	Lorinzer Clark, Central State (Oh.)
T	James Caldwell, Tennessee State
T	Theodore Benson, Morris Brown
G	Willie Bloxton, Xavier
G	Alphonso Varner, Florida A&M
C	James Straughter, Southern
QB	Raymond Thornton, Bethune-Cookman
HB	Henry Mosely, Morris Brown
HB	Willie Smith, West Virginia State
FB	Johnny Spinks, Alcorn

Defense:

E	Harold Turner, Tennessee State
E	Floyd Keene, Virginia State
T	Walter Hunter, North Carolina
T	Vince Reed, West Virginia State
G	Andrew Rodez, Virginia Union
G	Donald Thomas, Maryland State
C	William Kenchon, Florida A&M

QB	William Jackson, North Carolina A&T
HB	Sidney Parker, Central
HB	Robert Slocum, Savannah State
FB	Ray Don Dillon, Prairie View

1952

Offense:

E	Floyd Keene, Virginia State
E	Jack McClairen, Bethune-Cookman
T	James Caldwell, Tennessee State
T	Roosevelt Brown, Morgan State
G	James Black, Central
G	Rupert Curry, West Virginia State
C	Andrew Hinson, Bethune-Cookman
QB	Audrey Ford, Texas Southern
HB	Leo Lewis, Lincoln (Mo.)
HB	Matthew Maiden, Tennessee State
FB	Sherman Robinson, Southern

Defense:

E	Arthur Statum, North Carolina A&T
E	Charles Wright, Prairie View
T	Norman Day, Virginia State
T	Walter Hunter, North Carolina A&T
G	Alvin Neeson, Morris Brown
G	Harry Stokes, Lincoln (Mo.)
C	John Bundy, Delaware State
QB	Alkin Hepburn, Florida A&M
HB	Leon Wilson, Maryland State
HB	James Moore, Florida A&M
HB	Leo Miles, Virginia State

1953

E	Charles Wright, Prairie View
E	Willie Jordan, Maryland State
T	Norman Day, Virginia State
T	Sam Marshall, Florida A&M
G	Joe Person, North Carolina
G	Alvin Neeson, Morris Brown
C	Clyde Tillman, Texas Southern
QB	Charlies "Choo-Choo" Brackins, Prairie View
HB	Leo Lewis, Lincoln (Mo.)
HB	Roy Kimble, Tennessee State
FB	Clyde "Bull" Sanders, Bethune-Cookman

1954

E	Charles Wright, Prairie View
E	William Roach, Langston
T	Sherman Plunkett, Maryland State
T	Matthew Boone, North Carolina College
G	C. Brownley, Tennessee
G	E. Campbell, Xavier
C	Elroy Wise, Texas Southern
QB	Charlie "Choo-Choo" Brackins, Prairie View

HB	Leo Lewis, Lincoln (Mo.)
HB	Willie Galimore, Florida A&M
FB	Robert Dinkins, Southern

1955

E	Heron Tibbs, Prairie View
E	Peter Boston, Alcorn
T	Willie Davis, Grambling
T	Sherman Plunkett, Maryland State
G	Charles Patton, Tennessee State
G	Calvin Gladden, Florida State
C	Emmitt Simon, Southern
QB	Audrey Ford, Texas Southern
HB	Johnny Sample, Maryland State
HB	Edward Murray, Grambling
FB	Willie Galimore, Florida A&M

1956

E	Hollis Felder, Texas Southern
E	Vernon Vaughn, Maryland State
T	John Baker, North Carolina State
T	Charles Gavin, Tennessee
G	Alfred Luster, Langston
G	Carl Crowell, Florida A&M
C	Leon Larce, Grambling
B	Fay Mitchell, Tennessee State
B	Willie Galimore, Florida A&M
B	Aldophus Frazier, Florida A&M
B	Edward Murray, Grambling

1957

E	William "Rock" Glossom, Texas Southern
E	Leon Jamison, Tennessee State
T	Vernon Wilder, Florida A&M
T	John Baker, North Carolina Central

29th Courier All-America Grid Team Biggest in History

G	Gentris Hornsby, Prairie View
G	Carl Crowell, Florida A&M
C	Ray Self, Jackson
QB	Floyd Iglehart, Wiley
HB	John Sample, Maryland State
HB	John Bradley, Lincoln (Mo.)
FB	Herbert Drummond, Central State

1958

E	Burnie McQueen, North Carolina A&T
E	William "Rock" Glossom, Texas Southern
T	Willie Wyche, Florida A&M
T	George McGee, Southern
G	Henry Eiland, Jackson
G	Gentris Hornsby, Prairie View
C	Herman O'Neil, Lincoln (Mo.)
QB	John Thomas, Southern
HB	Clifton Jackson, North Carolina Central
HB	Leroy Hardee, Florida A&M
FB	Calvin Scott, Prairie View

1959

E	Charles Walker, Sr., Tennessee State
E	Willie Richardson, Fr., Jackson
T	Jimmy Hunt, Sr., Prairie View
T	Roger Brown, Sr., Maryland State
G	Gentris Hornsby, Sr., Prairie View
G	Louie Bing, Sr., Morris Brown
C	Raymond Ross, Sr., Southern
QB	Bobby Rowe, Sr., Winston-Salem
HB	Hezekiah Braxton, Jr., Virginia Union
HB	Clarence Childs, Jr., Florida A&M
FB	Preston Powell, Jr., Grambling

1960

E	Hiram Wilson, Jr., Wiley
E	Willie Richardson, Soph., Jackson
L	James Brewington, North Carolina Central
L	Ernest Ladd, Jr., Grambling
L	Lorenzo Stanford, Sr., North Carolina A&T
L	George Balthazar, Sr., Tennessee A&I
C	Charlie Malone, Sr., Prairie View
QB	Cyrus Lancaster, Sr., Southern
HB	Hezekiah Braxton, Sr., Virginia Union
HB	Clarence Childs, Sr., Florida A&M
FB	Preston Powell, Sr., Grambling

1961

End	Willie Richardson, Jr., Jackson
End	Pettis Norman, Sr., J.C. Smith
Tackle	Charles Hinton, Sr., North Carolina Central
Tackle	David Evans, Sr., Southern
Guard	Garland Boyette, Sr., Grambling
Guard	Robert Young, Jr., Sr., Morgan
Center	Curtis Miranda, Sr., Florida A&M
QB	Roy Curry, Jr., Jackson State
HB	Robert Paremore, Jr. Florida A&M
HB	Guthrie Nelson, Sr., Winston-Salem
FB	Charles Holmes, Sr., Maryland State

1962

E	Alfred Denson, Jr., Florida A&M
E	Willie Richardson, Sr., Jackson State
T	Ben McGee, Jr., Jackson
T	Junious "Buck" Buchanan, Sr., Grambling
G	Clarence Wells, Sr., Wiley
G	Joe Henderson, Sr., North Carolina A&T
C	Junious Simon, Sr., Southern
QB	Roy Curry, Sr., Jackson State
HB	Homer Jones, Sr., Texas Southern
HB	Robert Paramore, Sr., Florida A&M
FB	J.D. Garrett, Sr., Grambling

1963

E	Alfred Denson, Sr., Florida A&M
E	Warren Wells, Sr., Texas Southern
T	Ben McGee, Sr., Jackson State
T	Carl Robinson, Sr., Prairie View
G	Luther Woodruff, Sr., North Carolina A&T
G	Phillip Gainous, Sr., Morgan State
C	Carl Woodard, Sr., Texas Southern
QB	James Tullis, Sr., Florida A&M
HB	Ezell Seals, Sr., Prairie View
HB	Robert Currington, Sr., North Carolina Central
FB	Smith Reed, Jr., Alcorn State

1964

E	Herman Driver, Sr., Texas Southern
E	Arthur Robinson, Jr., Florida A&M
T	Alphonse Dotson, Sr., Grambling
T	Verlon Biggs, Sr., Jackson State
G	George Dearborne, Sr., Prairie View
G	Robert Reed, Sr., Tennessee A&I
C	Archie Williams, Sr., Florida A&M
QB	Jimmy Kearney, Sr., Prairie View
HB	Emerson Boozer, Jr., Maryland State
HB	Smith Reed, Sr., Alcorn
FB	Henry Dyer, Jr., Grambling

1965

E	Kirby McDaniels, Sr., Tuskegee
E	John Robinson, Jr., Tennessee State
T	Frank Cornish, Sr., Grambling
T	David Daniels, Sr., Florida A&M
G	James Carter, Sr., Tennessee State
G	Clinton Vasser, Sr., Mississippi Valley
C	Pete Barnes, Jr., Southern
QB	Eldridge Dickey, Soph., Tennessee State
HB	Emerson Boozer, Sr., Maryland State
HB	Kenneth Duke, Sr., Morgan State
FB	Henry Dyer, Sr., Grambling

1966

E	Harold Jackson, Jr., Jackson State
E	John Eason, Jr., Florida A&M
T	Claude Humphrey, Jr., Tennessee A&I
T	Elvin Bethea, Jr., North Carolina A&T
G	Willie Lanier, Sr., Morgan
G	Norman Davis, Sr., Grambling
C	Pete Barnes, Sr., Southern
QB	Eldridge Dickey, Jr., Tennessee A&I
HB	Willie Ellison, Sr., Texas Southern
HB	Charles "Monk" Williams, Jr., Arkansas AM&N
FB	Bill Tucker, Sr., Tennessee State

1967

Offense

E	John Eason, Sr., Florida A&M
E	Elmo Maples, Sr., Southern
T	Tommy Funches, Sr., Jackson State
T	Arthur Shell, Sr., Maryland State
G	Henry Davis, Sr., Grambling
G	Willie Banks, Sr., Alcorn
C	David Snead, Sr., Tuskegee
QB	Eldridge Dickey, Sr., Tennessee State
HB	Charles Williams, Sr., Arkansas AM&N
HB	David McDaniels, Sr., Miss. Valley
FB	Edward Tomlin, Sr., Hampton

Defense

E	Alfred Beauchamp, Sr., Southern
E	Henry Sharper, Sr., Virginia State
T	Claude Humphrey, Sr., Tennessee State
T	Carlton Dabney, Sr., Morgan
G	William Kindricks, Sr., Alabama A&M
G	Elvin Bethea, Sr., North Carolina A&T
C	Robert Reeves, Jr., Souther Carolina State
DB	John Outlaw, Sr., Jackson
DB	Major Hazelton, Sr., Florida A&M
DB	Robert Atkins, Sr., Grambling
DB	Daryl Johnson, Sr., Morgan

1968

Offense

TE	Elbert Drungo, Sr., Tennessee State
WE	Edward Cross, Sr., Arkansas AM&N
T	Clarence Williams, Sr., Prairie View
T	Eugene Ferguson, Sr., Norfolk State
G	Willie Peake, Sr., Alcorn
G	Percy Griffin, Sr., Jackson
C	Kenneth Page, Sr., North Carolina A&T
QB	James Harris, Sr., Grambling
HB	Willie Pearson, Sr., North Carolina A&T
Flanker	Charlie Joiner, Sr., Grambling
FB	Moses Denson, Soph., Maryland State

Talent Galore On 41st All America Team

Juniors Dominate Annual Selections

Defense

E	Richard Neal, Sr., Southern
E	Roger Finnie, Sr., Florida A&M
T	James Mitchell, Jr., Virginia State
T	Doug Wilkerson, Jr., North Carolina Central
MG	Ernest Calloway, Sr., Texas Southern
LB	Harold McClinton, Sr., Southern
LB	Rayford Jenkins, Jr., Alcorn
LB	Robert Reeves, Sr., South Carolina State
CB	James Marsalis, Sr., Tennessee State
CB	Johnny June, Sr., Virginia Union
S	William Thompson, Sr., Maryland State
S	Edward Hayes, Sr., Morgan

1969

Offense

SE	Julian Martin, Sr., North Carolina Central
TE	Ken Burrough, Sr., Texas Southern
T	Doug Wilkerson, Sr., North Carolina Central
T	Willie Young, Sr., Alcorn
G	Horace Lovett, Sr., Florida A&M
G	Claude Brumfield, Sr., Tennessee State
C	Jimmy McCaskill, Sr., Florida A&M
QB	Marvin Weeks, Sr., Alcorn
FL	Frank Lewis, Jr., Grambling
RB	William Dusenbery, Sr., J.C. Smith
RB	Hubert Ginn, Sr., Florida A&M

Defense

DE	Alden Roche, Sr., Southern
DE	Joe Jones, Sr., Tennessee State
T	Charles Blossom, Sr., Texas Southern
T	James Mitchell, Sr., Virginia State
MG	Sam Singletary, Sr., North Carolina Central
LB	Rayford Jenkins, Sr., Alcorn
LB	Merl Code, North Carolina A&T
CB	Melvin Blount, Jr., Southern
CB	Glen Alexander, Sr., Grambling
S	David Hadley, Sr., Alcorn
S	Bivian Lee, Jr., Prairie View

1970

Offense

TE	David Davis, Sr., Tennessee State
WE	Ray Jarvis, Sr., Norfolk State
T	Vernon Holland, Sr., Tennessee State
T	Harold Bell, Sr., Morgan State
G	Sam Holden, Sr., Grambling
G	Melvin Holmes, Sr., North Carolina A&T
C	Charles Ellis, Sr., Jackson
FL	Frank Lewis, Sr., Grambling

RB   Tim Beamer, Sr., J.C. Smith
RB   Steve Davis, Sr., Delaware State
QB   Joe Gilliam, Jr., Jr., Tennessee State

Defense
E   Arthur May, Sr., Tuskegee
E   Richard Harris, Sr., Grambling
T   Maulty Moore, Sr., Bethune-Cookman
T   Anthony McGee, Sr., Bishop
MG   Ernie Holmes, Sr., Texas Southern
LB   Isiah Robertson, Sr., Southern
LB   Ralph Coleman, Jr., North Carolina A&T
CB   Bivian Lee, Sr., Prairie View
CB   Willie Alexander, Sr., Alcorn
S   Nathaniel Allen, Sr., Texas Southern
S   Cleo Johnson, Sr., Alcorn

1971
Offense
TE   Luther Palmer, Sr., Virginia Union
WE   Allen Dunbar, Sr., Southern
T   Lonnie Leonard, Sr., North Carolina A&T
T   Robert Penchion, Sr., Alcorn
G   Louis White, Sr., Alcorn
G   Robert Woods, Jr., Tennessee State
C   Kerry Grant, Sr., Grambling
RB   Franklin Roberts, Sr., Alcorn
RB   Eldrie Turner, RB, Grambling
QB   Joe Gilliam, Jr., Sr., Tennessee State
FL   Jerome Barkum, Sr., Jackson State

Defense
E   Lester Sims, Sr., Alabama State
E   Harry Gooden, Sr., Alcorn
T   Tommy Gay, Sr., Arkansas AM&N
T   Charles Burrell, Sr., Arkansas AM&N
CB   Ron Bolton, Sr., Norfolk State
CB   Cliff Brooks, Sr., Tennessee State
LB   John Mendenhall, Sr., Grambling
LB   Ralph Coleman, Sr., North Carolina A&T
LB   Waymond Bryant, Soph., Tennessee State
S   Charles Neugent, Sr., Tuskegee
S   Mike Holmes, Jr., Texas Southern

1972
Offense
TE   Terry Nelson, Sr., Ark. AM&N
SE   James Thaxton, Sr., Tennessee State
FL   Ollie Smith, Sr., Tennessee State
T   Leon Gray, Sr., Jackson State
T   Robert Woods, Sr., Tennessee State
G   Henry Lawrence, Jr., Florida A&M
G   Bracy Bonham, Sr., North Carolina Central
C   Dennis Thomas, Jr., Alcorn

QB   Matt Reed, Sr., Grambling
RB   Walter Payton, Jr., Jackson State
RB   Jeff Inmon, Sr., North Carolina Central

Defense
E —   Exil Bibbs, Jr., Grambling
T   Ed "Too Tall" Jones, Jr., Tennessee State
T   Barney Chavous, Sr., South Carolina State
E   William Wideman, Sr., North Carolina A&T
LB   Walter Baisy, Sr., Grambling
LB   Stanley Cherry, Sr., Morgan State
LB   Waymond Bryant, Jr., Tennessee State
CB   Donnie Walker, Sr., Central State
S   Van Green, Sr., Shaw
S   Mike Holmes, Sr., Texas Southern
CB   Charles McTorry, Sr., Tennessee State

1973
Offense
WR   John Holland, Sr., Tennessee State
WR   Kenneth Payne, Sr., Langston
WR   John Stallworth, Sr., Alabama A&M
T   Henry Lawrence, Sr., Florida A&M
T   Gregory Kindle, Sr., Tennessee State
G   Jimmy Davis, Sr., Alcorn
G   James Wilson, Sr., Clark
C   Dennis Thomas, Sr., Alcorn
RB   Walter Payton, Jr., Jackson State
RB   Randy Walker, Jr., Bethune-Cookman
QB   Prienson Poindexter, Sr., Langston

Defense
E   Donald Reese, Sr., Jackson State
E   Ed "Too Tall" Jones, Sr., Tennessee State
T   Gary "Big Hands" Johnson, Jr., Grambling
T   Billy Howard, Sr., Alcorn
LB   Godwin Turk, Sr., Southern
LB   Waymond Bryant, Sr., Tennessee State
LB   John Tate, Sr., Jackson State
DB   Maurice Spencer, Sr., North Carolina
      Central
DB   Bobby Brooks, Sr., Bishop
DB   William Bryant, Sr., Grambling
DB   Donnie Shell, Sr., South Carolina State

1974
Offense
WR   Robert Gaddis, Sr., Mississippi Valley
WR   Larry Dorsey, Jr., Tennessee State
TE   Bob Cook, Sr. Tuskegee
T   Alonzo Pickett, Sr., Texas Southern
T   James Wilson, Sr., Clark
G   Herbert Scott, Sr., Virginia Union
G   Joe Moore, Sr., Tuskegee

C   John Butler, Sr., Tennessee State
HB   Walter Payton, Sr., Jackson State
FB   John Bradford, Sr., Central State
QB   William Wooley, Sr., Alcorn

Defense
E   Charles Smith, Sr., North Carolina Central
E   Cleveland Elam, Sr., Tennessee State
T   Gary "Big Hands" Johnson, Sr.,
      Grambling
T   Robert Barber, Sr., Grambling
MLB   Robert Brazile, Sr., Jackson State
OLB   Harry Carson, Jr., South Carolina State
OLB   Lawrence Pillers, Jr., Alcorn
DB   Frank Oliver, Sr., Kentucky State
DB   Mike Jones, Sr., Virginia Union
DB   Morris McKie, Sr., North Carolina A&T
DB   James Hunter, Jr., Grambling

1975
Offense
TE   Loaird McCreary, Sr., Tennessee State
FL   Larry Dorsey, Sr., Tennessee State
T   Melvin Mitchell, Sr., Tennessee State
T   Arthur Gilliam, Sr., Grambling
G   Jackie Slater, Sr., Jackson State
G   Darius Helton, Jr., North Carolina Central
C   Charles Young, Sr., Florida A&M
RB   Sammie White, Sr., Grambling
RB   Andrew Bolton, Sr., Fisk
FB   David Bohannon, Jr., Prairie View
QB   Parnell Dickinson, Sr., Mississippi Valley

Defense
E   Harry Carson, Sr., South Carolina State
E   Carl Hairston, Sr., Maryland State
T   Willie Lee, Sr., Bethune-Cookman
T   Perry Brooks, Sr., Southern
OLB   Frankie Poole, Sr., Florida A&M
MLB   Robert Pennywell, Sr., Grambling
OLB   Lawrence Pillers, Sr., Alcorn
DB   James Hunter, Sr., Grambling
DB   Anthony Leonard, Sr., Virginia Union
DB   Tim Baylor, Sr., Morgan State
DB   Al Simmons, Jr., Texas Southern

1976
WR   Carlos Pennywell, Jr., Grambling
WR   Leon Sherrod, Sr., Jackson State
TE   Andre Samuels, Sr., Bethune-Cookman
T   Fred Dean, Sr., Texas Southern
T   Darius Helton, Sr., North Carolina Central
G   William Light, Sr., Morgan State
G   Darrell Hill, Sr., Virginia Union

C	Robert Weeks, Sr., Winston-Salem	DB	Mike Harris, Sr., Grambling		(Offensive Player of the Year)
QB	Douglas Williams, Jr., Grambling	DB	Oliver Davis, Sr., Tennessee State	QB	Joe "747" Adams, Soph., Tennessee State

C   Robert Weeks, Sr., Winston-Salem

QB   Douglas Williams, Jr., Grambling
(Offensive Player of the Year)

RB   Charles White, Sr., Bethune-Cookman

RB   Nathan Simpson, Sr., Tennessee State

Defense

E   Johnny Jackson, Sr., Southern

E   Ezra Johnson, Sr., Morris Brown

T   Robert Sims, Sr., South Carolina State
(Defensive Player of the Year)

T   Ken Mullens, Sr., Florida A&M

T   Larry Warren, Sr., Alcorn

LB   Andre Jones, Sr., Southern

LB   Rudolph Bryant, Sr., South Carolina State

DB   Johnny Stoutamire, Jr., Livingstone

DB   Mike Harris, Sr., Grambling

DB   Oliver Davis, Sr., Tennessee State

DB   Dexter Curry, Sr., Norfolk State

1978

Offense

TE   Bill Murrell, Sr., Winston-Salem

WR   John Smith, Sr., Tennessee State

T   Dwight McNeil, Jr., Texas Southern

T   James Williams, Jr., Mississippi Valley

G   Arthur Prescott, Sr., South Carolina State

G   Tyrone McGriff, Sr., Florida A&M

C   Kaiser Lewis, Jr., Florida A&M

HB   Judge Thomas, Sr., Virginia Union

HB   Jeffrey Moore, Sr., Jackson State

FB   Timmy Newsome, Jr., Winston-Salem

(Offensive Player of the Year)

QB   Joe "747" Adams, Soph., Tennessee State

Defense

E   Dwaine Board, Sr., North Carolina A&T

E   Bruce Radford, Sr., Grambling

T   James White, Sr., Albany State

T   Robert Hardy, Sr., Jackson State

LB   Plummer Bullock, Jr., Virginia Union

LB   Harrell Oliver, Sr., Florida A&M

LB   George Small, Sr., North Carolina

DB   Charles Johnson, Sr., Grambling
(Defensive Player of the Year)

DB   Don Rose, Sr., Hampton

DB   Joe Fowlkes, Sr., Morgan State

DB   Anthony Young, Sr., Jackson State

SHERIDAN BLACK NETWORK ALL-TIME BLACK COLLEGE FOOTBALL TEAM

Offense

QB   Doug Williams, Grambling

RB   Walter Payton, Jackson State
      Tank Younger, Grambling

WR   Jerry Rice, Mississippi Valley State
      John Stallworth, Alabama A&M
      Charlie Joiner, Grambling

OL   Art Shell, Maryland State
      Rayfield Wright, Ft. Valley State

      Jackie Slater, Jackson State
      Larry Little, Bethune-Cookman
      Ernie Barnes, North Carolina Central

Defense

DL   Willie Davis, Grambling
      Ed "Too Tall" Jones, Tennessee State
      David "Deacon" Jones, Mississippi Vocational

      L.C. Greenwood, Arkansas AM&N

LB   Robert Brazille, Jackson State
      Harry Carson, South Carolina State
      Willie Lanier, Morgan State

DB   Mel Blount, Southern
      Lem Barney, Jackson State
      Donnie Shell, South Carolina State
      Everson Walls, Grambling

MILTON ROBERTS ALL-TIME BLACK COLLEGE FOOTBALL SQUAD

1892-1900

End	George F. Porter, Atlanta University
End	Walter L. Smith, Howard
Guard	L.W. Baldwin, Tuskegee/Meharry Medical
Guard	Lawrence B. Ellerson, Biddle
Guard	James Phillips, Lincoln
QB	Pulaski O. Holt, Fisk
QB	Frank W. Avant, Howard/Lincoln
QB	Dwight O.W. Holmes, Howard
HB	John W. Work, Fisk
HB	Cain P. Cole, Lincoln
HB	Elmer C. Campbell, Howard
HB	Robert H. Scott, Lincoln
FB	William J. Trent, Livingston
FB	John H. Love, Shaw
FB	William C. Matthews, Tuskegee

1900-1910

End	Augustus M. Fisher, Lincoln
End	Richard "EPH" Morris, Lincoln
End	Harry Matanga, Lincoln
End	Livingstone Mzimba, Lincoln
Tackle	William H. Washington, Howard
Tackle	Banjamin B. Church, Livingstone
Guard/HB	Benjamin S. Jackson, Howard

Guard/Tackle	Victor C. Turner, Atlanta Baptist (Morehouse)
Guard	Frederick D. Smith, Atlanta U./Howard
Center	Sandy M. Jackson, Atlanta Baptist
Center	Tom Williams, Alabama State
QB	Manuel Taylor, Shaw
QB	Henry E. Barco, Virginia Union/Howard
QB	Charles H. Wesley, Fisk
QB	Edwin A. Harleston, Atlanta University
QB	Augustus A. Marquess, Fisk
QB	Paul V. Smith, Hampton
HB	Floyd "Terrible" Terry, Talladega/Meharry/Howard
HB	Edward B. Gray, Howard
HB	John L. McGriff, Shaw/Meharry/Howard
HB	Emory Peterson, Virginia State
HB	Luke Lowdog, Hampton
HB	Clarence "Gene" Allen, Roger Williams/Howard/Atlanta Baptist
HB	Robert M. Turner, Atlanta Baptist
HB	George M. King, Tuskegee/Fisk
HB	William H. Craighead, Tuskegee

1910-1920

End	Fred M. Slaughter, Howard
End	Ulysses "Lyss" Youang, Lincoln
End	George Gilmore, Howard

End	James "Pop" Gayle, Hampton		QB	Arthur Hendley, Tuskegee
End	Sam Holland, West Virginia State		QB	Tom L. Zuber, Atlanta Baptist/Meharry
End	Edward P. Hurt, Lincoln/Howard		QB	Henry Hucles, Virginia Union
End	George D. Brock, Morehouse		QB	Henry Collins, Lincoln
End	Henry A. Kean, Fisk		QB	George Brice, Howard
End	Samuel B. Taylor, Virginia Union		QB	Jimmy Webster, Wiley
End	Booker T. Washington, Jr., Fisk		QB	Fred Bender, Hampton
Tackle	John M. Clelland, Howard		HB	William Ziegler, Fisk
Tackle	C.B. Dowdell, Howard		HB	Charles Lewis, Atlanta University
Tackle	James Meeks, Livingstone		HB	Leigh Maxwell, Atlanta University
Tackle	Zanas Tantsi, Shaw		HB	Henry Merchant, Howard/Fisk
Tackle	Andrew Savage, Talladega/Atlanta Baptist		HB	Charleston B. Cox, Talladega
Tackle	Dick Richardson, Shaw		HB	William K. Kindle, Fisk
Guard	Island Johns, Shaw		HB	Hannibal Howell, Virginia Union
Guard	John Goodgame, Talladega/Atlanta Baptist		HB	Charles Pinderhughes, Howard
Guard	Reggie Beamon, Howard		HB	Benjamin C. Gregory, Virginia Union
Center	Edward L. Dabney, Hampton		HB	Joseph Brown, Shaw
Center	Zeal Dillon, Tuskegee/Prairie View		HB	James S. "Big" Bullock, Lincoln
Center	L.N. Bass, Walen/Meharry Medical		(Source: "A Hard Road To Glory")	
Center	Samuel Coles, Talladega		(Milton Roberts was a sports historian)	

SHERIDAN BLACK COLLEGE FOOTBALL ALL-AMERICAN TEAM

1987

Offense:

WR	Shannon Sharpe, Soph., Savannah State
WR	Davis Smith, Jr., Texas Southern
OL	Houston Hoover, Sr., Jackson State
OL	Gerald Perry, Sr., Southern
OL	Pat Boyd, Soph., Howard
OL	Tony Danzey, Sr., Delaware State
OL	Calvin Petties, Sr., Central State
TE	Jimmy Johnson, Jr., Howard
QB	Lee Debose, Jr., Howard
RB	Lewis Tillman, Jr., Jackson State
RB	Harvey Reed, Sr., Howard
PK	Gabriel Uriri, Sr., Jackson State

Defense:

DL	Albert Goss, Sr., Jackson State
DL	Curtis Maxey, Sr., Grambling
DL	Brian Brewer, Soph., Florida A&M
DL	Lybrant Robinson, Jr., Delaware State
LB	Andre Lloyd, Sr., Jackson State
LB	Lafayette Kemp, Sr., Alabama A&M
LB	Dennis Conner, Sr., Jackson State
DB	Kevin Dent, Jr., Jackson State
DB	Conrad Austin, Sr., Howard
DB	Vince Buck, Soph., Central State (Ohio)
DB	Ed Hooker, Sr., North Carolina A&T
P	Fred McRae, Fr., Jackson State

Offensive Player of the Year: Harvey Reed, RB, Howard

Defensive Player of the Year: Andre Lloyd, LB, Jackson State

Coach of the Year: Houston Markham, Alabama State

1988

Offense:

WR	Shannon Sharpe, Jr., Savannah State
WR	Johnnie Barnes, Soph. Hampton
OL	Bryan Herd, Sr., Central State (Ohio)
OL	Tim Brown, Jr., Jackson State
OL	Patrick Boyd, Sr., Howard
OL	Dareen Peebles, Sr., Winston-Salem State
OL	Ken Perry, Sr., Va. Union
TE	Jimmy Johnson, Sr., Howard
QB	Earl Harvey, Sr., N.C. Central
RB	Lewis Tillman, Sr., Jackson State
RB	Fred Killings, Jr., Howard
PK	James Vertuno, Soph., Florida A&M

Defense:

DL	Harold Hogue, Sr., Central St. (Ohio)
DL	Tony Robinson, Jr., Morris Brown
DL	Charles Jackson, Sr., Jackson State
DL	Bryan Brewer, Jr., Florida A&M
LB	Cammie Collins, Sr., Jackson State
LB	Darion Conner, Jr., Jackson State
LB	Rod Reed, Sr., Tennessee State
DB	Steve Calhoun, Jr., Morris Brown
DB	Stacy Sanders, Sr., Hampton
DB	Kevin Dent, Sr., Jackson State
DB	Vince Buck, Jr., Central State (Ohio)
P	Vaughn Wilson, Sr., Florida A&M

1989

Offense:

WR	Shannon Sharpe, Sr., Savannah State

WR	Barry Wagner, Sr., Alabama A&M	
OL	Taymond Smith, Jr., Grambling	
OL	Tim Brown, Sr., Jackson State	
OL	Willie Felder, Sr., Howard	
OL	Eric Douglas, Sr., South Carolina State	
OL	Darrell Ryals, Sr., Hampton	
TE	David Jones, Jr., Delaware State	
QB	Clemente Gordon, Sr., Grambling State	
RB	Walter Dean, Jr., Grambling State	
RB	Amir Rasul, Jr., Florida A&M	
PK	Ike Ayozie, Jr., Jackson State	

Defense:

DL	Henry Blades, Jr., Grambling State
DL	Sam Butler, Sr., Alcorn State
DL	Wilbert Jack Cooper, Sr., Albany State
DL	Anthony Pleasant, Sr., Tennessee State
LB	Demetrius Harrison, Sr. North Carolina A&T
LB	Darion Conner, Sr., Jackson State
LB	Royal Reed, Sr., Morris Brown
DB	Aeneas Williams, Sr., Southern
DB	Vince Buck, Sr., Central State (Ohio)
DB	Mario Black, Jr., Fort Valley State
DB	Garry Lewis, Sr., Alcorn State
P	Fred McCrae, Jr., Jackson State

Offensive Player of the Year: Barry Wagner, WR, Alabama A&M
Defensive Player of the Year: Demetrius Harrison, LB, N.C. A&T
Coach of the Year: Bill Davis, Savannah State

1990

WR	Jake Reed, Sr., Grambling State
WR	Chris Holder, Jr., Tuskegee
OL	Raymond Smith, Sr., Grambling State
OL	Charles Hope, Jr., Central State (Ohio)
OL	Eric Williams, Sr., Central State (Ohio)
OL	Terry Beauford, Sr., Florida A&M
OL	Rod Daniels, Sr., Norfolk State
TE	David Jones, Sr., Delaware State
QB	Maurice Heard, Jr., Tuskegee
RB	Walter Dean, Sr., Grambling
RB	Ivory Lee Brown, Sr., Arkansas Pine-Bluff
PK	Ike Ayozie, Sr., Jackson State

Defense:

DL	Eric Elzy, Sr., Jackson State
DL	James Dozier, Sr., Morgan State
DL	Leon Crenshaw, Sr., Tuskegee
DL	Henry Blades, Sr., Grambling
LB	David Woulard, Sr., Miss. Valley State
LB	Eddie Robinson, Jr., Jr., Alabama State
LB	Simon Shanks, Soph., Tennessee State
DB	Aeneas Williams, Sr., Southern
DB	Mario Black, Sr., Fort Valley State

DB	Ricky Hill, Jr., South Carolina State
DB	Robert Turner, Fr., Jackson State
P	Colin Godfrey, Soph., Tennessee State

Offensive Player of the Year: Walter Dean, RB, Grambling
Defensive Player of the Year: Aeneas Williams, DB, Southern
Coach of the Year: Bill Hayes, North Carolina A&T

1991
Offense:

WR	Chris Holder, Sr., Tuskegee
WR	Cedric Tillman, Sr., Alcorn State
OL	Jackie Rowan, Sr., Alabama State
OL	Patrick Johnson, Sr., Alabama State
OL	Charles Hope, Sr., Central State (Ohio)
OL	Shaun Archer, Sr., Alcorn State
OL	Greg Ellison, Sr., Fort Valley State
TE	Craig Thompson, Sr., North Carolina A&T
QB	Steve McNair, Fr., Alcorn State
RB	Eric Gant, Soph., Grambling
RB	Michael Murray, Sr., Delaware State
PK	Gilad Landau, Fr., Grambling

Defense:

DL	Robert Porcher, Sr., South Carolina State
DL	Kevin Little, Sr, North Carolina A&T
DL	Knox Thompson, Jr., North Carolina A&T
DL	Everette McIver, Jr., Elizabeth City State
LB	Eddie Robinson, Jr., Sr., Alabama State
LB	Charles Ray Davis, Sr., Jackson State
LB	Marvin Pope, Sr., Central State (Ohio)
DB	Ashley Ambrose, Sr., Mississippi Valley State
DB	Leroy Haynesworth, Sr., Norfolk State
DB	Ricjy Hill, Sr., South Carolina State
DB	William Carroll, Jr., Florida A&M
P	Colin Godfrey, Jr., Tennessee St.

Offensive Player of the Year: Steve McNair, QB, Alcorn State
Defensive Player of the Year: Eddie Robinson, Jr., LB, Alabama State
Coach of the Year: Houston Markham, Alabama State

1992
Offense:

WR	Terry Mickens, Jr., Florida A&M
WR	Doug Grant, Jr., Savannah State
OL	Herman Arvie, Sr., Grambling
OL	Lester Holmes, Sr., Jackson State
OL	Kwame Kilpatrick, Sr., Florida A&M
OL	Robert Carpenter, Sr., Howard
OL	Orlando Brown, Sr., South Carolina State
TE	Isiah Elias, Jr., Jackson State
QB	Steve McNair, Soph., Alcorn State
RB	Eric Gant, Sr., Grambling

RB	Rob Clodfelter, Jr., Livingstone		LB	Perry Hall, Sr., Tennessee State
PK	Gilad Landau, Soph., Grambling		DB	William Carroll, Sr., Florida A&M
			DB	Alonza Barnett, Sr., North Carolina A&T
Defense:			DB	Joseph Best, Jr., Fort Valley State
DL	Michael Strahan, Sr., Texas Southern		DB	Sean Wallace, Jr., Southern
DL	Everett McIver, Sr., Elizabeth City State		P	Colin Godfrey, Sr., Tennessee State
DL	Damien Moses, Sr., South Carolina State			
DL	LeRoy Thompson, Sr., Delaware State			
LB	Rodney Edwards, Sr., North Carolina A&T			
LB	Marlo Perry, Jr., Jackson State			

Offensive Player of the Year: Steve McNair, QB, Alcorn State

Defensive Player of the Year: Michael Strahan, LB, Texas Southern

Coach of the Year: Joe Taylor, Hampton

SOURCE MATERIALS

Aside from numerous extensive interviews, material for this book was culled from the Pittsburgh *Courier* newspaper, *Sports View* magazine, the respective conference and school football media guides and game programs, the National Collegiate Athletic Association (NCAA), National Association of Intercollegiate Athletics (NAIA), National Football League team media guides and league record book, the Pro Football Hall of Fame, and National Football Foundation and College Hall of Fame.

Book sources included:

—Louise M. Rountree, *Blue Bear Trax*, 1967.

—Dwight Lewis and Susan Thomas, *A Will to Win*, Cumberland Press, 1983.

—*This Fabulous Century*, Time-Life Books, 1970.

—David Wallechinsky and Irving Wallace, *The People's Almanac,* Doubleday, 1975.

—Geoffrey C. Ward, with Ric Burns and Ken Burns, *The Civil War*, Knopf, 1990.

—*The College Game*, Bobbs-Merrill, 1974.

—Arthur R. Ashe, Jr., *A Hard Road to Glory*, Warner Books, 1988.

—Collie J. Nicholson, *Black College Football Yearbook*, Vol. 1, No. 1, Alphonse Jackson publisher, 1979.

—David Hall, masters thesis for Florida State University School of Music, *William P. Foster, American Music Educator*, 1989.

C o m m i

*Some people
shy away
from
commitments...*

at State Farm we don't.
Especially in supporting education.

We are committed to the concept that the future of our country depends on the education of our youth. That's why in ...

- 1963 we founded the State Farm Companies Foundation.
- 1972 we started a Summer Minority Internship Program.
- 1990 we began our program to recognize special educators with the Good Neighbor Award for Teachers.

State Farm is There.®

D e d i c

Recipient Joseph Sweeney, Jackson Heights, New York and his "Graffiti Busters." Joseph's students used their math skills by organizing data from a survey they took to curb graffiti.

Truly Dedicated.

That describes State Farm's commitment to education and a trait of the teachers who receive State Farm's Good Neighbor Award.

Outstanding elementary and secondary teachers who demonstrate extraordinary creativity and innovation in the classrooms are recognized through this award.

At State Farm, we feel this award is a way to provide well-deserved recognition and financial support to dedicated teachers.

Like a Good Neighbor,

a t i o n

Since 1990, monthly recipients have received a $5,000 check payable to the educational institution of their choice, a commemorative plaque and national advertising recognition in major publications, such as *Life*, *Time*, *National Geographic* and *USA Today*.

This is our way to highlight dedicated teachers who are shaping the lives of our nation's youth.

Recipient Sarah Wiggins, Roxboro, North Carolina and her 9th and 10th grade student writers. Sarah created "The Great Mail Race" to motivate her students to improve their writing.

A c h i e v

"Quite an Achievement"

Many students probably hear this statement after the announcement that they have been chosen to receive one of the State Farm Foundation's scholarships.

The foundation was established in 1963 with the same goals today... to encourage high-potential men and women to prepare themselves for leadership roles in industry and society... to stimulate insurance-related research and the development of new insurance knowledge... to encourage the pursuit of insurance-related careers, including insurance teaching... and promote educational activities related to the business world.

Like a Good Neighbor,

State Farm awards over a hundred scholarships each year and donates to other scholarship foundations, like the United Negro College Fund, the NAACP Special Contribution Fund and the Consortium for Graduate Study in Management (MBA's for Minorities).

S u c c

Students who participate in State Farm's Summer Minority Internship Program don't have to wait long for success to find them.

Through this program, State Farm's goal is to provide students with productive employment and solid work experience. In addition to on-the-job projects, interns meet with employees on career development insights and participate in weekly Toastmasters meetings to improve public speaking and interpersonal communication skills.

State Farm's president, Ed Rust Jr., commented: "Since the inception of our program more than 20 years ago, we have established a tradition of success that provides a quality opportunity for the people involved. In fact, we currently have more than 300 people on board today who are graduates of that program. With results like that, it is easy to say that this program works exceptionally well for everyone."

Success… it's right around the corner.

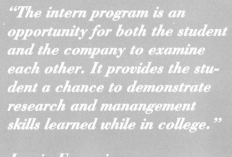

"The intern program is an opportunity for both the student and the company to examine each other. It provides the student a chance to demonstrate research and manangement skills learned while in college."

Louis Francisco,
Agency Manager
Summer Intern 1976

"Today, more than ever, it is important that we continue to identify talented young people and create the environment for them to be successful in our organization. The intern program provides such an opportunity; a two-way opportunity... for the students and for the company. People are our most valuable asset."

Shirley Gordon,
Deputy Regional Vice President
Summer Intern 1973

STATE FARM
Auto
Life Fire
INSURANCE ®

State Farm Insurance Companies
Home Offices:
Bloomington, Illinois

State Farm is There. ®

ABOUT THE AUTHOR

Photograph by Robert Hanashiro

Michael Hurd, was a sportswriter for fourteen years. He is a Vietnam veteran, who served eight years in the U.S. Air Force (one year, 1971, at Phu Cat Air Base, Vietnam). After military service, he attended the University of Texas-Austin, though both his late mother, Emily (Bishop College) and his father, James (Virginia State University), attended historically black colleges, as did several other relatives.

Michael Hurd was born in Texarkana, Texas, January 17, 1949, and grew up in Houston, graduating from Evan E. Worthing High School in 1967. He has worked at the Houston *Post*, where his primary responsibility was covering small colleges, including the Southwestern Athletic Conference (SWAC). He later wrote for the Austin *American-Statesman*, before moving to *USA Today* as a member of the paper's original staff in 1982. For the last 10 of his eleven years at *USA Today*, he worked from the paper's West Coast bureau in Los Angeles. However, he recently returned to the *American-Statesman* as an assistant city editor. He has covered an extremely wide variety of sports events—from auto racing to horse shows to volleyball and surfing, but most notably, events involving the National Basketball Association (including 10 Finals), National Football League (2 Super Bowls), Major League Baseball, National Hockey League, college football (Rose, Cotton, Fiesta Bowls, et al.) and basketball (postseason tournaments, including Final Four).

Hurd, a resident of Austin, Texas, is divorced and the father of two sons, Jeremy (age 8) and Jason (6)